IMAGES
of America

SEARCY

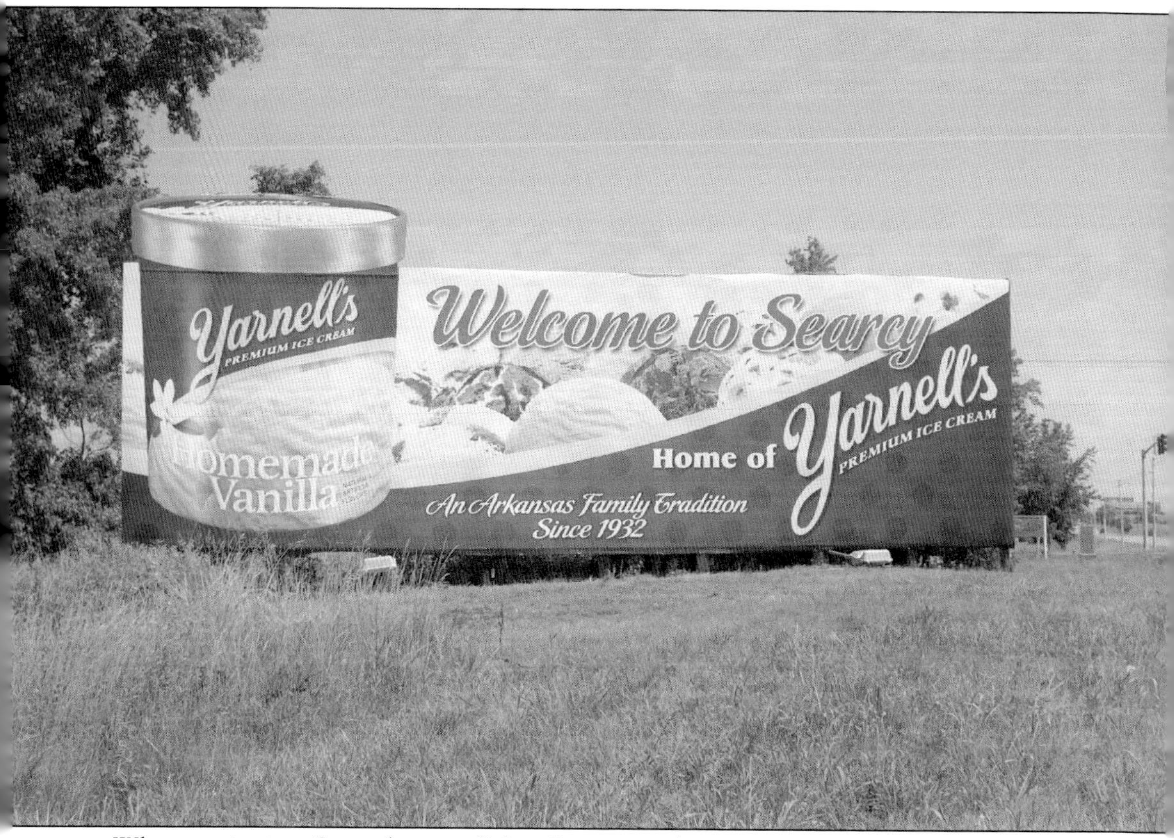

When coming into Searcy by way of Main Street, people were greeted by this Yarnell's Ice Cream billboard, a welcome sight on hot and humid summer days in Arkansas. Yarnell's, an Arkansas institution, was owned and operated by several generations of the Yarnell family before it closed in 2011. (Courtesy Carolyn Boyles.)

ON THE COVER: Searcy Bank, established by William Watkins in 1904, was located on the corner of Arch and Spruce Streets on the west side of the courthouse square. A fire during its first year forced operations to be temporarily moved across the street. In 1906, the name of the bank was changed to the Bank of Searcy. In 1967, upon being accepted into the National Banking Association, the name was changed again, becoming First National Bank. Because of its prime location, this has always been one of the busiest blocks in Searcy. Note the man on the power-line pole and the dirt street. (Courtesy Leon and Sherry Person.)

IMAGES
of America

SEARCY

Carolyn Boyles and Patsy Pipkin

ARCADIA
PUBLISHING

ISBN 978-0-7385-9101-8

Published by Arcadia Publishing
Charleston, South Carolina

Printed in the United States of America

Library of Congress Control Number: 2011930734

For all general information, please contact Arcadia Publishing:
Telephone 843-853-2070
Fax 843-853-0044
E-mail sales@arcadiapublishing.com
For customer service and orders:
Toll-Free 1-888-313-2665

Visit us on the Internet at www.arcadiapublishing.com

In memory of Jean Gipson, Col. Steven Joe Stone (US Army), and Mary Elizabeth Daniels Hamilton

Contents

Acknowledgments

We want to acknowledge and give our sincere thanks to the many people who have given their support and lent to us their treasured photographs as we compiled this book. We are sorry that we could not use all of the photographs we received, but space was limited.

There are so many who helped us with this project. They know who they are, but to show our appreciation again, we would like to mention them: Marilyn Collins, for suggesting the idea of doing a book and helping with the initial stages; Leon and Sherry Person, for the Ivan Quattlebaum collection and personal photographs; Mayor David Morris, for his continued encouragement and support, and his assistant, Lillie Cook, for her photographs of the city; Mary Beth Waters, president, and Shelly Keech, secretary, of the White County Historical Society (WCHS); WCHS board of directors and members, especially those who work in the office downtown; and Nancy Williams Showalter, who shared the Roger Williams collection and her "who's-who" knowledge.

Also, Amy Burton of Main Street Searcy; First Security Bank marketing department and Kathryn Sims; Kayla Osborne and Regions Bank; Phil Pyeatt, for photographs and the history of Searcy Bank; Buck Layne and the Searcy Regional Chamber of Commerce; Darla Ino, director of the Searcy and White County Regional Library; Don Harlan and staff at Arkansas State University–Searcy; Leon and Lynn Van Patten; Betsy Bailey at Searcy Public Schools; Jeff Montgomery at Harding University; John Baker at John Baker Photography; Mary Lou Dunn, director of the Sunshine School; Albert and Doris Yarnell, for their photographs and insight into Searcy's history; the many others who so graciously shared their personal and family photographs; and last but definitely not least, our friends Eloise Muncy, for her husband's book and photographs and helping edit our work, and Barbara Duncan, for her editing and knowledge of Searcy history.

The help we have received from our Arcadia editors Amy Perryman and Simone Monet-Williams has been invaluable.

Above all, we appreciate our husbands and our friends who continued to express an interest in this project while sometimes finding us ignoring them. Having always had an interest in history, we fear we have made this book our major focus during the previous year. It has been a wonderful experience, and we have learned so much.

The images in this volume appear courtesy of friends and family as noted, Searcy Regional Chamber of Commerce (SRCC), and White County Historical Society (WCHS).

INTRODUCTION

In 1817, a tall, redheaded, ambitious young man with piercing gray eyes came by flatboat down the Tennessee, Ohio, and Mississippi Rivers to the Missouri Territory. His name was Richard Searcy ("sur-see").

Rapidly progressing from Lawrence County clerk to Davidsonville postmaster to Independence County clerk in a matter of a few years, Searcy went on to read law and was admitted to the Arkansas bar. In 1823, Pres. James Monroe appointed him to the superior court of the territory; he was assigned to the Fourth District. Land fraud crowded the court of the day, and Searcy earned the respect of all around him by settling the cases quickly and in a manner that satisfied all parties involved. Searcy died at age 36, in 1832, at the height of his career.

In 1835, the General Assembly of the Territory of Arkansas passed an act that took in 1,027 square miles of land from Pulaski, Independence, and Jackson Counties to create White County. When the county seat was established in 1837, the legislature named the county after Richard Searcy. At the time, there were approximately 874 citizens in White County. The latest census (2010) recorded 77,076 in White County and 22,558 in Searcy.

Establishing a homestead in this area of Arkansas was not without its challenges. Searcy is located approximately 100 miles west of the Mississippi River and near both the White and Little Red Rivers. Most early settlers came by way of the rivers and referred to the area, when they first arrived, as Searcy Landing. Despite the challenges, early settlers found Searcy to be a good location to make their homes—near the waterways and surrounded by plentiful game and fertile land. The sulphur springs in the area caused many of the first settlers to call the area White Sulphur Springs.

Israel M. Moore, a talented surveyor from Philadelphia, came to Searcy a few years after the settlement began and was assigned the responsibility of laying out the city streets. Moore was constrained by the Territorial Land Ordinance of 1785 to lay out streets running due north, south, east, and west, which divided the land into townships of 36 square miles. He chose to name the streets after the city streets in Philadelphia.

Searcy's early settlers were true pioneers. They worked hard, cleared the land, and spent their money wisely when, and if, they chose to spend it. They depended on their religious faith to guide them through hard times, resulting in Searcy sometimes being referred to as "a city of churches."

As transportation improved, new settlers came in wagons by land and in steamboats on the Mississippi and White Rivers. When gold was discovered in California in 1849, many families packed up and headed west to look for new opportunities in unsettled land, but when some arrived in Arkansas, they decided they had found what they were looking for and stayed.

As the second half of the 19th century came and went, settlers continued to move into Searcy. The first brick buildings, made from clay found near the Little Red River, were erected. As evidenced by the many old homes and other buildings in Searcy, the brick structures were constructed to last by determined craftsmen.

Hotels were built to accommodate the many who came to Searcy to take advantage of the curative powers of the sulphur springs. Doctors, dentists, and druggists who noticed people heading toward Searcy seeking "cures for what ailed them" also flocked to the growing town.

One of the most popular springs was located in the center of town in Spring Park, another, Armstrong Springs, was a few miles away. A shuttle service transported people between the two locations, and boardinghouses and hotels stayed occupied. The springs in Searcy continued to draw visitors until the early 1940s, when nearby drilling for a new water supply accidentally tapped into the springs' underground storage basin, causing them to run dry.

Brig. Gen. Dandridge McRae was Searcy's most famous son during the Civil War. He entered the war as a captain and advanced rapidly. Searcy survived the Civil War and Reconstruction but suffered its share of need. Most of the people were hardy and able to keep their families fed, but the community did help, providing lodging and food for widows and orphans. There was little funding for civil needs because of the inability of the Arkansas General Assembly to pass an act to legalize the levying of taxes, which the assembly finally did in 1876. Unpaved city streets were dusty in the summer and muddy when it rained, and streets remained unlit until 1878.

In the late 19th century, now that the city had paved streets, streetlights, a fire company, and other improvements, growth picked up again. Brick churches were constructed all over town. Well-to-do citizens built palatial homes, and education became very important. People from other communities moved to Searcy to take advantage of the schools and colleges, which grew at a steady pace. The Searcy Male and Female Institute became the Searcy Male and Female College, and Galloway Female College attracted many families with young ladies seeking education in social graces. Harding College, founded in 1924, took over the Galloway Female College campus and is now known as Harding University.

Searcy continued to grow through the early part of the 20th century as electricity became feasible and widespread. As paved roads and cars grew to be commonplace, Searcy became a shopping center for people from throughout the area.

Medical care improved during the 1920s and 1930s, and industry grew. During the Great Depression, many local businesses not only survived, they flourished. In the late 1930s, a young county judge, Wilbur Mills, set the stage to make Searcy a household word when he was elected to Congress in 1939. Mills became powerful during the 1960s, when the Democrats controlled the country. Between 1940 and 1974, Searcy was the third largest city in Arkansas and was featured in *Forbes* magazine.

In the early 1950s, the city began to attract new industries offering employment for people in Searcy. This boom lasted for several decades. When the economy forced Searcy companies to consolidate or close in the early part of the 21st century, the town started to benefit from economic fortunes of a different kind: vast reserves of natural gas discovered in what is known as the Fayetteville Shale. Many White County citizens have benefited from the discovery.

Despite the massive growth in population, Searcy has managed to keep the feel of a small town. The citizens like to boast that Searcy is "where thousands live as millions wish they could." The late Dr. Jimmy Carr, assistant to former president of Harding College (now Harding University), Joe Pryor, is said to have coined the phrase.

One

Historic Life and People

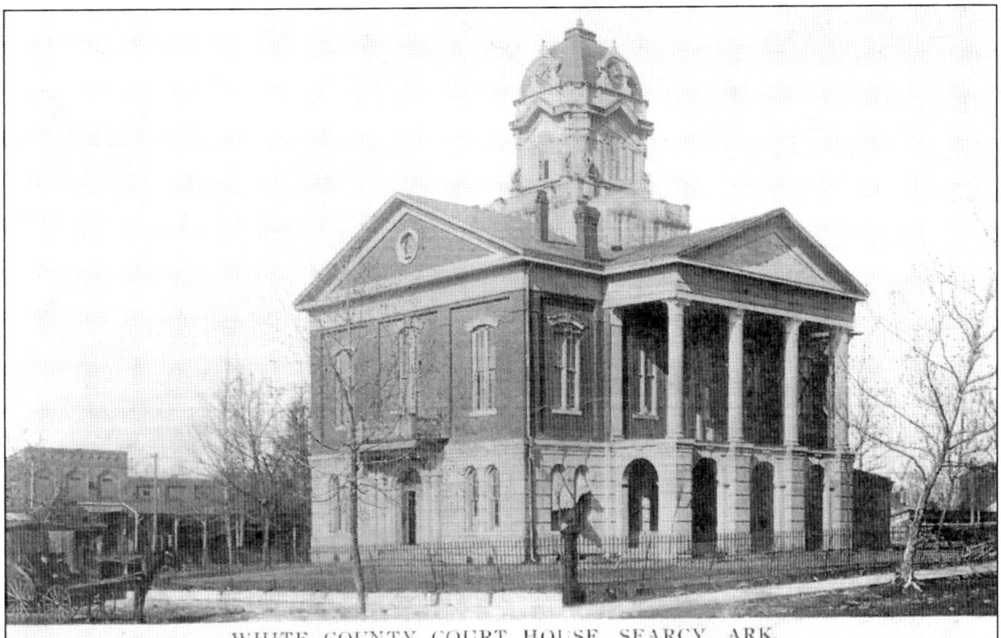

This is a view of White County Courthouse, as it appeared in 1908, in the center of the square in downtown Searcy. The fence surrounding the courthouse has been removed, as have some of the trees, although additional landscaping has been added. (Courtesy WCHS.)

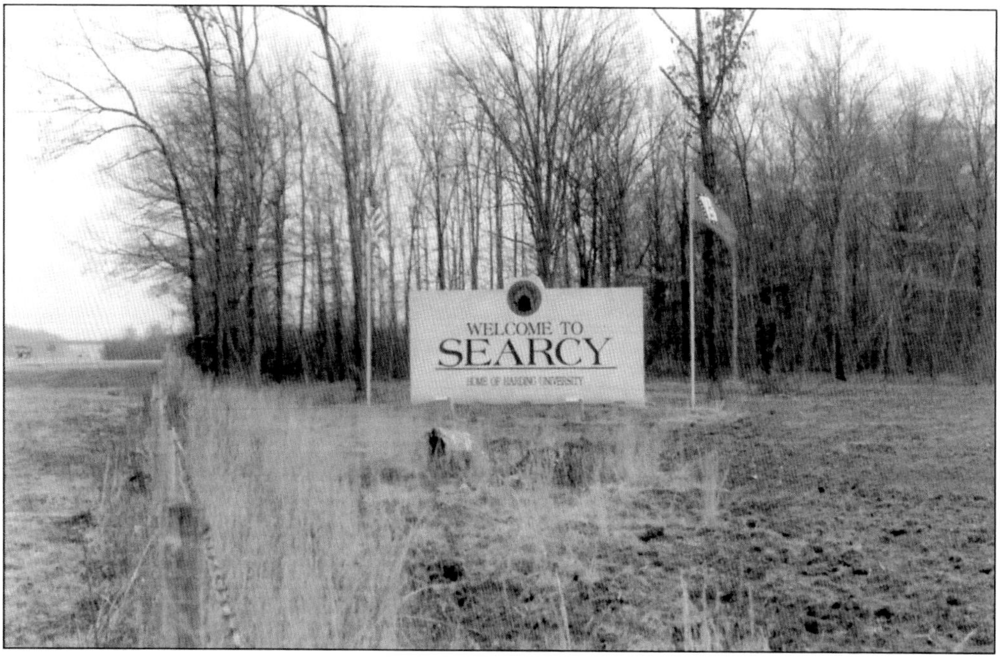

The Searcy welcome sign has changed through the years, but a warm welcome is in store when one turns off US Route 67/167 and enters the Searcy city limits. Searcy has always been a great place to live. In the 1950s, Lela Duncan, a teller at the Searcy Bank, was given a lot in the Cloverdale subdivision after winning a contest to name the new housing development. (Both, courtesy SRCC.)

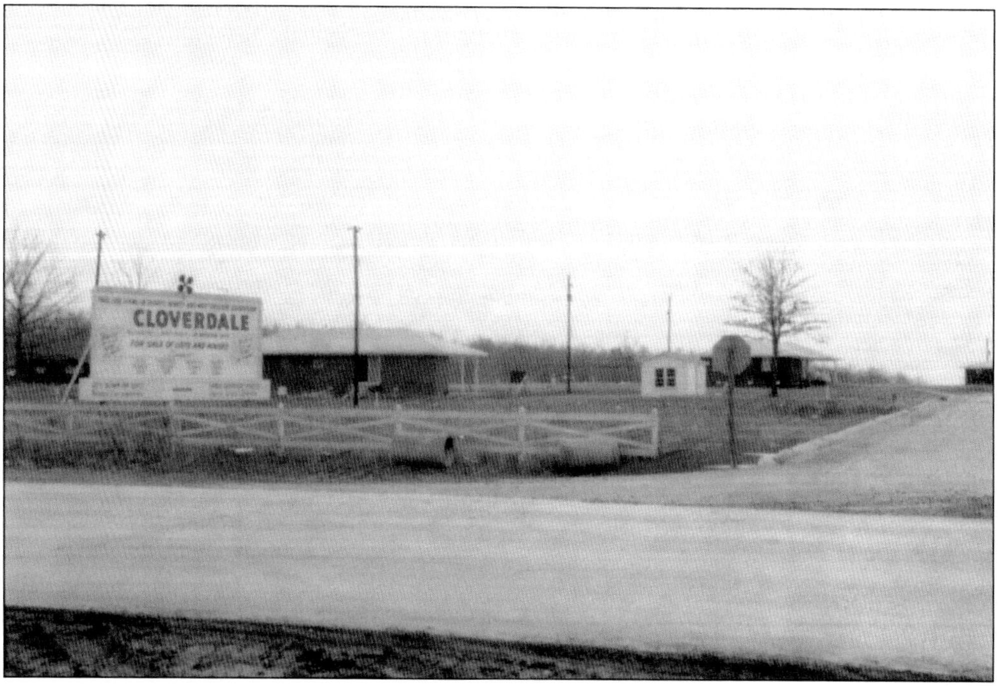

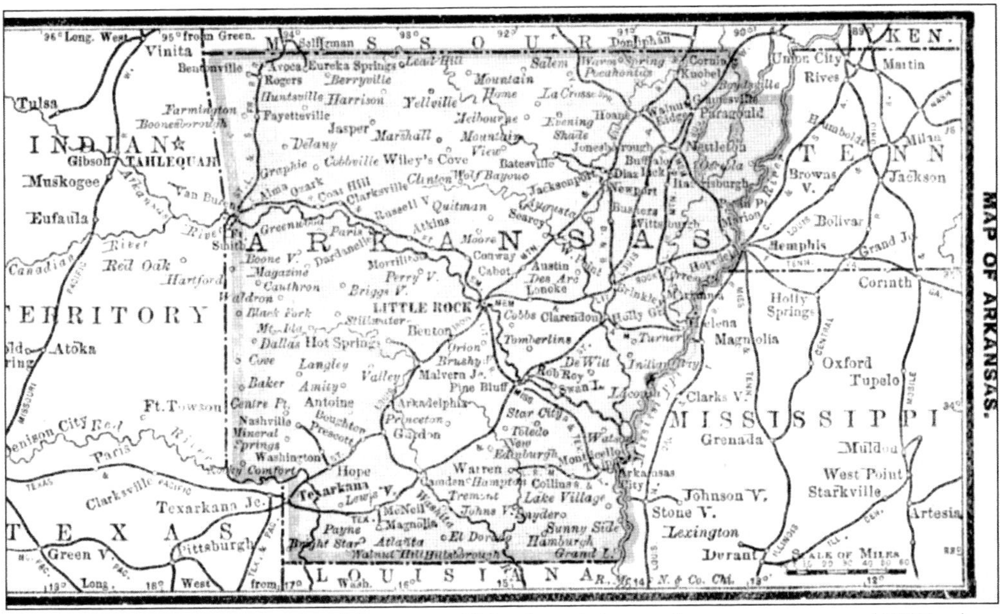

This early Arkansas map is dated between 1836, when Arkansas became a state, and 1907, when Oklahoma officially became part of the United States. Searcy is located just above and to the right of the "N" in Arkansas. The heavy lines within the state boundaries are not highways but railroad routes. Little Rock, in all capitals, is the state capital, while Texarkana appears in bold, presumably designating it as a major population center. Jonesboro, in the northeast corner, appears with its early spelling: "Jonesborough." This map clearly depicts Tahlequah, Oklahoma, as the capital of the Indian Nation. (Courtesy WCHS.)

This 1976 photograph of the Little Red River shows where the Gin and Deener Creeks empty into the river at Searcy Landing. Some believe the landing was a short distance upriver, near the present-day Highway 16 cutoff. Stern-wheelers made their way up the muddy river to unload cargo near what is now Oak Grove Cemetery, and steamboats traveled the Mississippi and White Rivers to arrive at Searcy Landing. (Courtesy Eloise Muncy.)

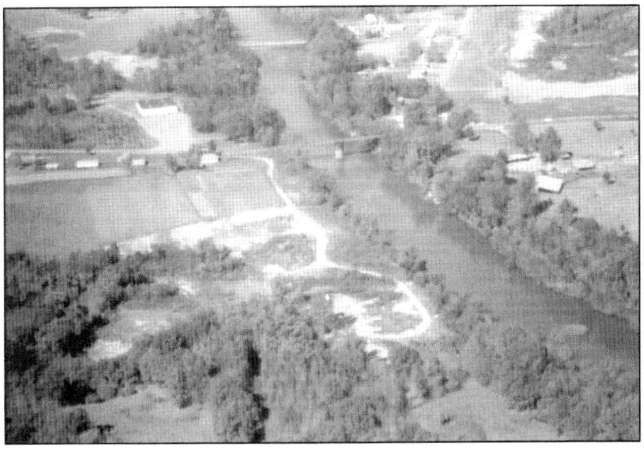

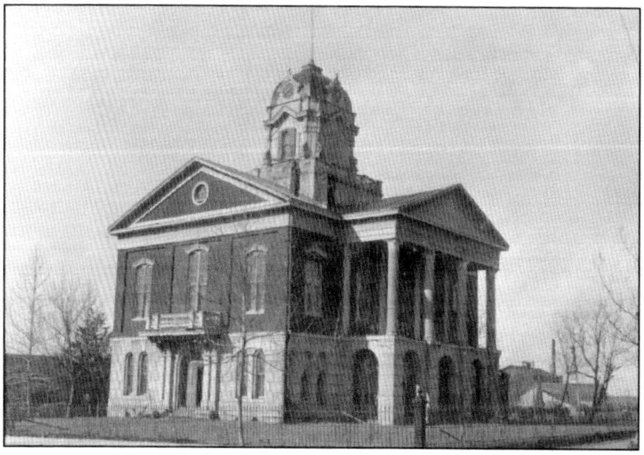

In 1837, two years after the creation of White County, Searcy was laid out as the permanent county seat. The courthouse, completed in 1871, has a bell tower with a bell dated 1855. The bell resembles the Liberty Bell in Philadelphia. A remodeling of the courthouse took place in 1912. This is one of the earliest known images of the White County Courthouse, which is the oldest courthouse still functioning in Arkansas. (Courtesy Leon and Sherry Person.)

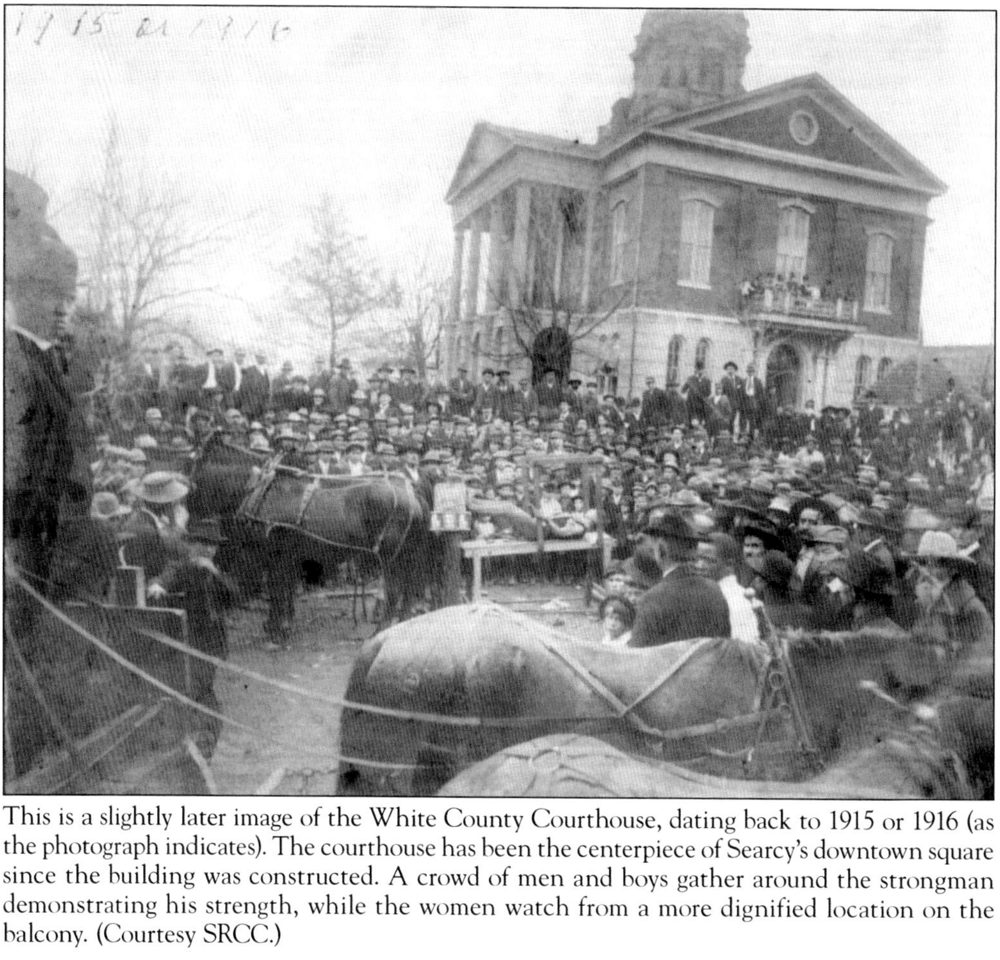

This is a slightly later image of the White County Courthouse, dating back to 1915 or 1916 (as the photograph indicates). The courthouse has been the centerpiece of Searcy's downtown square since the building was constructed. A crowd of men and boys gather around the strongman demonstrating his strength, while the women watch from a more dignified location on the balcony. (Courtesy SRCC.)

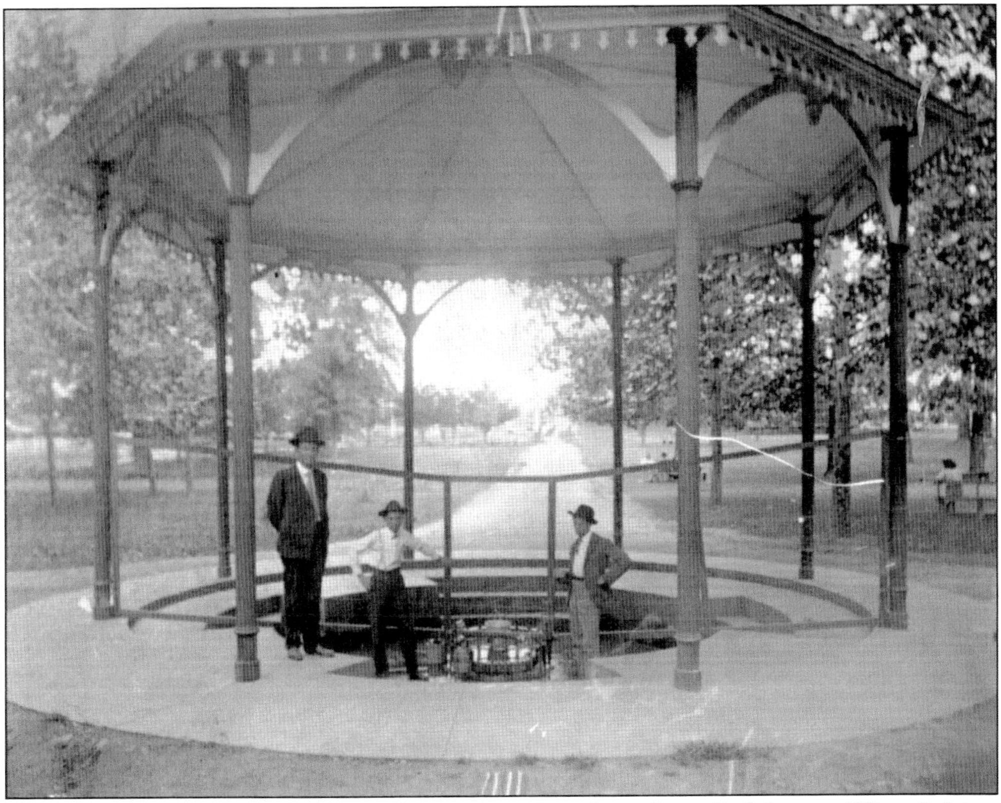

In recognition of the springs found in the Searcy area, early settlers called the area White Sulphur Springs. The springs, located in Searcy's Spring Park, are now closed. In the past, people came from near and far to bathe in the spring's healing waters or take water home for medicinal purposes. In the early days, animals were watered at the springs, then bathhouses and hotels were built in the area, and the park became a place for fun and dancing. In the photograph, three unidentified men stand near the spring under a large pavilion. (Courtesy Nancy Williams Showalter and SRCC.)

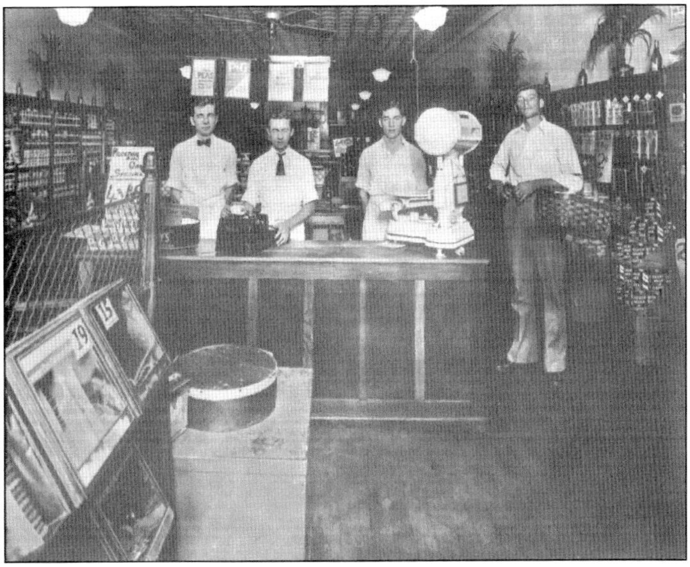

Four unidentified young men in the Robbins-Sanford Mercantile pose for a photograph. As seen on the counter sign, Proctor & Gamble was already a household name. Robbins-Sanford was in business as early as 1916. It closed during the 1950s. The Van Atkins store later occupied the same location. (Courtesy SRCC.)

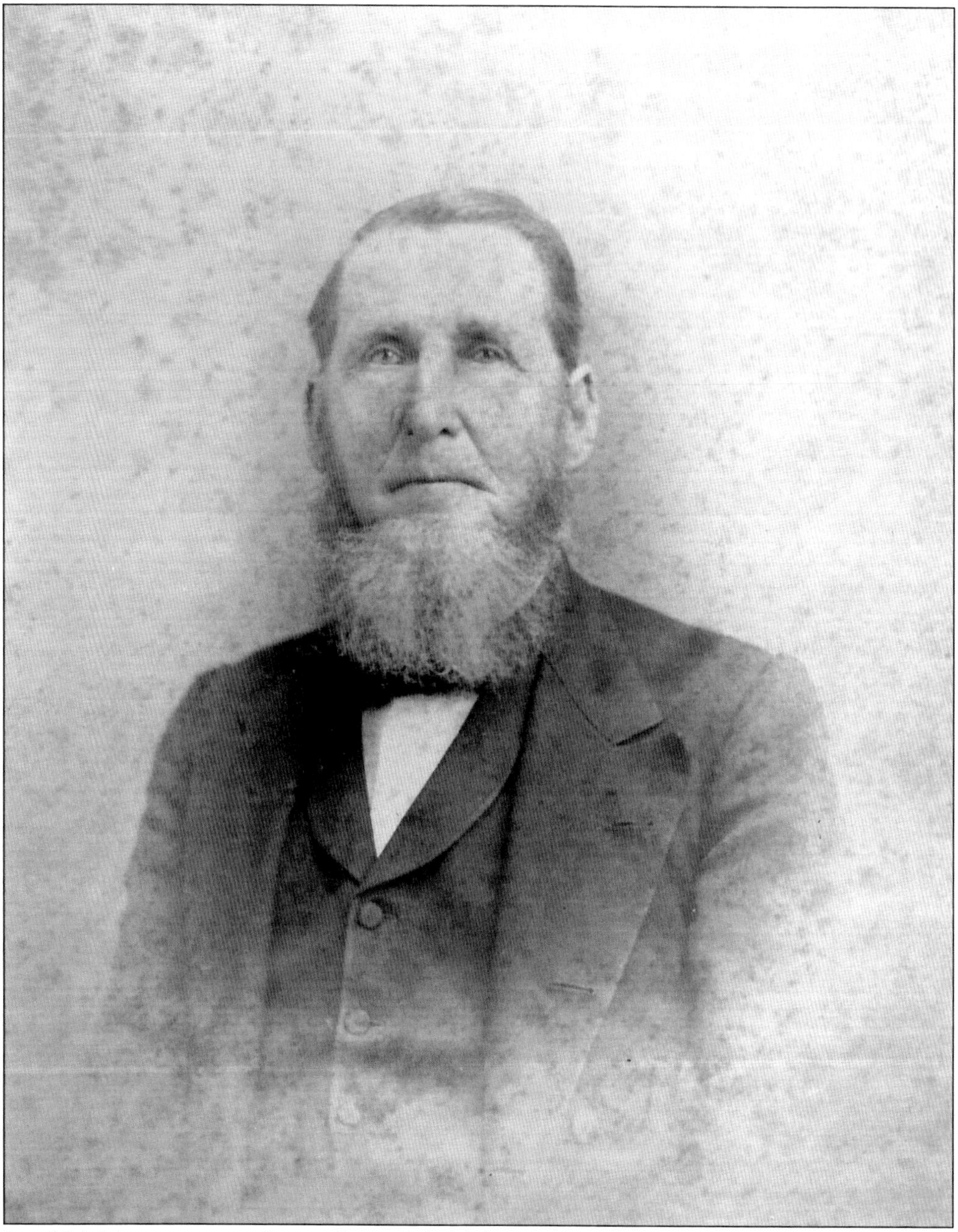

Israel M. Moore came to Searcy from Philadelphia in the late 1800s and purchased 160 acres of land for $1,215. He became involved in a land ownership dispute, which went all the way to the Arkansas Supreme Court. Moore was a surveyor by profession. He laid out the initial streets of Searcy and named them after the streets of his hometown—with the exception of Chestnut Street. Moore donated land to the city for the White County Courthouse, First Methodist Church, the junior high school, and Spring Park. For unknown reasons, Moore was ignored during the street-naming process until 1957, when North Line Street was renamed Moore Street. (Courtesy Mary Lou Dunn.)

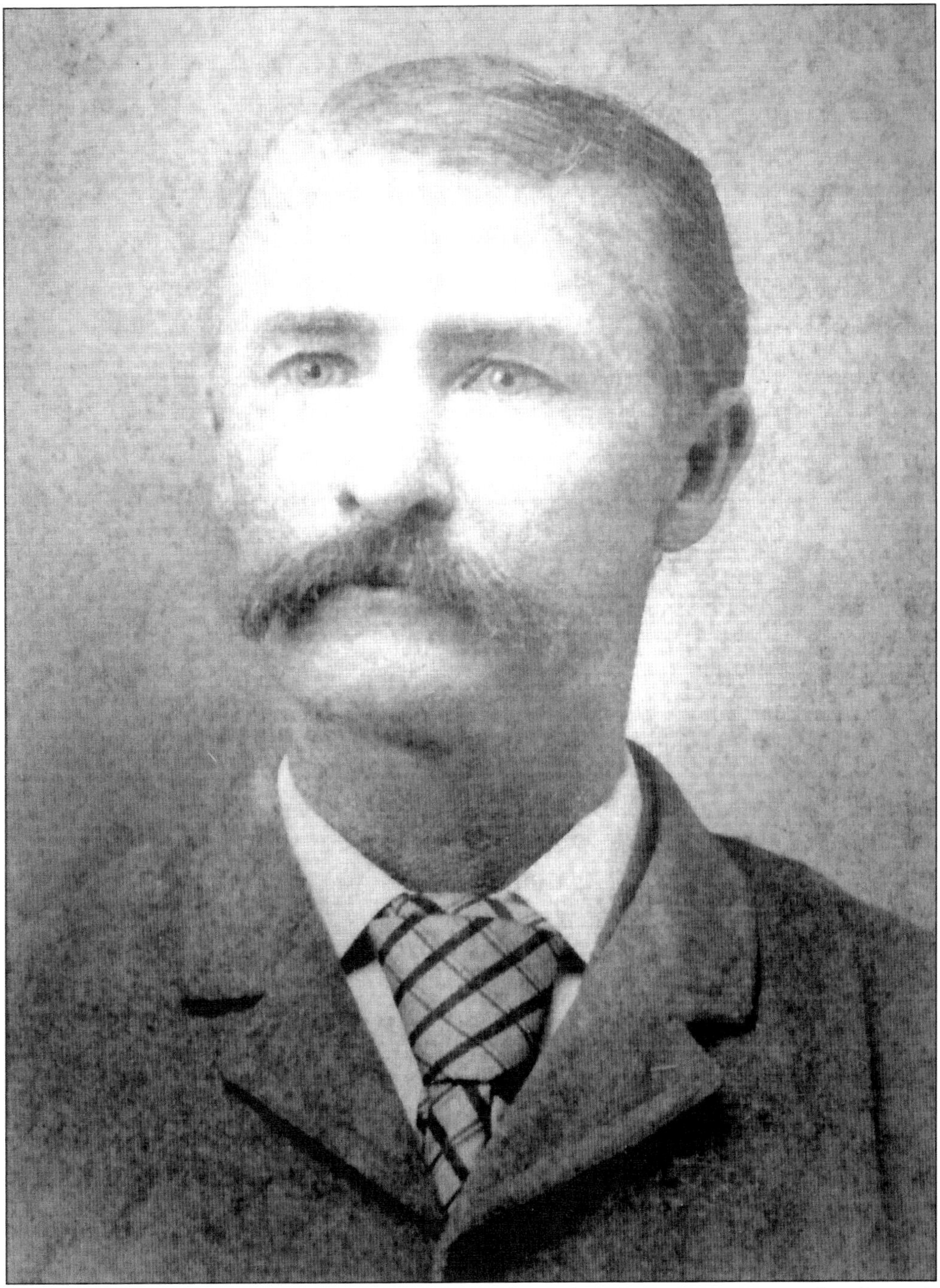

Benjamin Clayton ("B.C.") Black was another early settler who was instrumental in Searcy's history. During the Civil War, Black served as a captain for the Confederate States of America. Between 1886 and 1894, he was mayor. He also served as Searcy's sheriff, postmaster, and was on the board for the University of Arkansas. He donated land on the corner of Vine and Locust Streets to the Baptist church for a new brick meetinghouse. (Courtesy Eloise Muncy.)

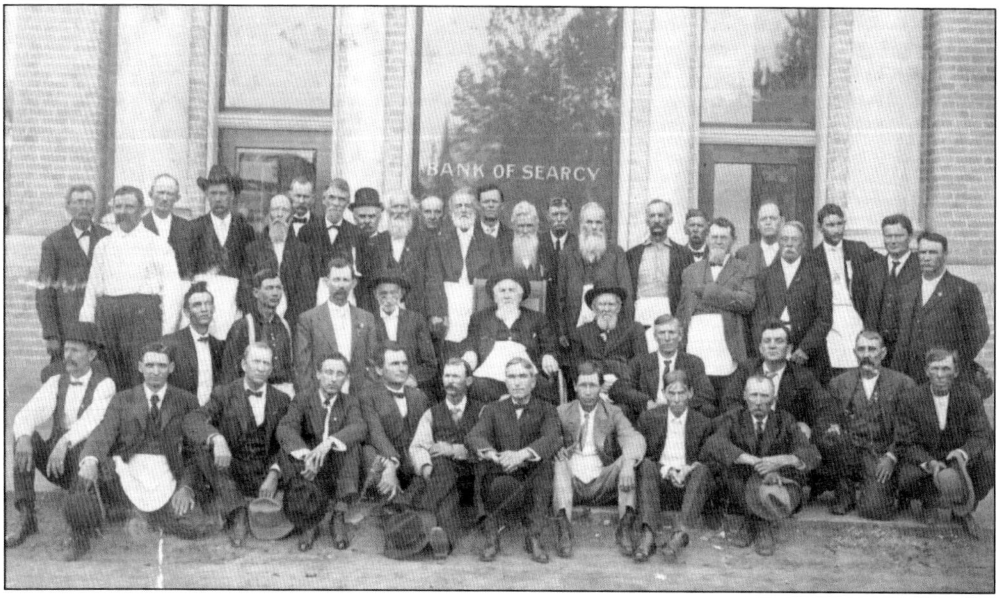

This photograph of the founding members of Searcy Masonic Lodge No. 49 was taken around 1906 in front of the Bank of Searcy. The lodge members met on Tuesday nights under a full moon. The first Masonic Lodge Hall was on the southeast corner of the square and often served as a courtroom. W.R. (Reiser) Stewart, who owned this photograph, wrote on the back: "I found this picture in a trash box about 1950, and found it again July 18, 1976 in the blue closet. I think it should be kept." (Courtesy Jiles Pagan and W.R. (Reiser) Stewart.)

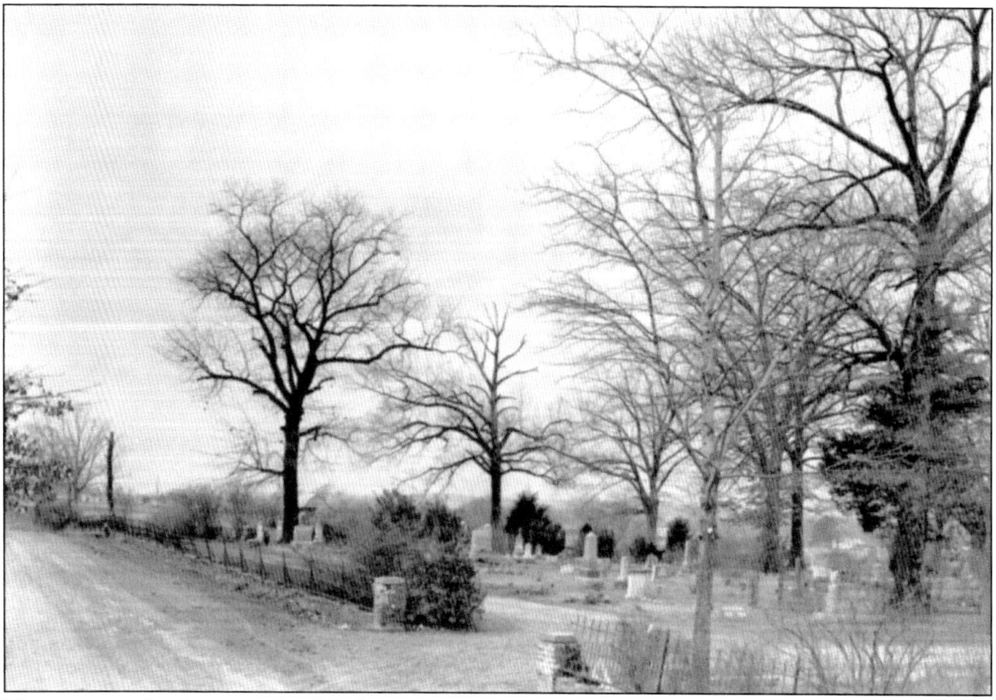

This is an early photograph of Oak Grove Cemetery on Moore Street. It was taken before the beautification project that added iron gates over the entrances. (Courtesy SRCC.)

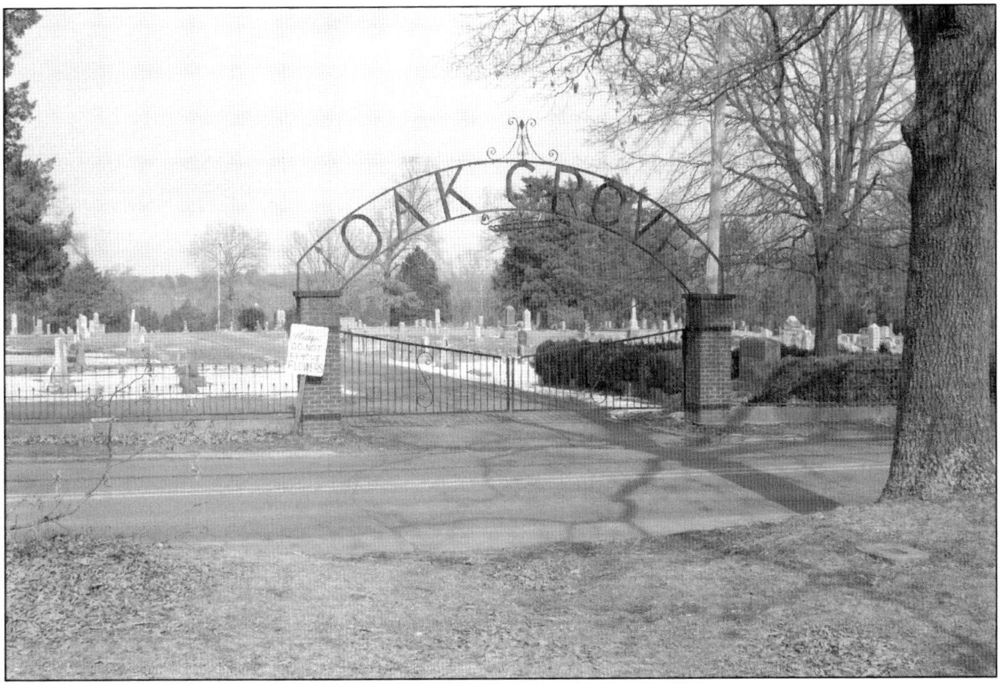

The Oak Grove Cemetery dates back to 1855, when Juliette Howerton sold 10 acres of land to White County to be used as a common burial ground. The photograph above shows one of the current entrances. (Courtesy Carolyn Boyles.)

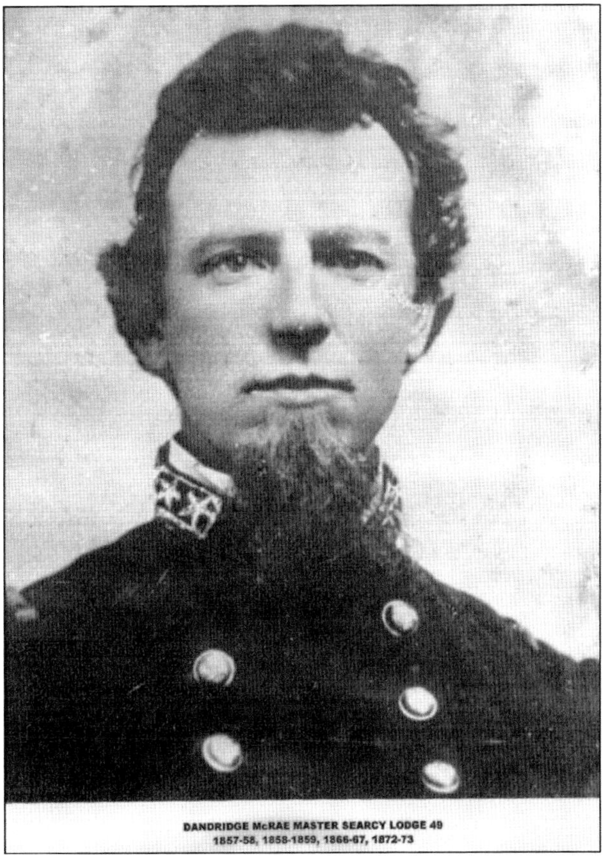

Confederate brigadier general Dandridge McRae came from Alabama to Searcy in 1853. Admitted to the bar in 1854, he served as county and circuit court clerk until the Civil War. After the war, he returned to Searcy, continued his law practice, and was appointed deputy secretary of state in 1881. He served as commissioner for the Arkansas exhibit at the World's Fair in New Orleans in 1886 and was a four-time master of Searcy Masonic Lodge No. 49. (Courtesy Jiles Pagan.)

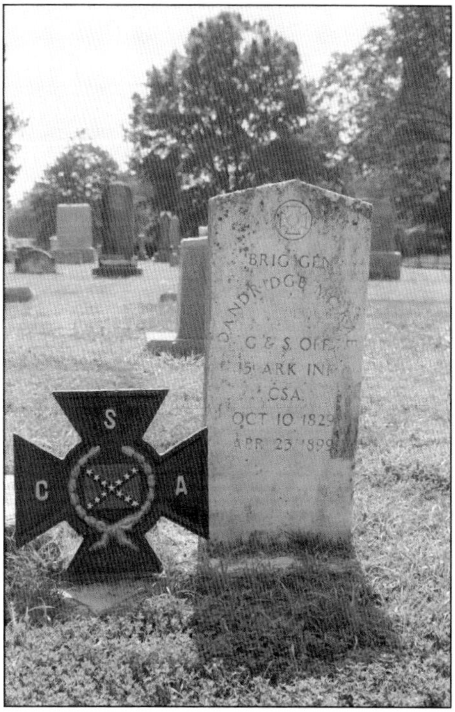

Brigadier General McRae is buried in Oak Grove Cemetery. McRae, Arkansas, and Searcy's McRae Elementary School are named for him. (Courtesy Carolyn Boyles.)

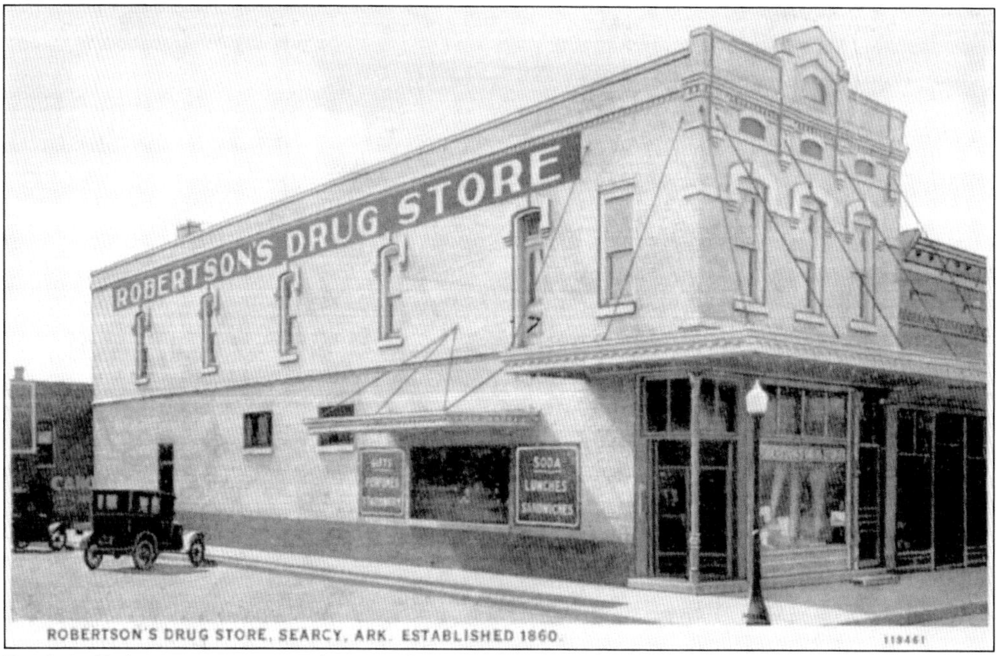

Dr. P.A. Robertson, a young druggist from Memphis, settled in Fort Smith before coming to Searcy in 1860. He relocated to Robertson's Drug Store on the southeast corner of the courthouse square after his original business outgrew its building. Stephen Brundidge Jr. constructed the larger building. Robertson sold more than just drugs; he owned the only glass-cutting machine in town and sold windowpanes, as well as paint, oil, and other household supplies. (Courtesy Nancy Williams Showalter.)

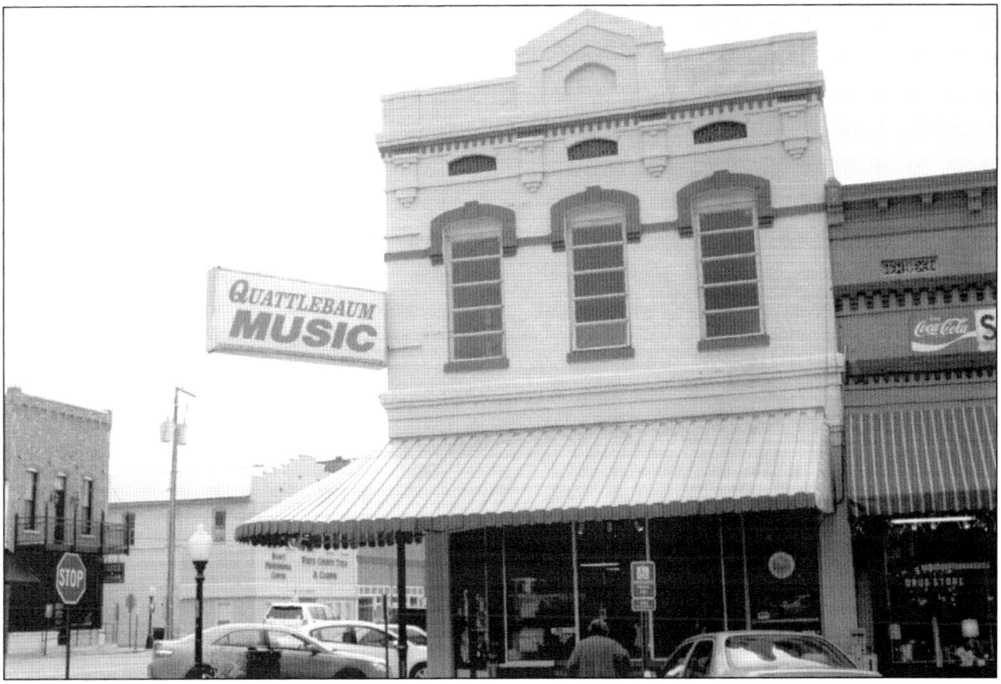

P.A. Robertson's Drug Store closed in the 1970s, and Quattlebaum Music has occupied the building since. Note the streetlight from the earlier photograph is still present on the corner. (Courtesy Carolyn Boyles.)

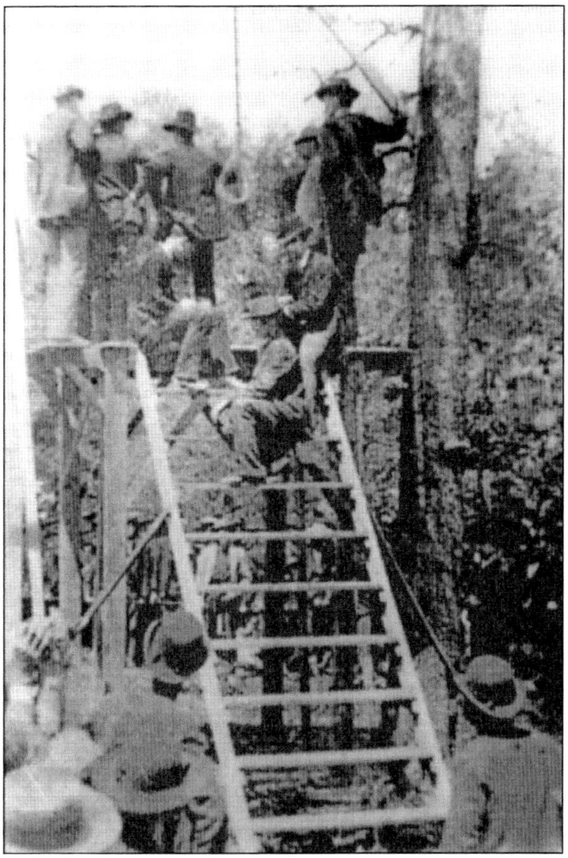

The last legal hanging in White County occurred on May 30, 1886, when George Carroll met his demise at the gallows. Carroll murdered his wife, Elizabeth, by pushing her into a well. His accomplice, Delvina ("Viney") Pool Tidwell, is alleged to have held Elizabeth Carroll underwater until she drowned. Delvina turned state's evidence and was released. The man resting one hand on the tree is Sheriff Ford, the executioner. The tree was near where the Searcy public swimming pool is today. (Courtesy Nancy Williams Showalter.)

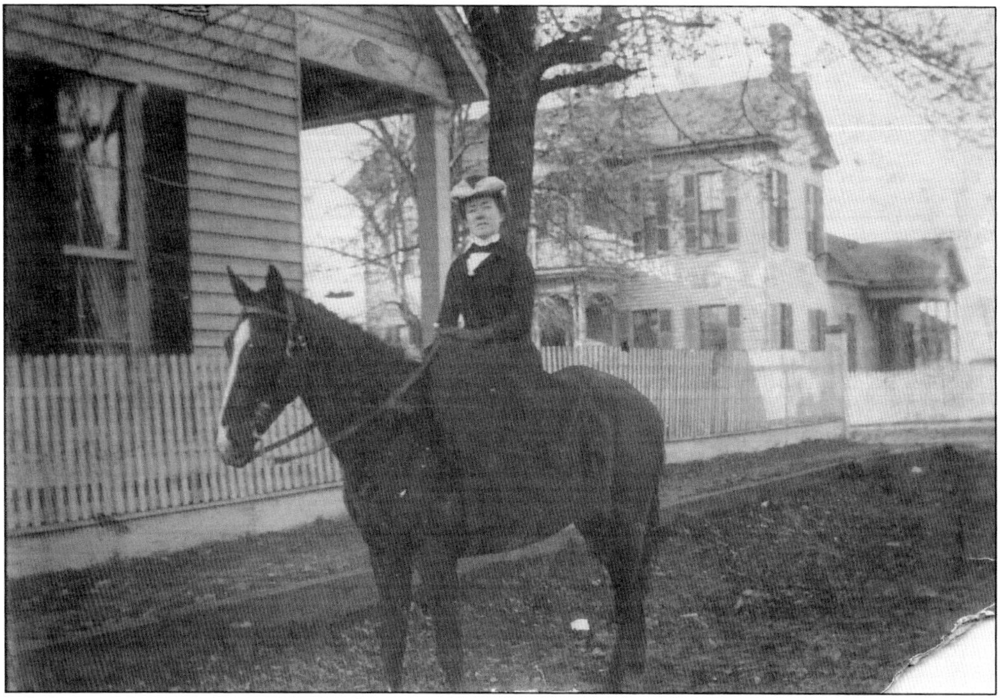

Miss McKennon was a music teacher at the Searcy Female Institute/Academy that, after being damaged by fire, reopened in 1868. The house in the background, on the corner of Race Avenue and North Main Street, was the home of Dr. S.T. (Thomas) Tapscott Sr. (Courtesy Nancy Williams Showalter.)

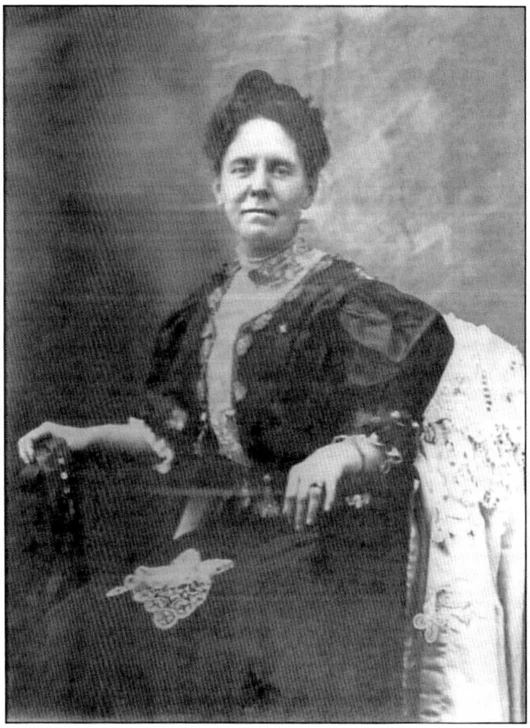

Mrs. Richard Willis, wife of the local Presbyterian minister, was co-owner and head teacher of Searcy Female Institute from 1891 to 1907. She came from a highly educated family. The school was founded by Mrs. Willis and Cora Tapscott, daughter of the local physician, Dr. S.T. Tapscott. The school emphasized instruction in both liberal and fine arts instead of more masculine pursuits like math and science. (Courtesy Eloise Muncy.)

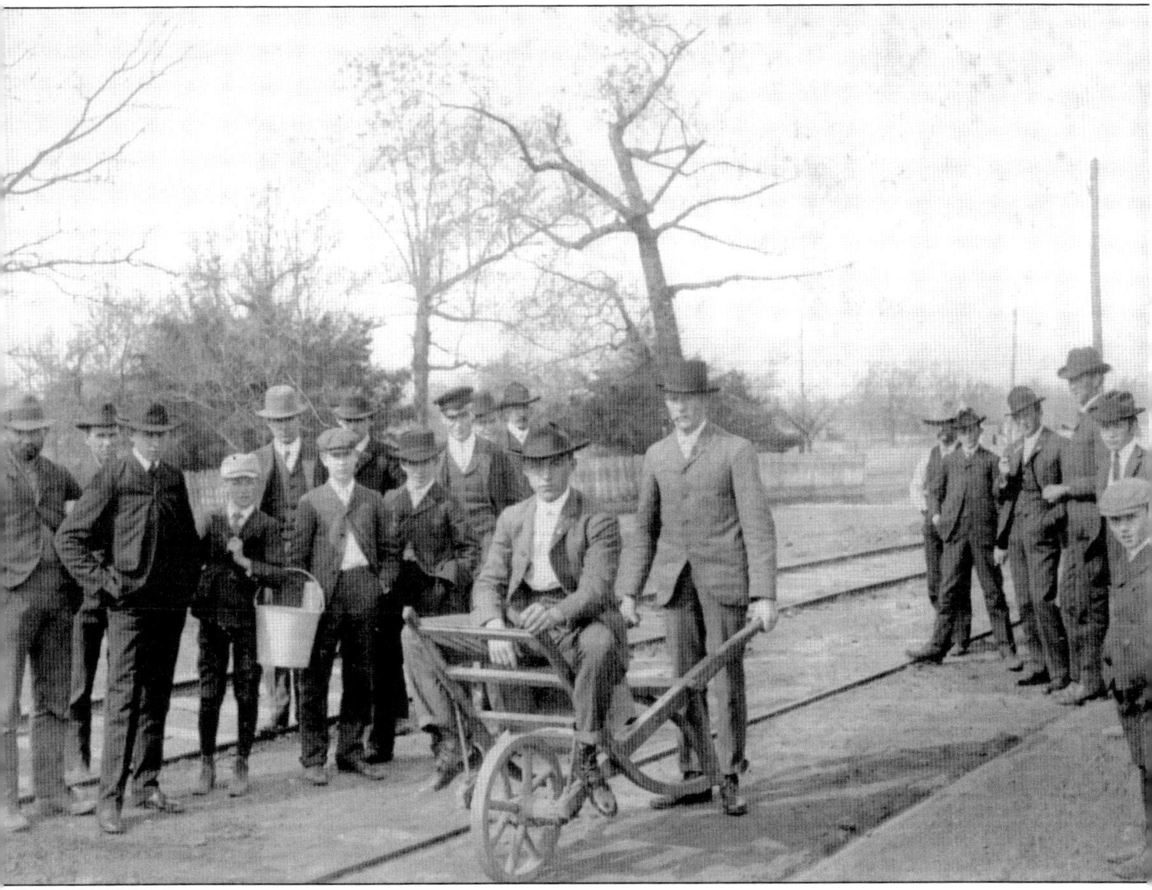

This c. 1900 photograph supposedly shows the results of a bet on an election. The man riding in the wheelbarrow is Missouri & Northern Arkansas (M&NA) Railroad conductor Ed Ferrell, who won the bet, and this was the payoff. Claude King is the wheelbarrow driver. King ran a dray service in town and played in the local brass band. The wheelbarrow supposedly came from the Henry Wrape Company's plant owned by Searcy Flooring & Lumber Company. The bearded man is "Whiskers" Simpson, a professional slaughterer for the town's many meat markets. The location is near the old Rock Island train depot. The fence in the background enclosed Spring Park. (Courtesy Eloise Muncy.)

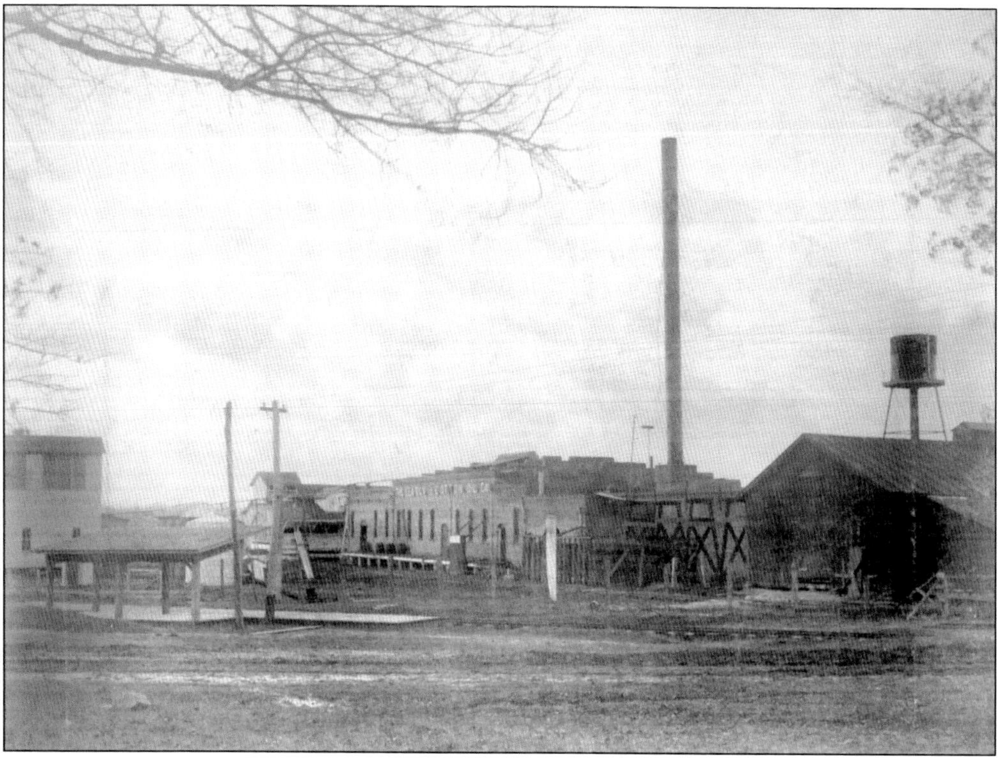

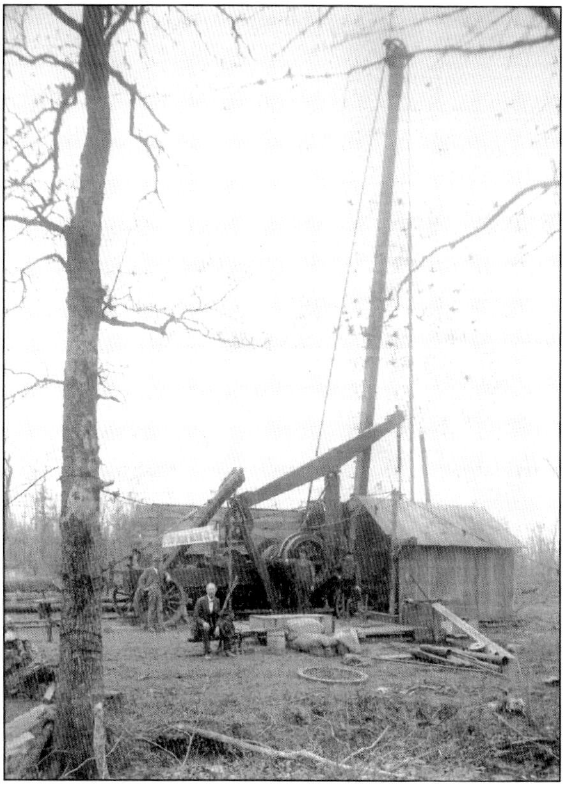

This photograph of the Searcy Cotton Oil Company was taken around 1900. The company was in business as late as 1932, according to the *American Fertilizer Hand Book*. (Courtesy WCHS.)

One of the first efforts to find gas and/or oil in White County was this test well drilled northwest of Four Mill Hill and Highway 16, near the Sidon community. It went down 1,400 feet before being abandoned. It was redrilled in 1923, but interest in the possibility about gas and oil in the Searcy area was abandoned until recent years, when modern drilling equipment and more sophisticated geological technical knowledge became available to locate and access underground natural gas deposits. (Courtesy Leon and Sherry Person.)

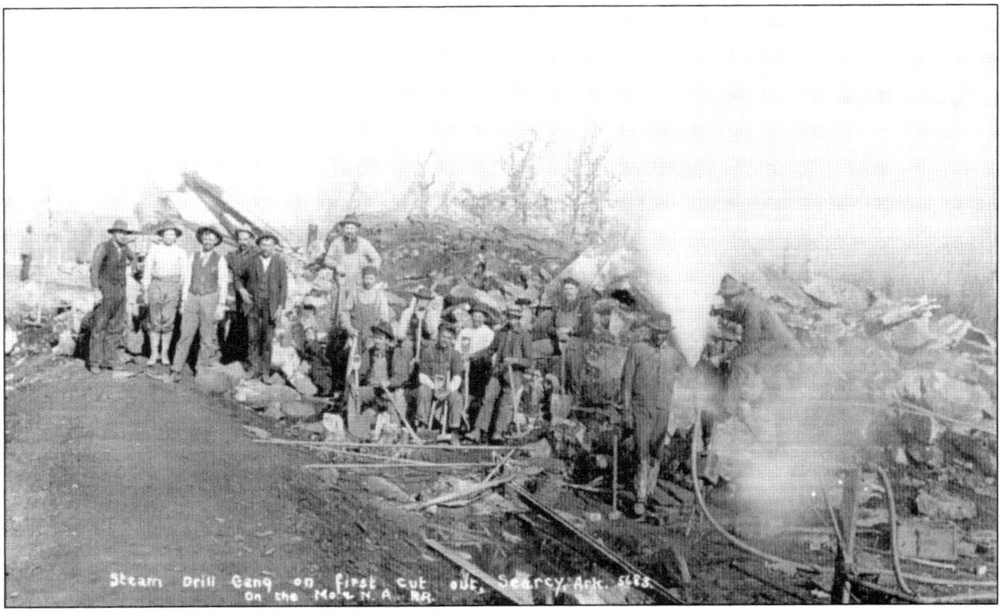

In 1910, local businessmen hired workers to build track for a connecting railroad shuttle between Kensett, Arkansas, and Searcy over M&NA Railroad tracks. This steam-drill gang worked on the first cut out. The Doniphan (Missouri), Kensett, and Searcy (DK&S) tracks connected Searcy to rail service. People in the area referred to the M&NA trains as "May Never Arrive." (Courtesy WCHS.)

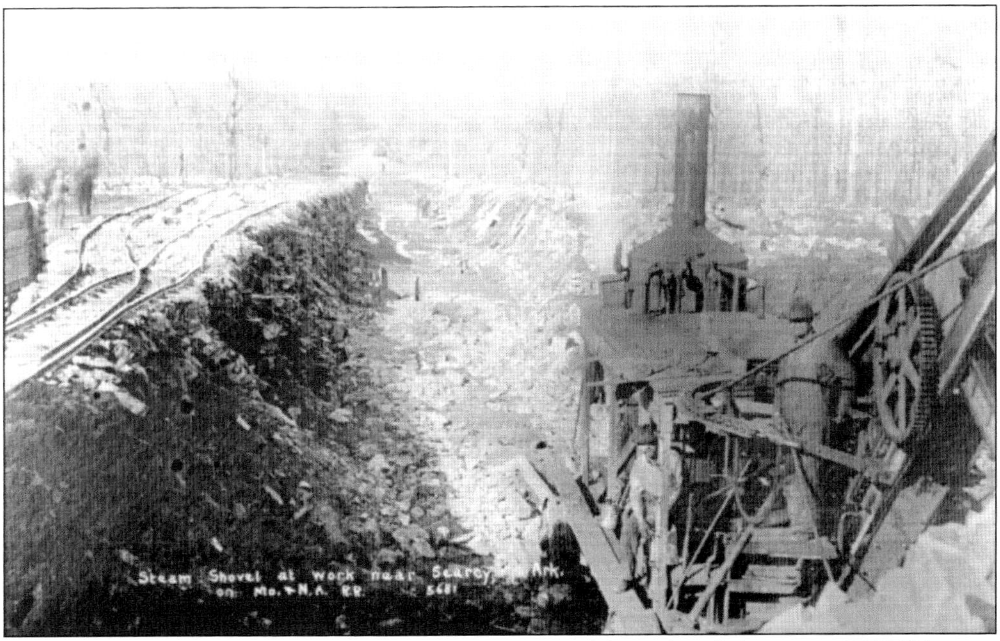

A man operates the steam shovel during construction of the railroad. (Courtesy WCHS.)

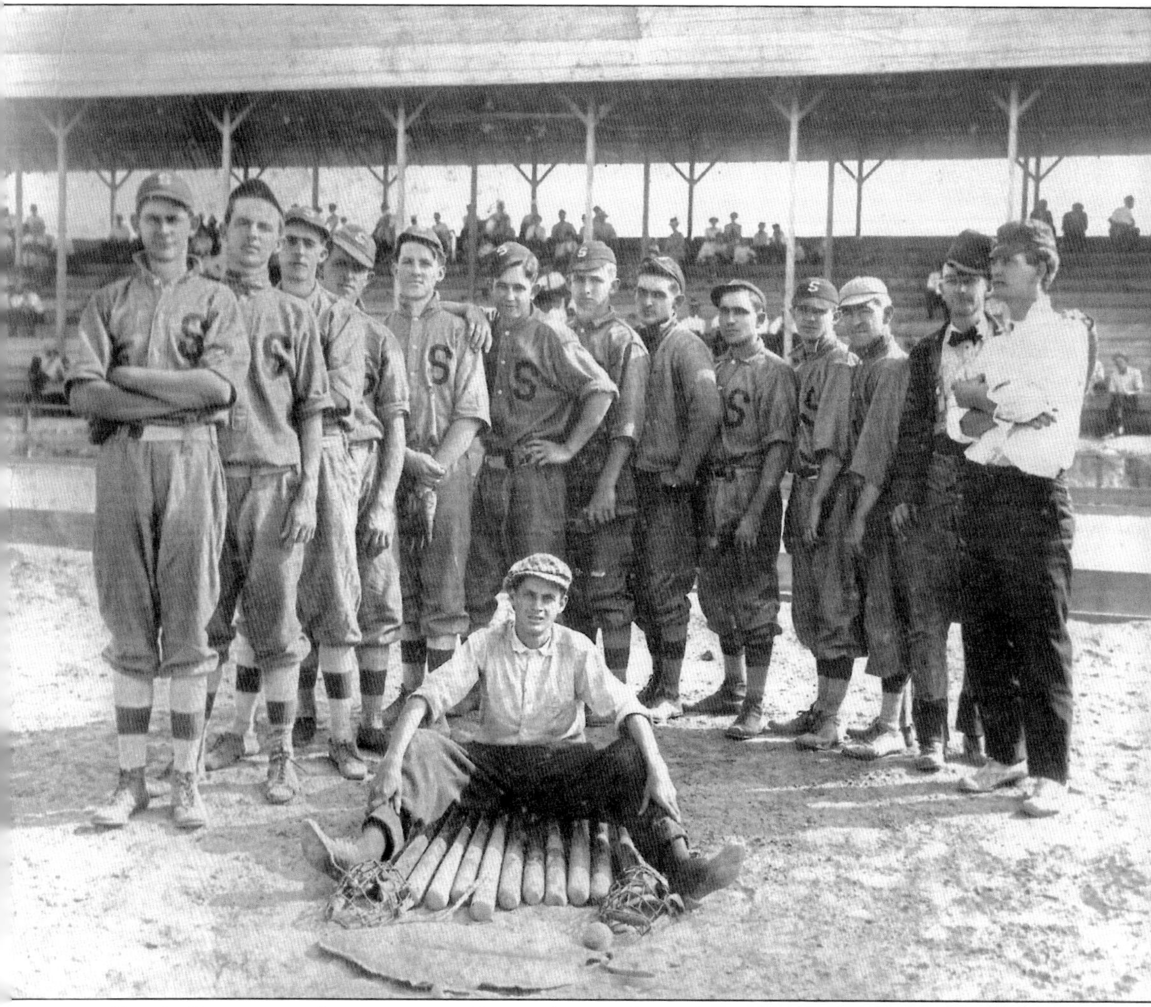

Baseball was a popular pastime in Searcy during the early part of the 20th century. The Searcy Bullets baseball team of 1912 is pictured here. They are, from left to right, Jordan Lambert, Will Yarnell, Chuck Stine, Oitho Ballew, Ben Mayo, Piggy Sinclair, James Skillern, captain Beule Welch, Green Booth, Ed Robbins, Son Sanford, manager Bill Black, Coach Hall, and mascot Papa Jack Griffin (seated). In the late 1920s, the team's name was changed to the Searcy Klondykes in recognition of a popular strawberry variety grown in and around Searcy. (Courtesy Nancy Williams Showalter.)

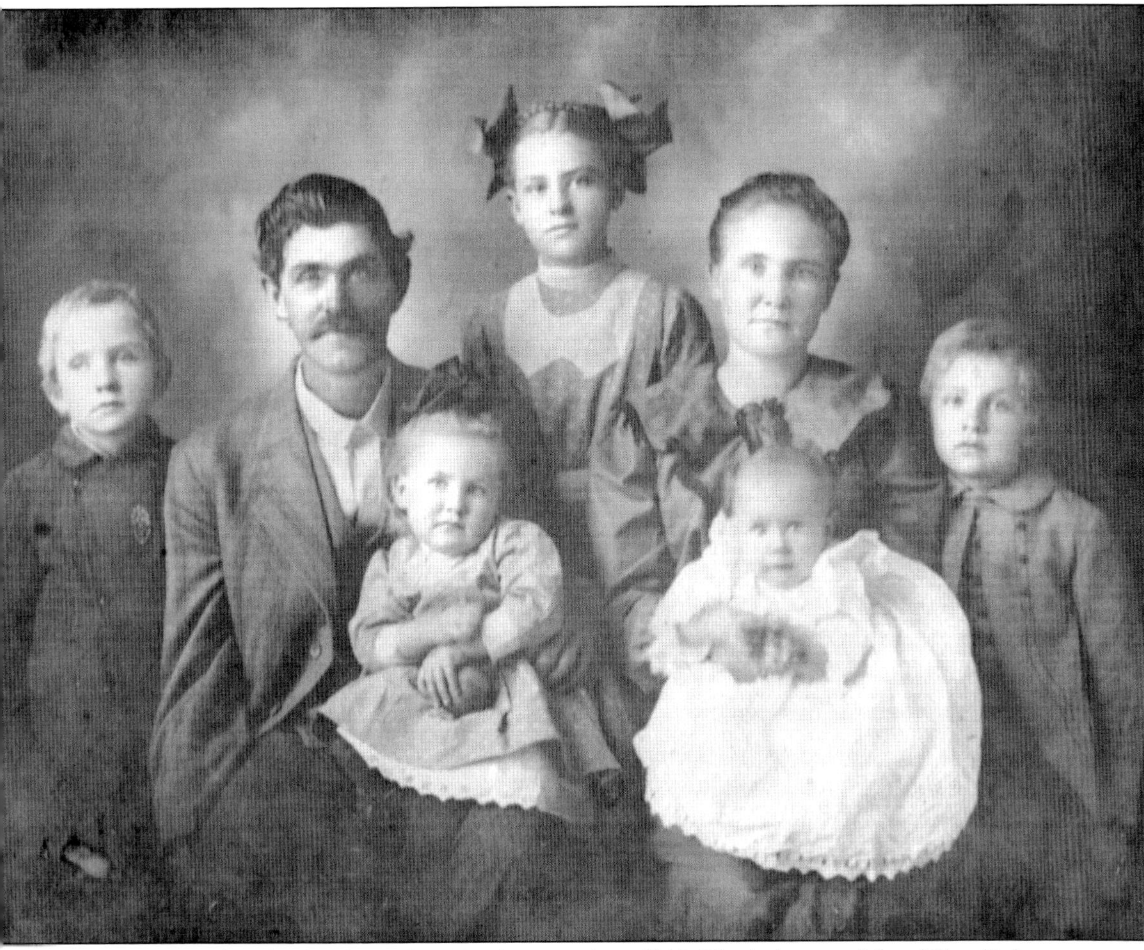

The John Samuel Coles family sat for this photograph in 1912. The babies are Mary Ellen Coles (left) and Irma Coles; the rest of the family, from left to right, is Cecil Coles, John Samuel Coles, Clara Coles, Ella Virgin Doyle Coles, and George Coles. Clara Coles Benson went on to own and manage the Benson Boarding House at 103 West Pleasure Avenue in Searcy in the 1940s. Mary Ellen Coles married Thomas J. Haynie. (Courtesy Nadine Haynie Birdwell.)

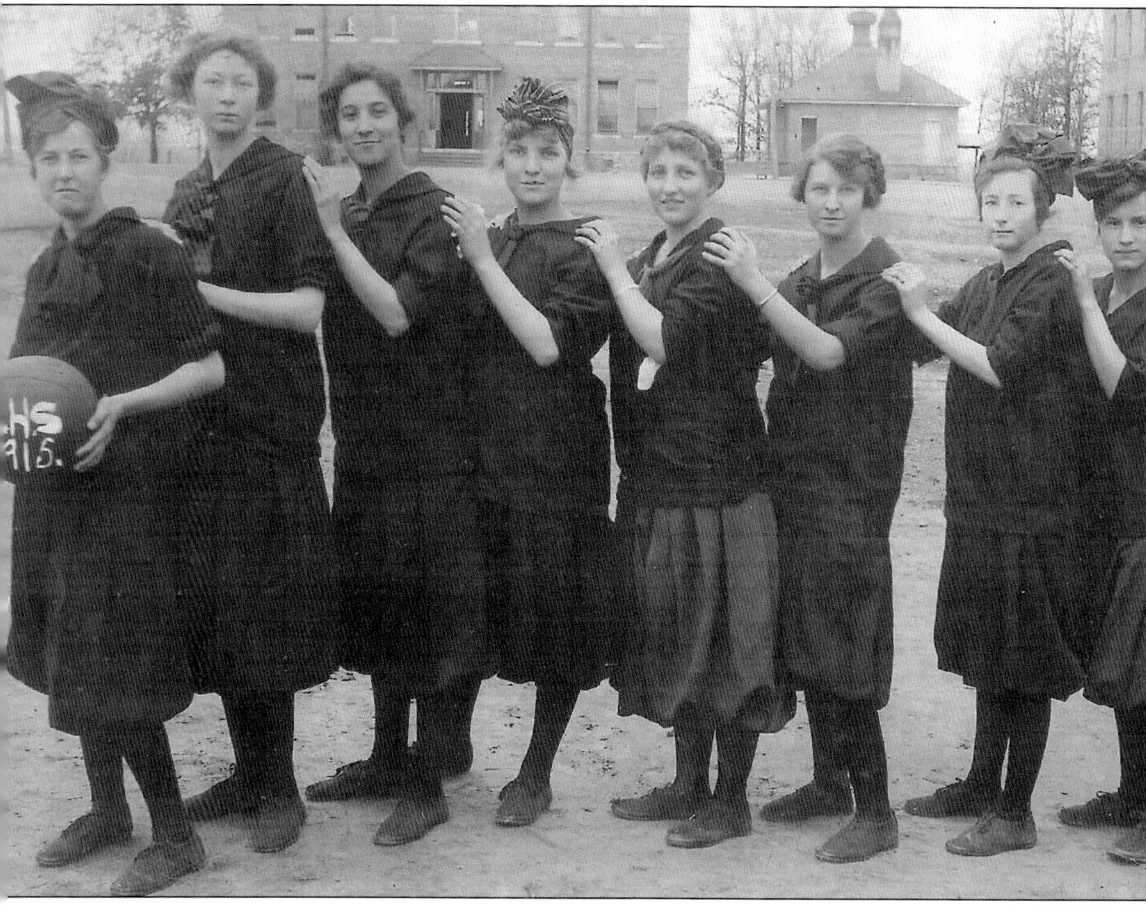

The 1915 Searcy High School girls' basketball team was a good-looking bunch, but they are unidentified. The big building directly behind the girls is said to have served as the sixth-grade building in later years, while the smaller building has been identified at various times as restrooms, the steam-heat building, and the superintendent's office. The building partially shown in the top right corner was identified as a public school in Searcy on a postcard addressed to Odeen Smith in Searcy, Arkansas. There is no postmark, but the message is signed "L.L.," and the card bears a 1¢ stamp. (Courtesy Betsy Bailey.)

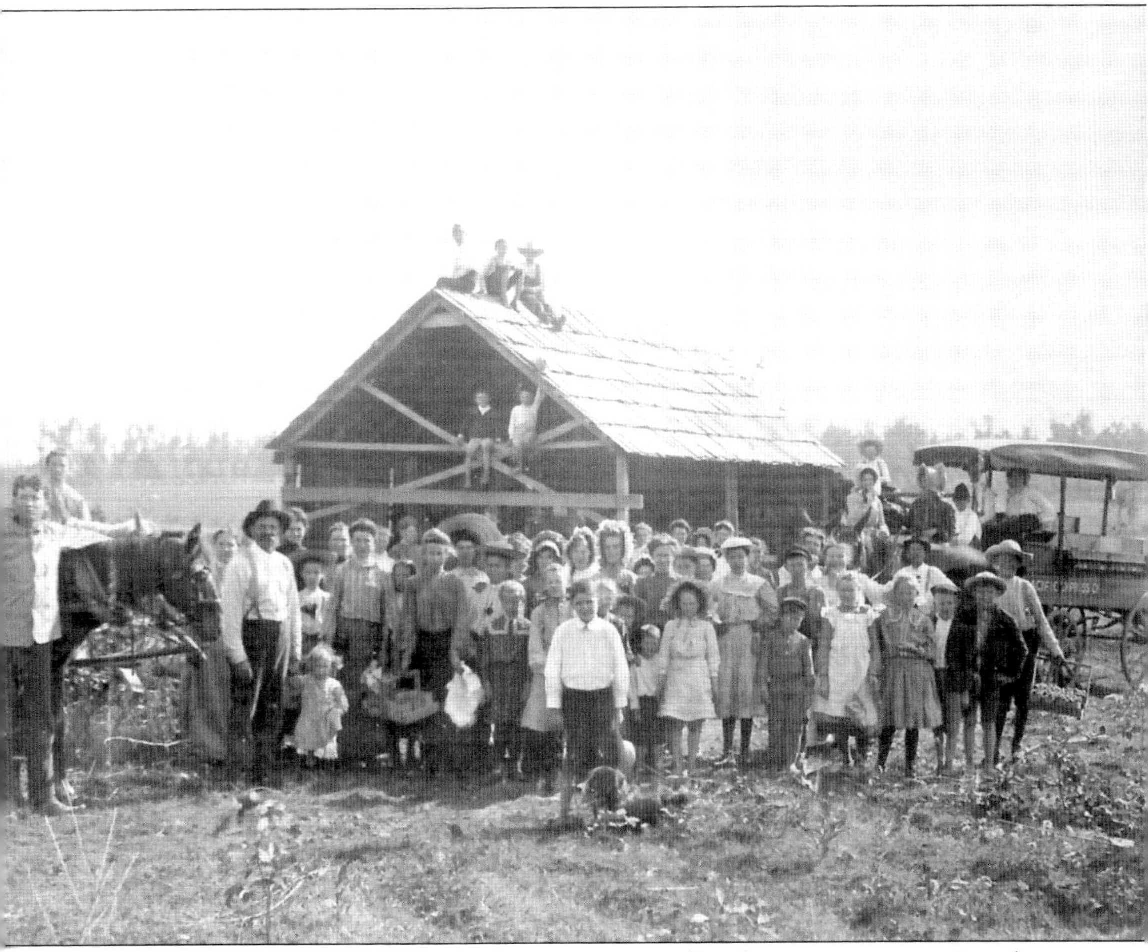

Strawberries have been a major crop in the Searcy area—as well as the entire country—since the 1920s. Between 1920 and 1930, two local strawberry growers' associations shipped 810,170 crates of strawberries nationwide. The going rate for picking strawberries was 3¢ per quart. Youngsters could make around $3 per day. Note the mule-drawn Pacific Express Company wagon, at right, standing by to take the daily picking to market. (Courtesy Eloise Muncy.)

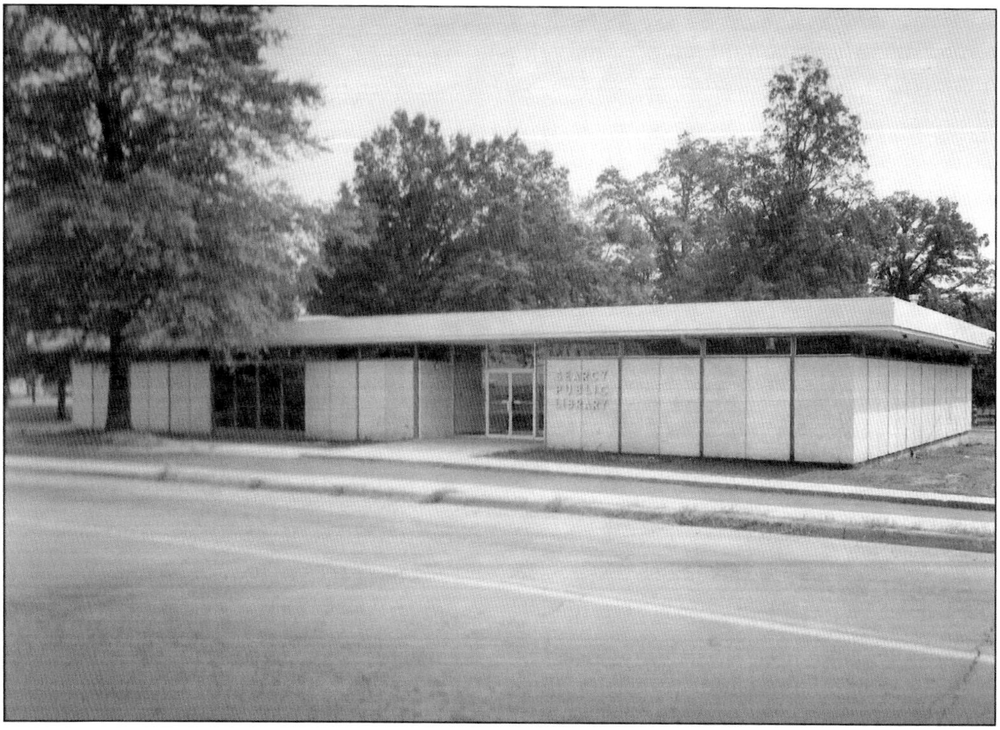

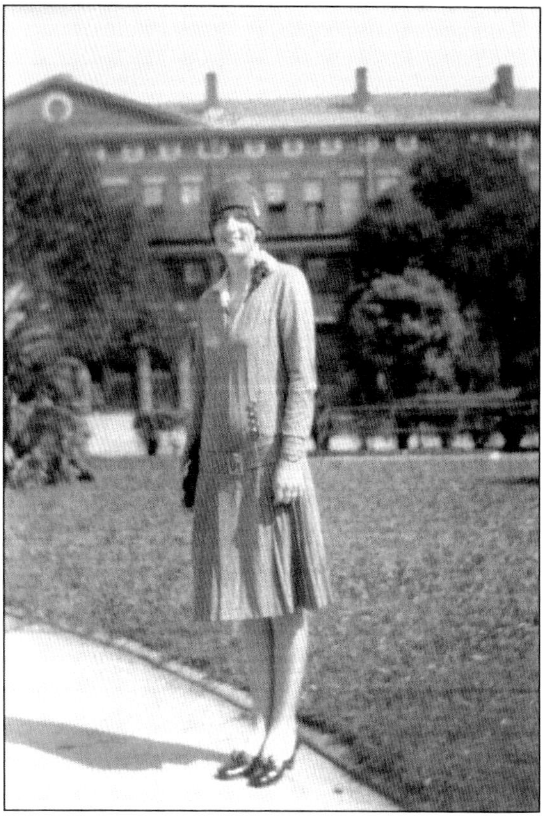

Searcy Public Library, which opened in 1966 in Spring Park, where the older library stood, is also the headquarters for the White County Regional Library System. The system includes seven branch libraries. The regional offices have now moved into the Ewing P. Pyeatt Building next to the library, which was vacated by the Searcy Regional Chamber of Commerce in 1999. The public library has an Arkansas room, a children's library, and a computer room. (Courtesy Darla Ino.)

Nancy Lee Yarnell Taylor, granddaughter of Israel M. Moore and mother of Mary Lou Taylor Dunn, was one of Searcy's most prominent citizens in the early part of the 20th century. She and Elmo Taylor were married in Searcy, and this photograph was taken in New Orleans while the couple was on their honeymoon. (Courtesy Mary Lou Dunn.)

Elmo Taylor was first Judicial District circuit judge for 26 years. When he retired on December 31, 1974, he had held the office longer than any other circuit judge in Arkansas. He was cochairman, with W.H. Roth, of Searcy's centennial celebration in 1937. (Courtesy Mary Lou Dunn.)

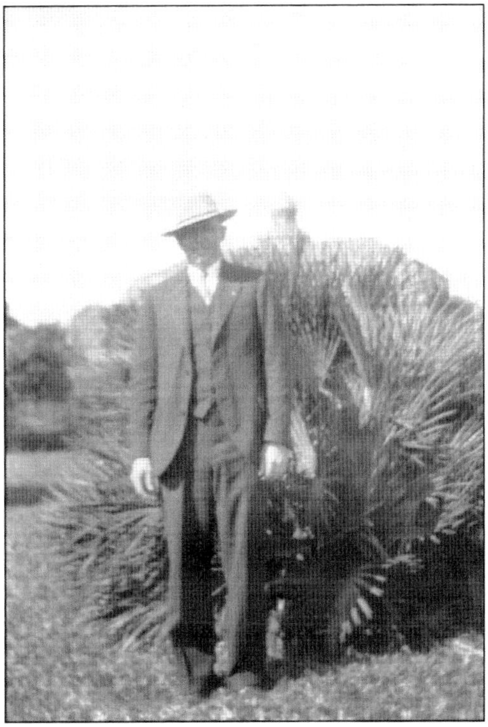

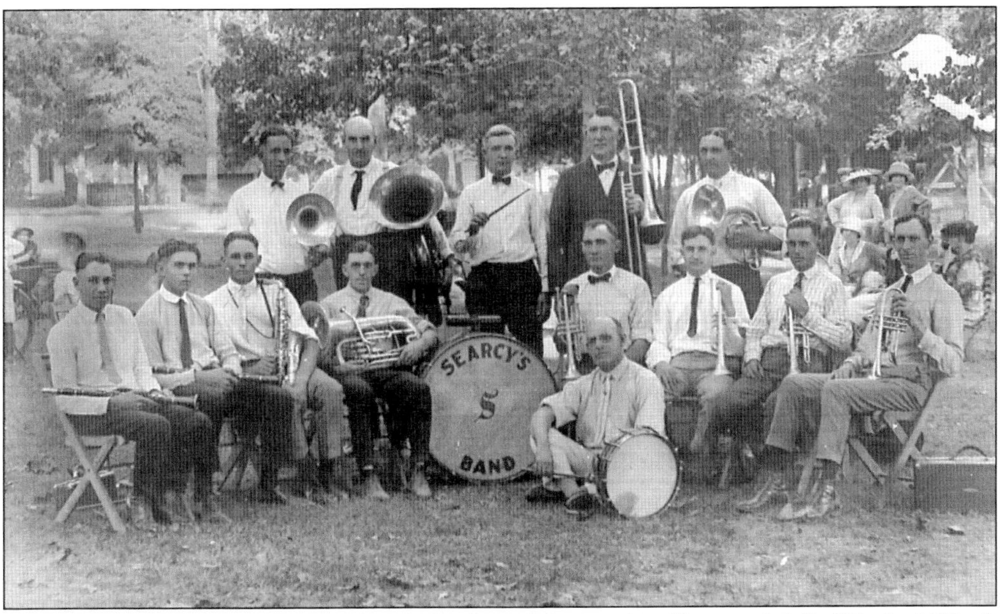

Members of this old Searcy Band include, from left to right, (first row) L.R. Winfred Word, Rowland Kingsley, Gerald Phillips, Karl Wilson, ? Dragoo (seated on the ground), John Carter, Dr. R.W. Toler, ? Ring, and A.T. Darnell; (second row) Neal Peebles, ? Cathcart, unidentified, Claude King, and Radney Phillips. Bands often played in Spring Park during the 1920s and 1930s. A Dragoo's Studio, where high school students would go to dance, was located on a second floor, above another business, during the 1920s. The Mr. Dragoo in this photograph may have been involved with its operation. (Courtesy Nancy Williams Showalter.)

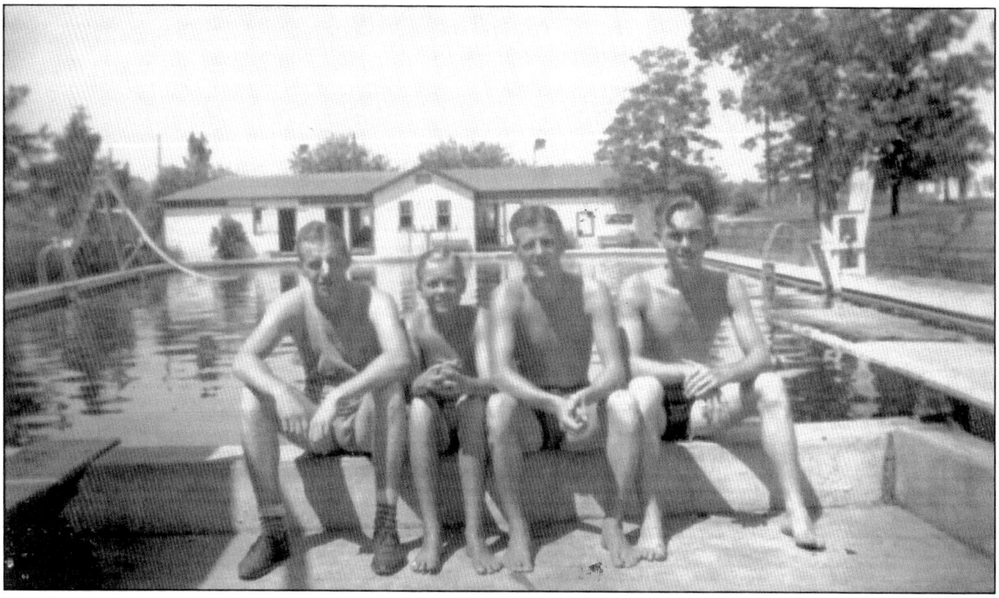

These young men cooled off during a typical humid Arkansas summer with a swim at the Searcy pool in 1935. From left to right are James Harris, Wayne "Pudney" Pasley, Bill Harris, and Jack Bomar. (Courtesy Nancy Williams Showalter.)

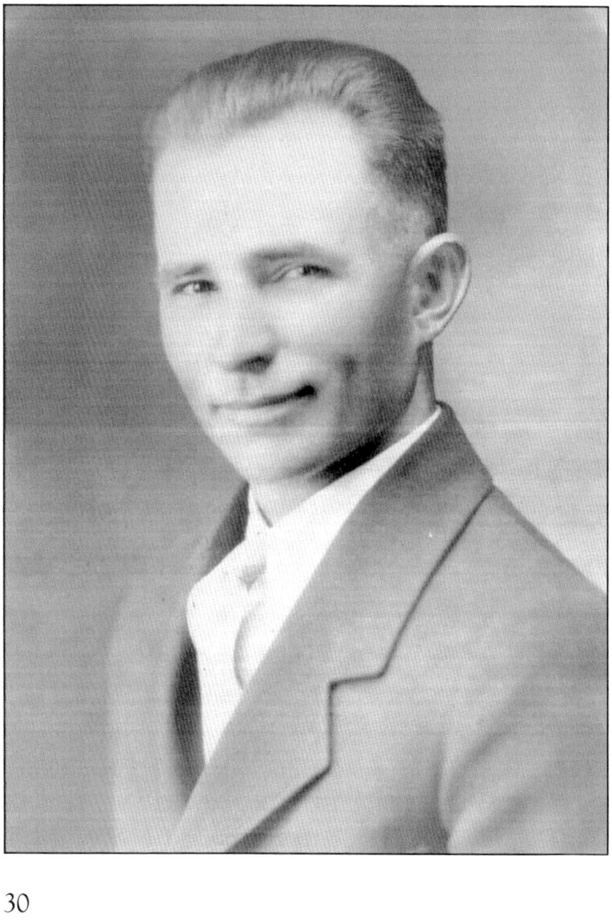

Hubert Lemuel Coward was notable in Searcy during the 1920s through the 1960s for a variety of reasons. A large tree existed on North Main Street, under which new arrivals to town would camp. In 1929, Coward tired of this practice and cut down the tree. As a new recruit to the Searcy Fire Department in 1943, he had the dubious honor of helping to extinguish a conflagration at the L.A. Thompson Cotton Company. He saved the town and eventually became fire chief. (Courtesy Mary Beth Weir Waters.)

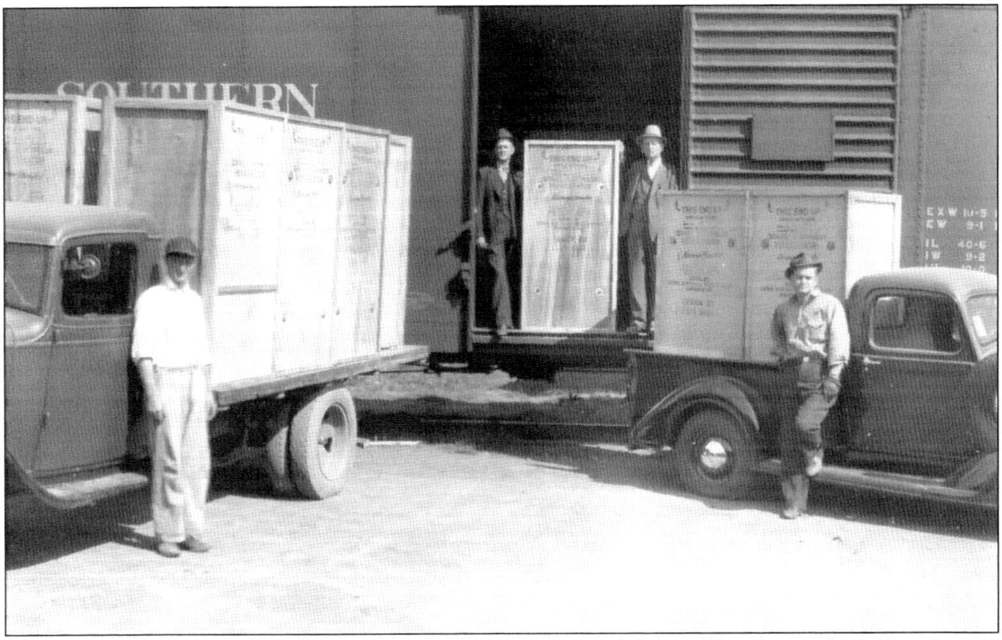

Men from Moye and Young Mercantile unload refrigerators from a boxcar on the railroad track that ran in front of Spring Park. The man on the left is unidentified, Otto Young and John Moye (right) are inside the boxcar, and Harold Moye is leaning against the truck on the right. (Courtesy Johnice Young Hearn.)

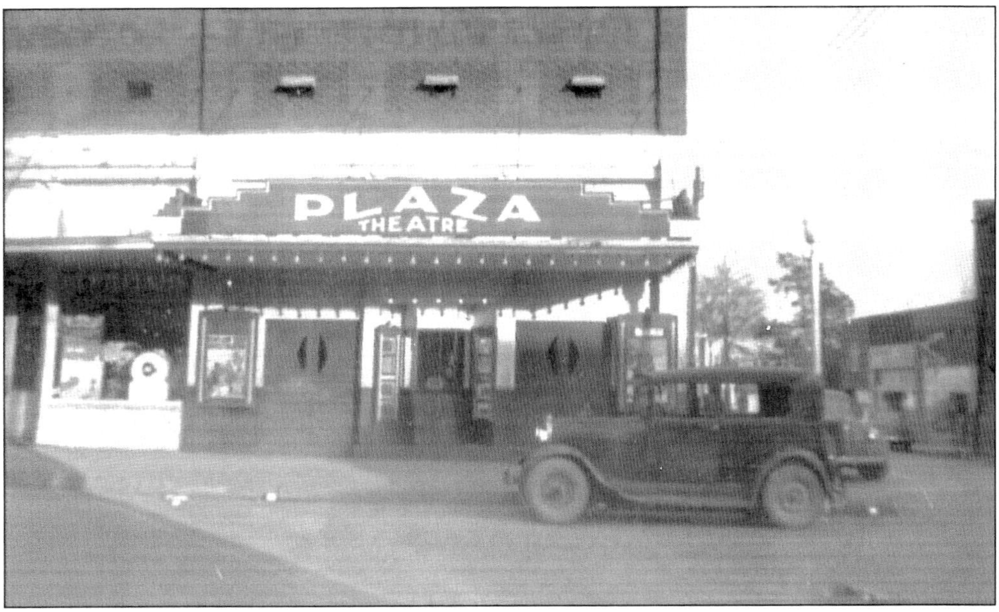

The Plaza Theatre was located on the corner of Spring and Center Streets, across from the Mayfair Hotel, in downtown Searcy in the 1930s. K.K. (Deacon) King, who came to Searcy from Batesville in 1937, owned the theater and had a contest to name it—Marie Hassell won the contest with her suggestion of "Plaza." (Courtesy Eloise Muncy.)

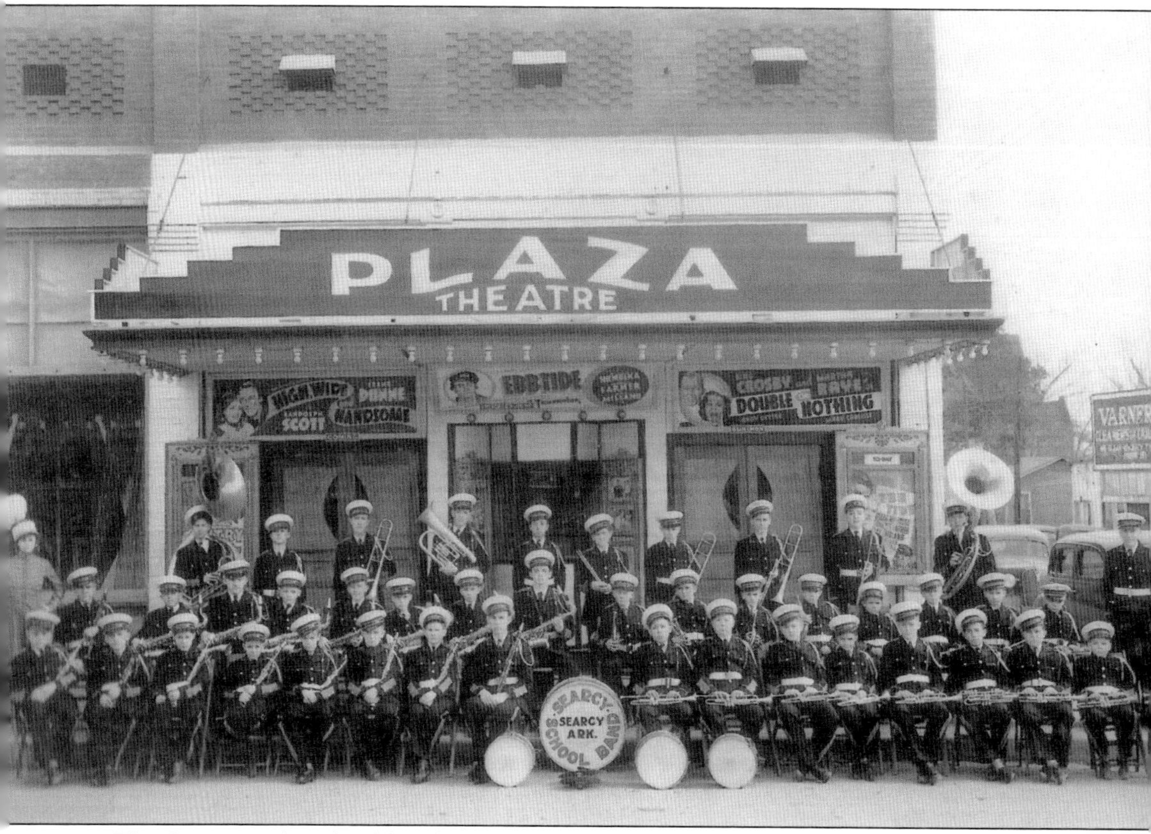

The Searcy High School band posed for this photograph outside the Plaza Theatre. School bands traditionally led parades through the city. Searcy's tradition of award-winning bands has continued through the years. Varner's Cleaners & Tailors was located on the side street across from the Plaza. The featured movies at the time were *High, Wide, and Handsome*, with Randolph Scott and Irene Dunne; *Ebb Tide*, with Oskar Homolka, Frances Farmer, and Ray Milland; and *Double or Nothing*, with Bing Crosby and Martha Raye—all of which date this photograph to 1937. (Courtesy Nancy Williams Showalter.)

Elwanda Hoofman and Lt. Robert Scott Bell were married on August 21, 1943, at Gentry Memorial Baptist Church on Spring Street (across from the Plaza Theatre). After being promoted to major, Bell died on March 23, 1951, when he disappeared while flying off the coast of Ireland during the Korean conflict. Bell is remembered for buzzing the courthouse as a young pilot. His sons, Robert Scott Bell Jr. and Arthur Watson Bell, live in Searcy. (Courtesy Jean Ann Bell.)

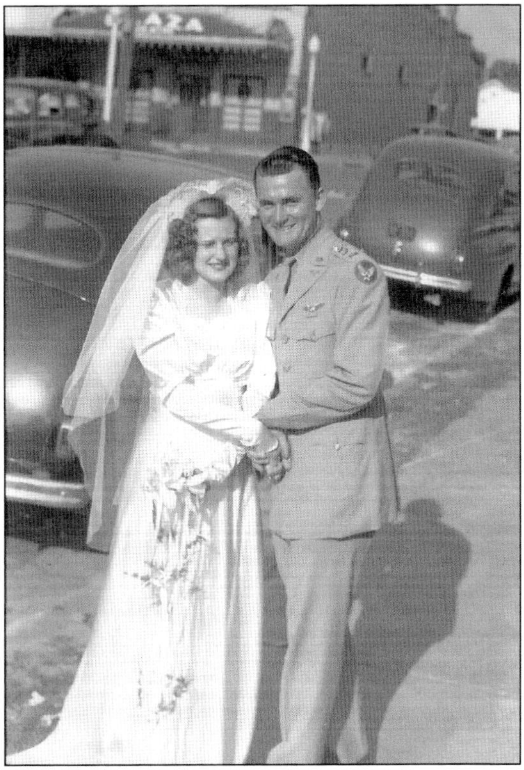

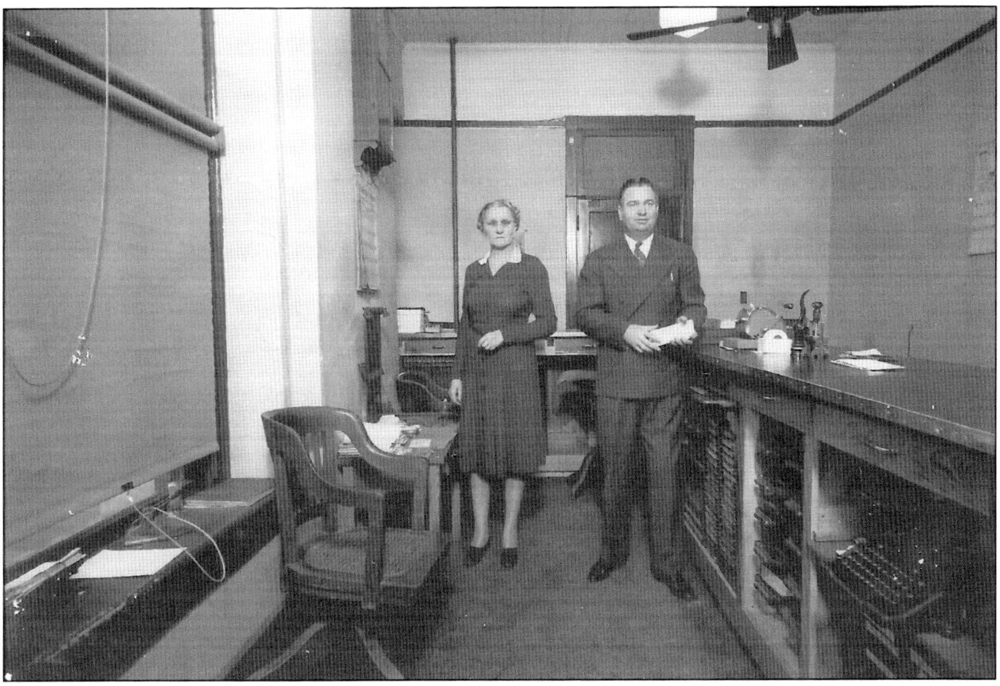

Mrs. Crockett and Floyd Bradberry pose for a photograph inside the tax collector's office at White County Courthouse. Bradberry worked as county clerk from 1936 through 1946 and served as tax collector from 1974 through 1980. (Courtesy Jim Bradberry.)

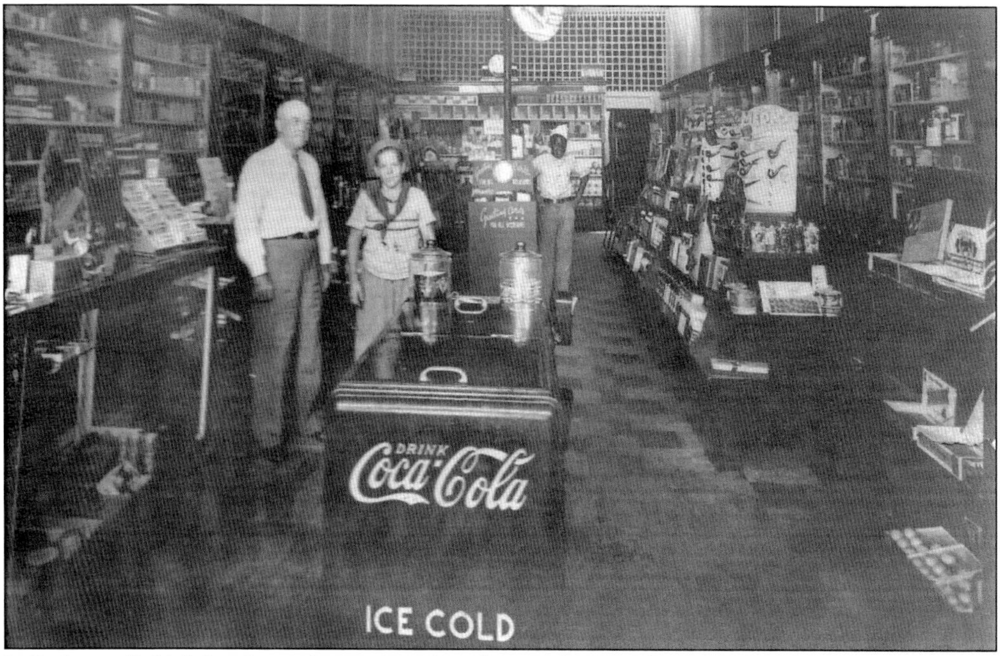

L.O. Stotts (left), John Stotts (center), and Willie Neeley stand inside Stotts Drug Store in 1938. L.O. Stotts came to Searcy in 1912. He was a graduate of the Atlanta College of Pharmacists, a member of the National Association of Retail Druggists, and a life member of the American Pharmaceutical Association. Stotts Drug Store is a familiar landmark on the square in Searcy. It was operated by L.O. Stotts' son-in-law Roger Williams until recently and is now operated by Williams' daughter Nancy Williams Showalter. (Courtesy Nancy Williams Showalter.)

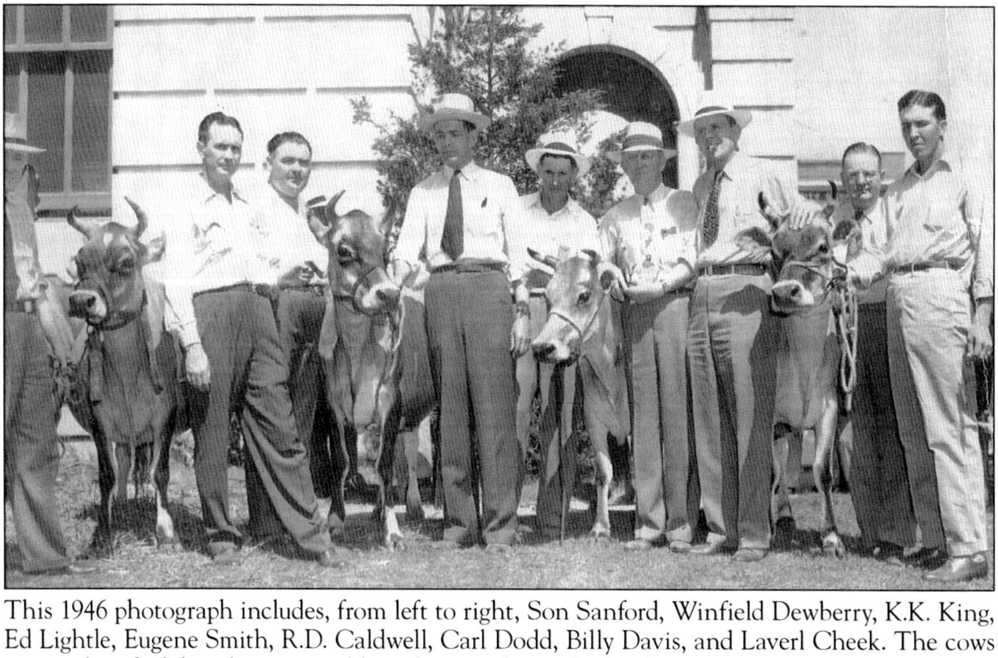

This 1946 photograph includes, from left to right, Son Sanford, Winfield Dewberry, K.K. King, Ed Lightle, Eugene Smith, R.D. Caldwell, Carl Dodd, Billy Davis, and Laverl Cheek. The cows are unidentified, but they were sold on the courthouse lawn after winning honors at the county fair. (Courtesy Nancy Williams Showalter.)

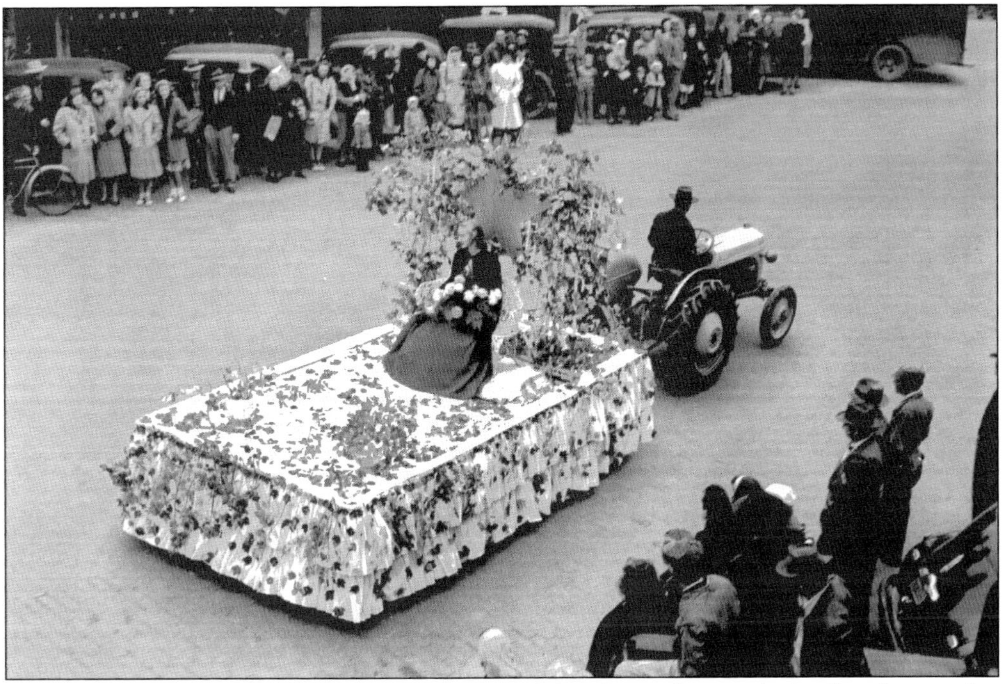

Searcy Fall Festival queen Tomile Abboud is paraded in front of a crowd of well-wishers in this image from the late 1940s. (Courtesy SRCC.)

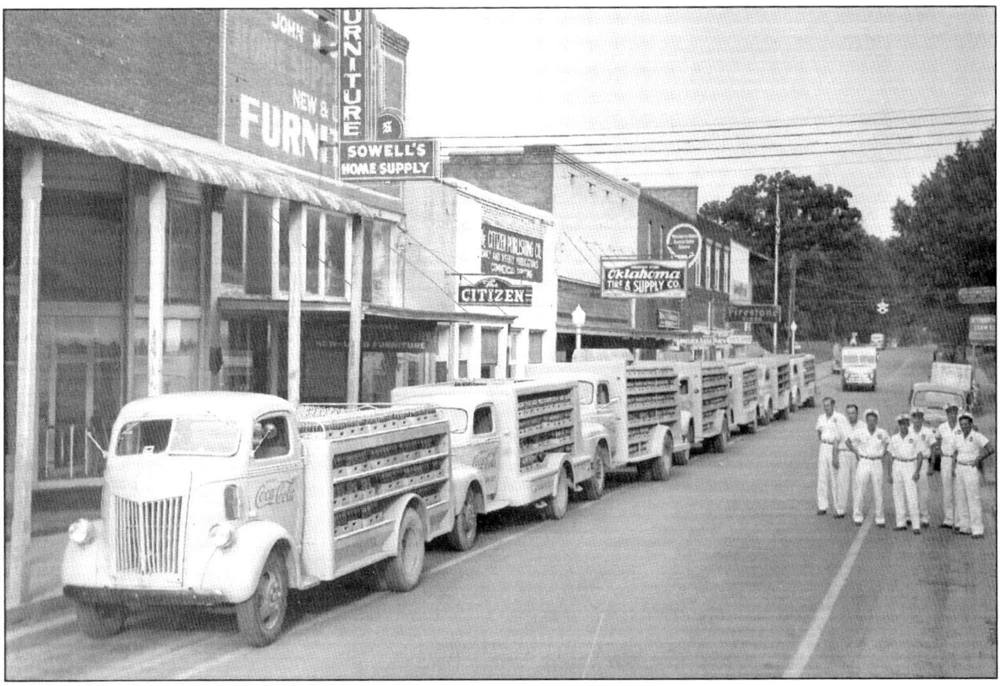

Employees of the Coca-Cola bottling plant on Arch Street in Searcy stand alongside the loaded delivery trucks across from the building in 1949. They are, from left to right, J.D. Greer, Oran West, Ocie Taylor, Richard Wooten, Buford Maddox, Lloyd Barratt, and Ralph Yearby. (Courtesy Buford Maddox.)

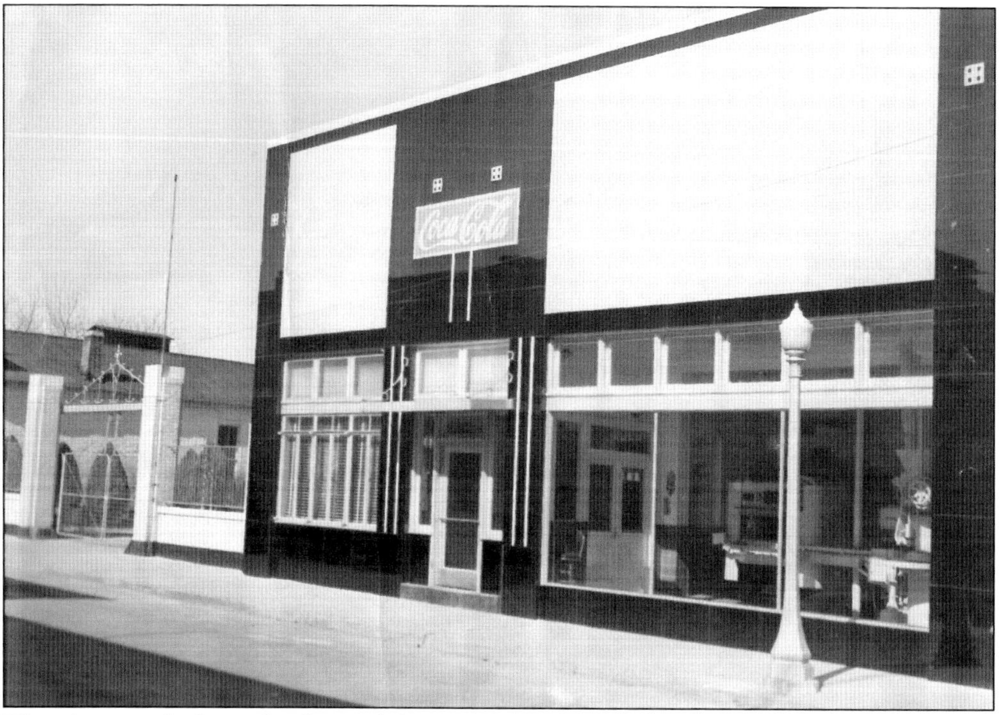

This photograph shows the front of the Coca-Cola plant. Sowell's Home Supply, the Citizen Publishing Company, and Oklahoma Tire and Supply Company were located across the street. (Courtesy Buford Maddox.)

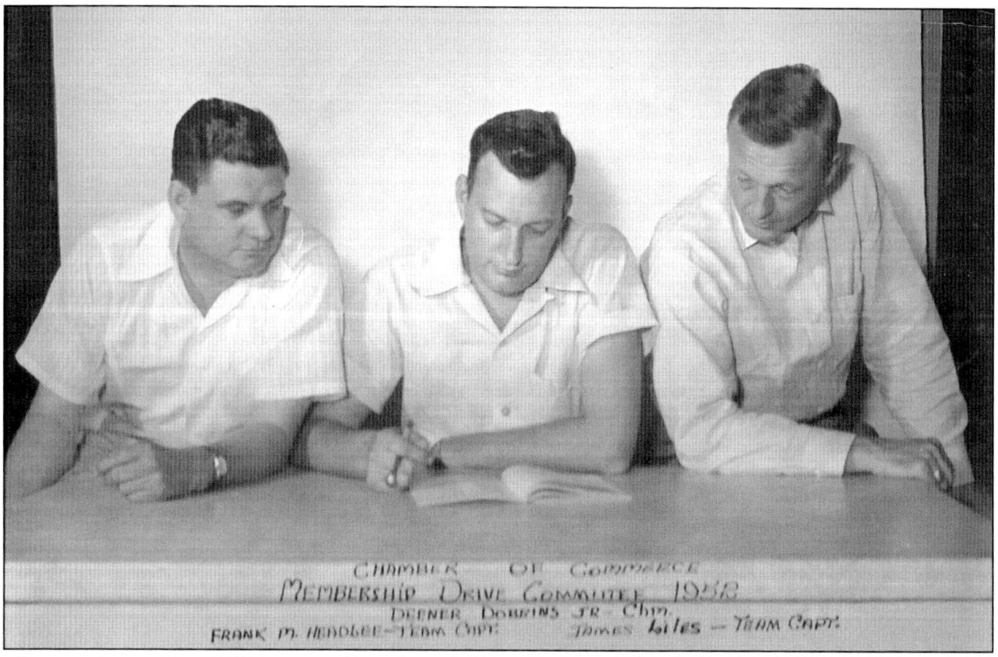

The members of the 1952 Searcy Chamber of Commerce Membership Drive Committee look over a publication. They are Deener Dobbins Jr. (left), Mayor Frank Headlee (center), and James Liles; Dobbins was the chairman, and Headlee and Liles were team captains. (Courtesy SRCC.)

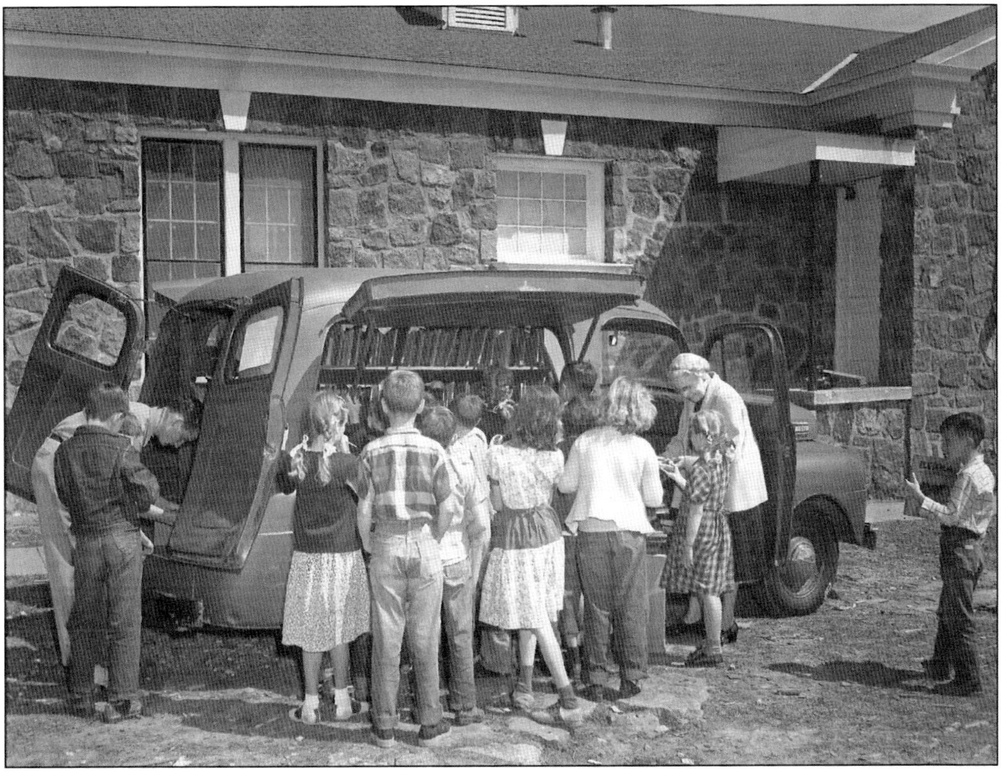

Inez Shannon Bishop, White County librarian, was instrumental in the growth of the Searcy Public Library. In 1955, she helped establish the first mobile library for children. The Bookmobile traveled through White County, offering books to both children and adults. Bishop served as librarian from 1952 through 1974. (Courtesy Darla Ino.)

Rodgers Perfection, World Grand Champion Tennessee Walking Horse in 1959, was trained and exhibited by Joe Webb. This horse was the third grand champion to come from the farm belonging to Dr. Porter Rodgers and his wife, Fern. The first was Old Glory's Big Man in 1950. The second was Go Boy's Shadow, who received the distinction in both 1955 and 1956. The Rodgerses held open house at their stables to acquaint people with their World Grand Champion Tennessee Walking Horse and to advertise the Arkansas State Horse Show. Proceeds from the Arkansas State Horse Show went to the Crippled Children's Colony of Arkansas. (Courtesy Hattie Mae Maddox.)

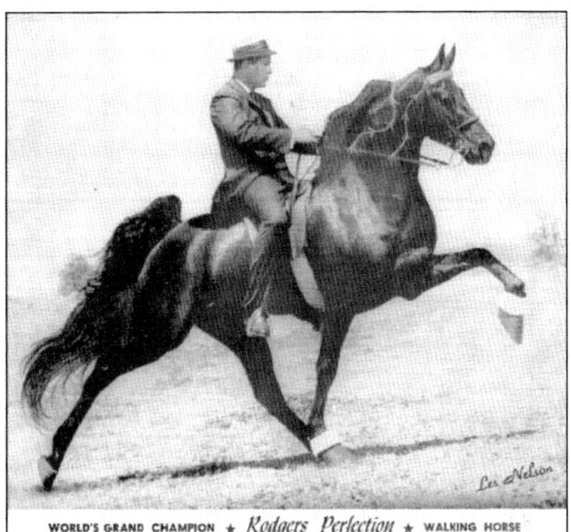

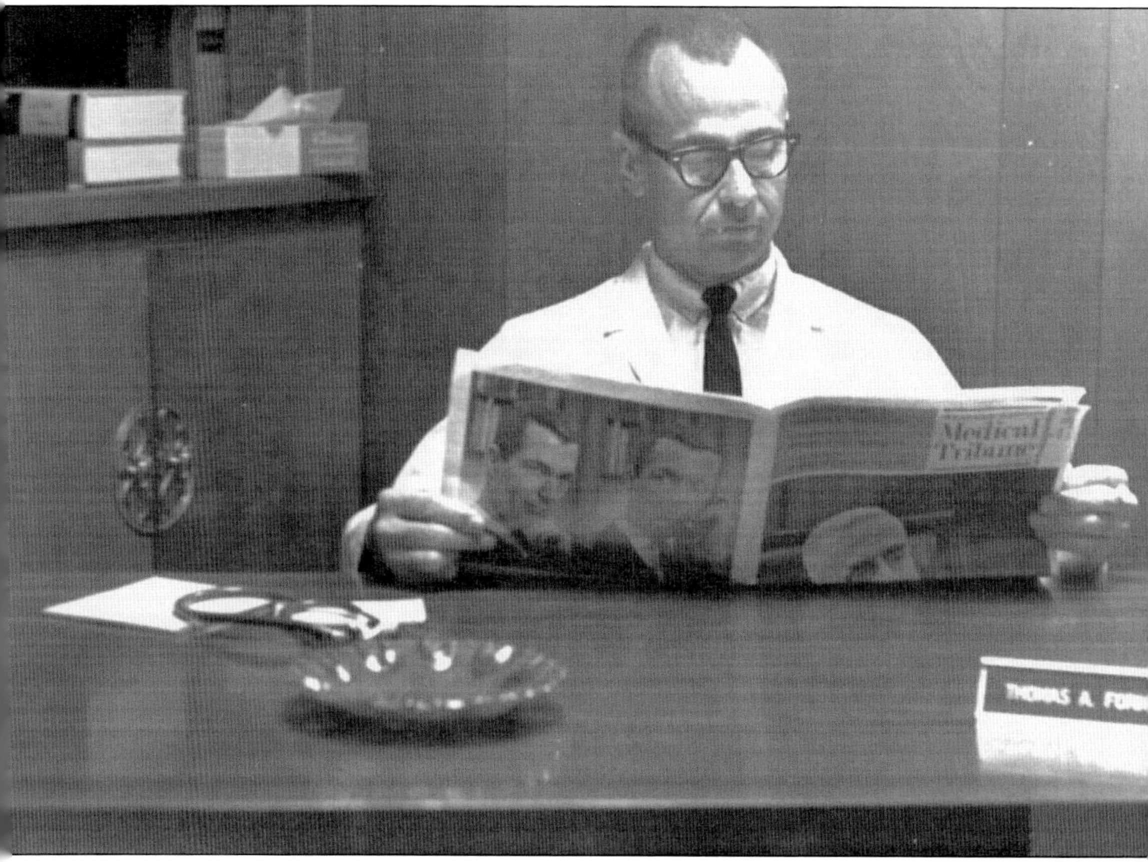

Dr. Thomas A. Formby enjoys his new office in the Searcy Clinic in 1960. Formby, along with Drs. A.R. Brown and William Davis, built the first modern health clinic in town. Dr. Formby came from Paragould to Searcy in 1953 to become associated with Dr. Martin Hawkins. The clinic was located at 910 East Race Avenue. It later merged with another clinic and became the Searcy Medical Center, which has grown to become the largest medical clinic in Searcy. (Courtesy Mary Formby.)

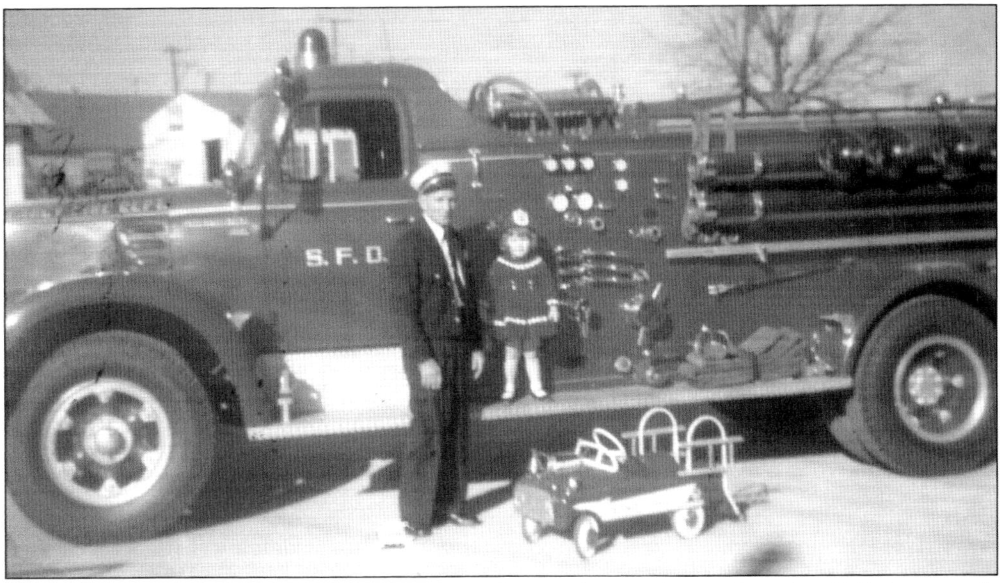

Searcy fire chief Hubert Coward stands next to the new Searcy fire truck in this 1961 photograph taken on Spruce Street. His granddaughter Mary Beth, age three, stands beside him admiring her own new pedal fire truck. (Courtesy Mary Beth Weir Waters.)

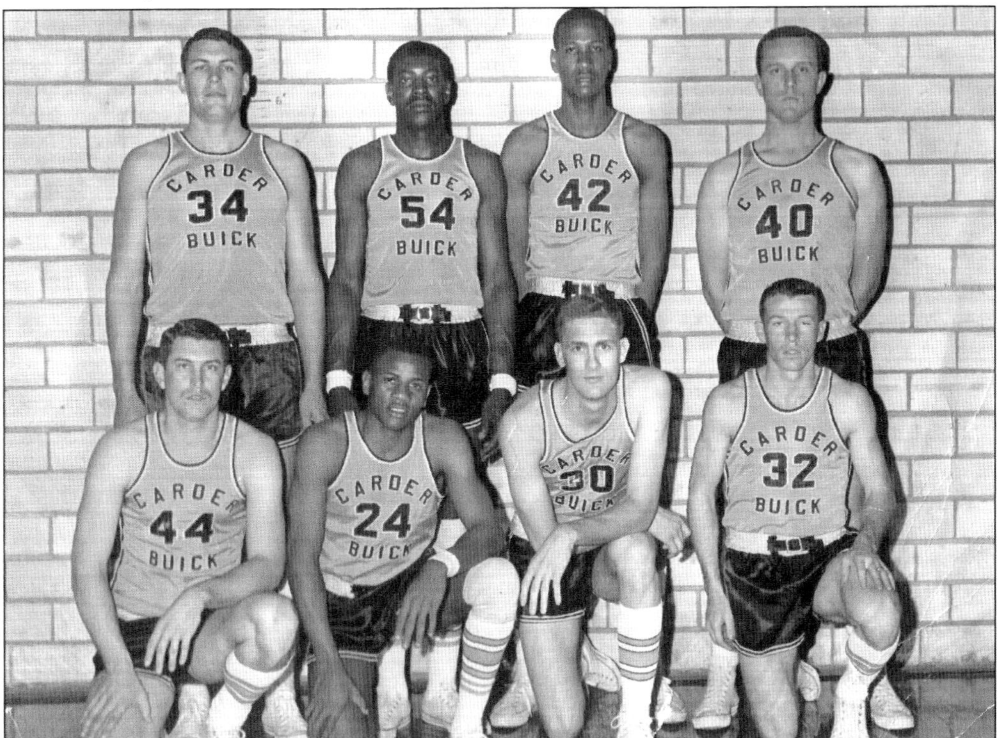

The Carder Buick Team from Searcy won the Arkansas Amateur Athletic Union Basketball Championship in 1969. The team members are, from left to right, (first row) Lavaughn Robertson, Donald Young, Bob Dobson, and Ned Boaz; (second row) David Seward, Napolian Cross, Grady Norman, and Jim Thompson. (Courtesy David and Mattie Seward.)

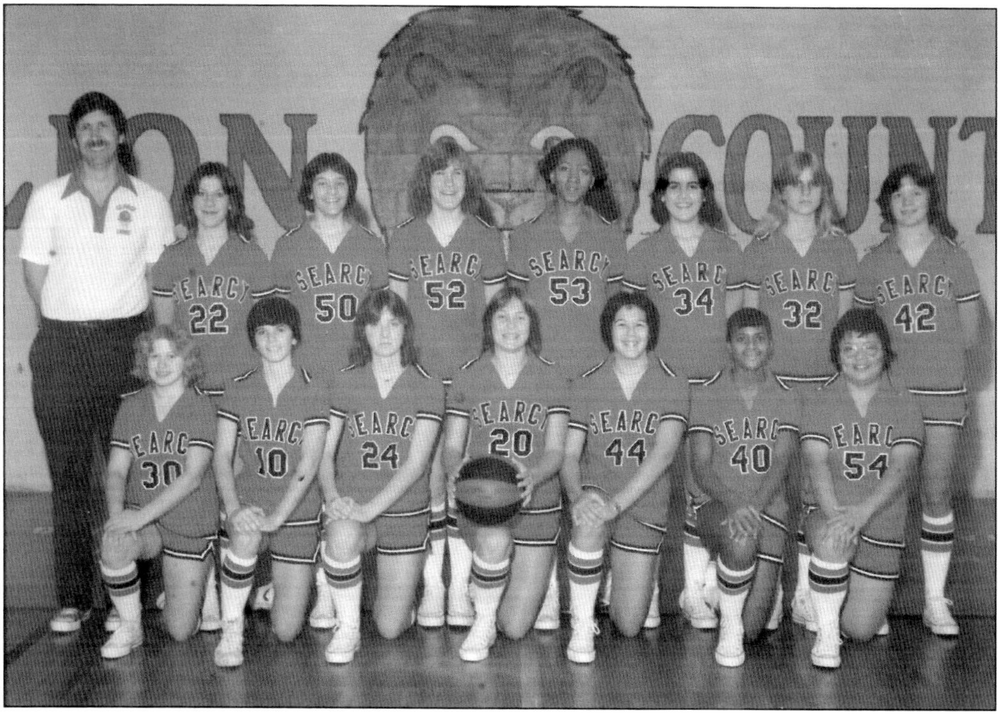

When Searcy High School brought back girls' basketball in 1980 after 20 years of nonparticipation in the sport, these young athletes were the first to wear the senior girls' uniforms. Pictured here are, from left to right, (first row) Anita Sewell, Judy Warren, Shelia McCoy, Stacy Youkers, Karen Jones, Paula Clay, and Angelia Lee; (second row) coach Danny Crow, Lyndy Bracki, Karla Cheatham, Lanita Parker, Beverly Gardner, Sandy Simpson, Cindy Nicholson, and Tammy Weir. (Courtesy Paula Clay Cleveland.)

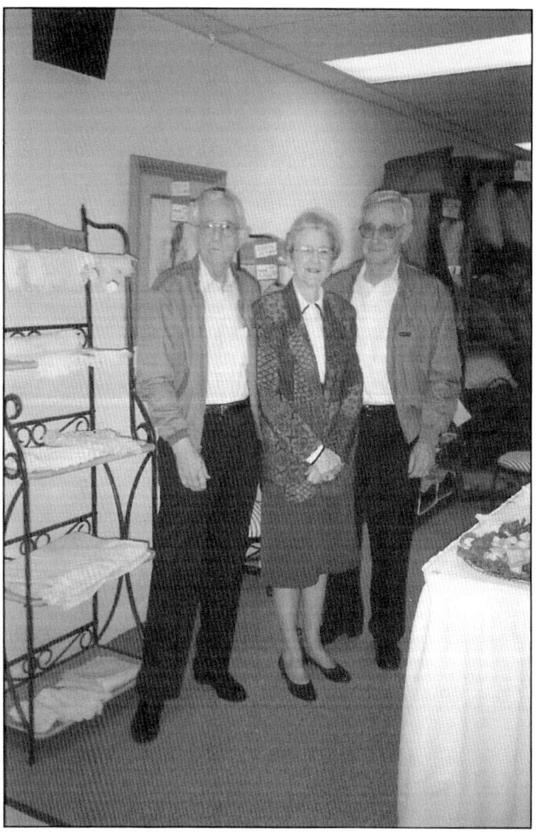

In 1945, John Sowell (left) opened Sowell's Home Supply at 207 West Arch Street in downtown Searcy. He was ready to celebrate, with refreshments for all visitors, on the 40th anniversary of the store. Standing with Sowell are Hattie Mae Maddox and Cecil Childers. (Courtesy Hattie Mae Maddox.)

Two

Downtown

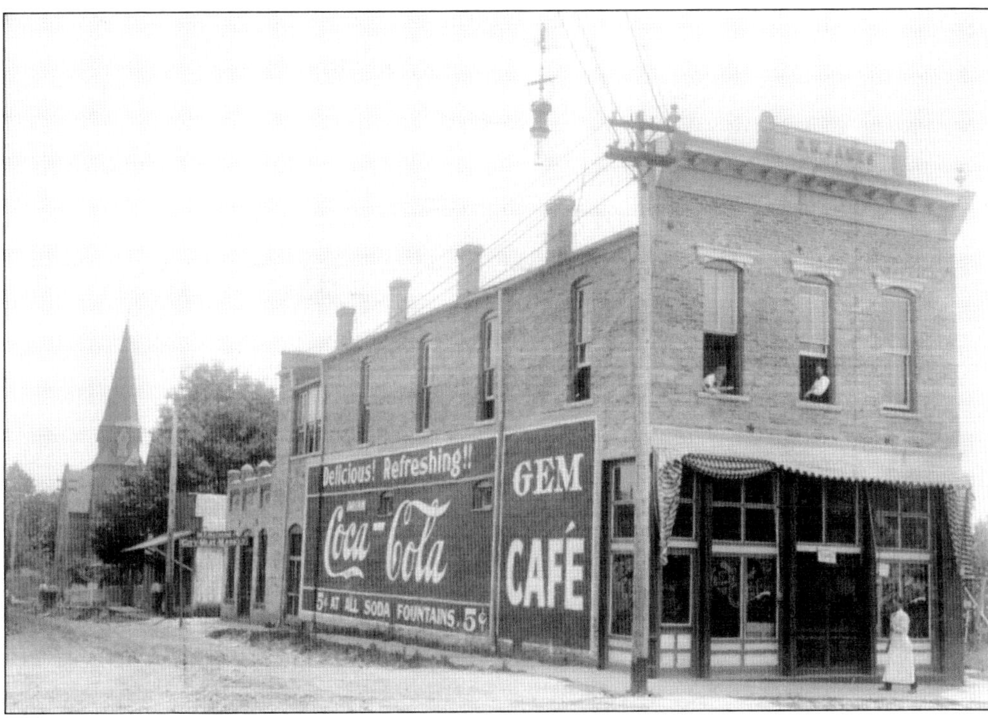

The Gem Café was located on the corner of Spring and Center Streets in the early 1900s. Giles Walker had a meat market directly behind the cafe, and the old First Presbyterian Church can be seen in the background. Searcy Lodge No. 49, F&A Masons, had a hall on the second floor of this building for many years. Between the meat market and the church, a wooden footbridge across Center Street is visible. (Courtesy Leon and Sherry Person.)

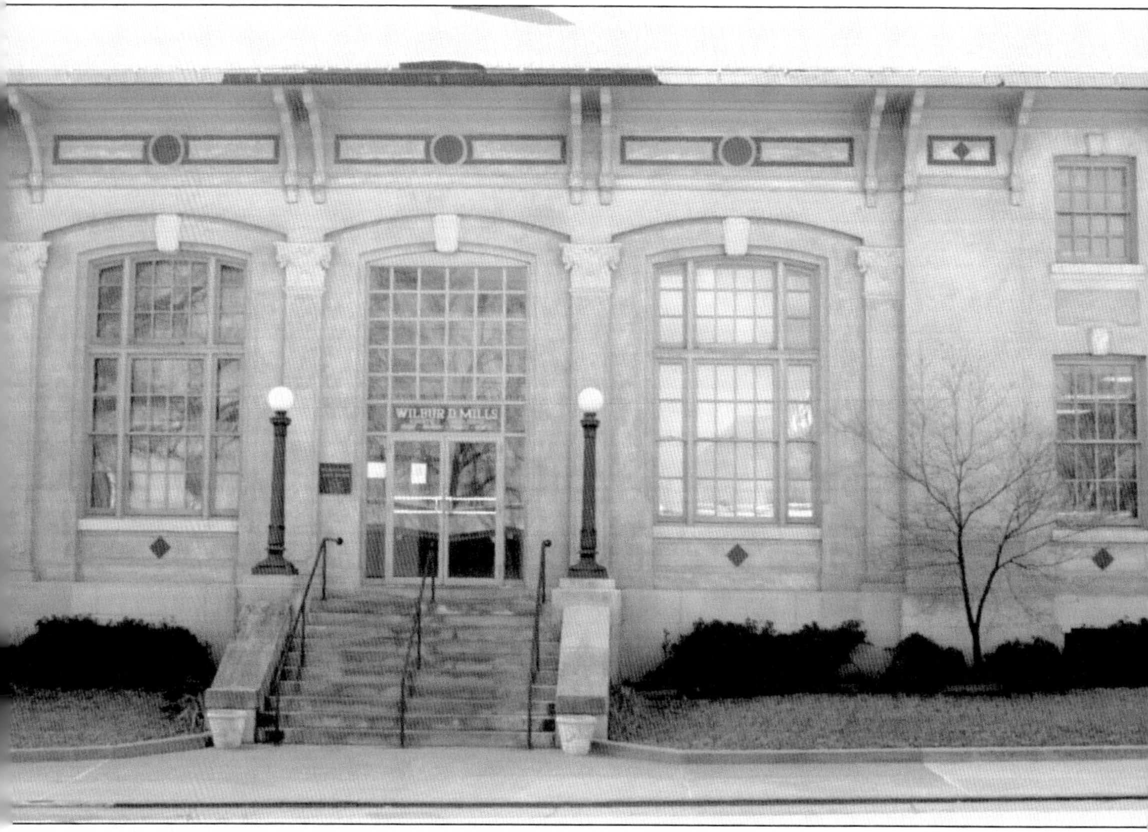

This building is commonly known as "the Post Office." Located at the corner of Gum and Arch Streets downtown, not far from the square, it was constructed in 1914 at a cost of $40,000. Judge Stephen Brundidge, elected to the US House of Representatives in 1902, is credited with getting the federal government to approve funding for the post office. Searcy was one of the first small cities in the country to have a post office. The building was expanded in 1959. In 1974, the post office was relocated to a new structure. This building is now the Wilbur D. Mills Court Building. (Courtesy Carolyn Boyles.)

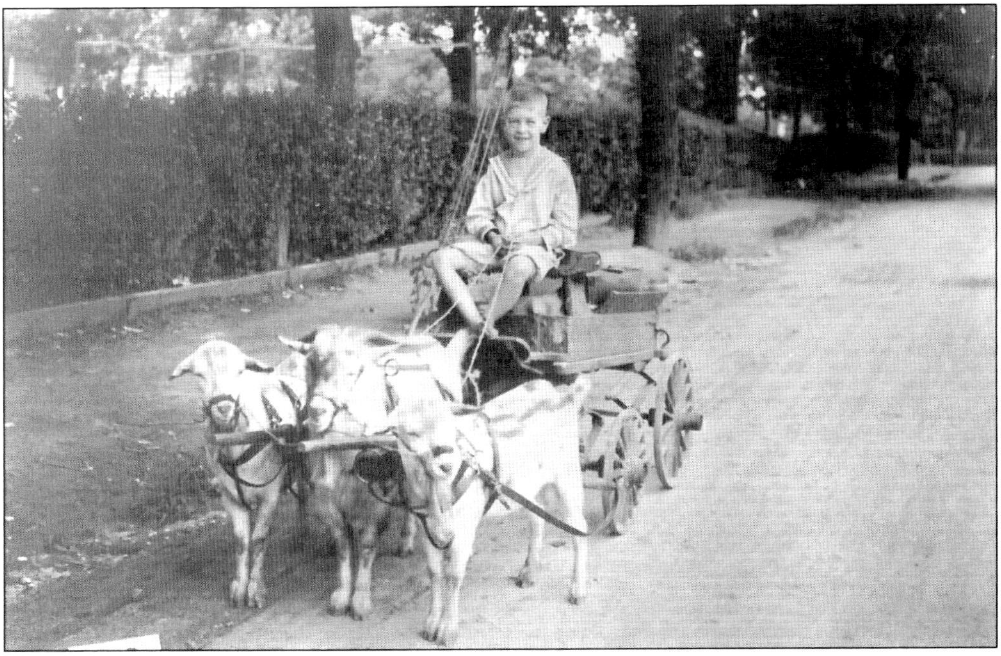

Young Bill Biggs drives his goat cart down Race Avenue in 1919, long before traffic demanded paved streets and stoplights. Race Avenue was unpaved and much narrower than it is today. (Courtesy Eloise Muncy.)

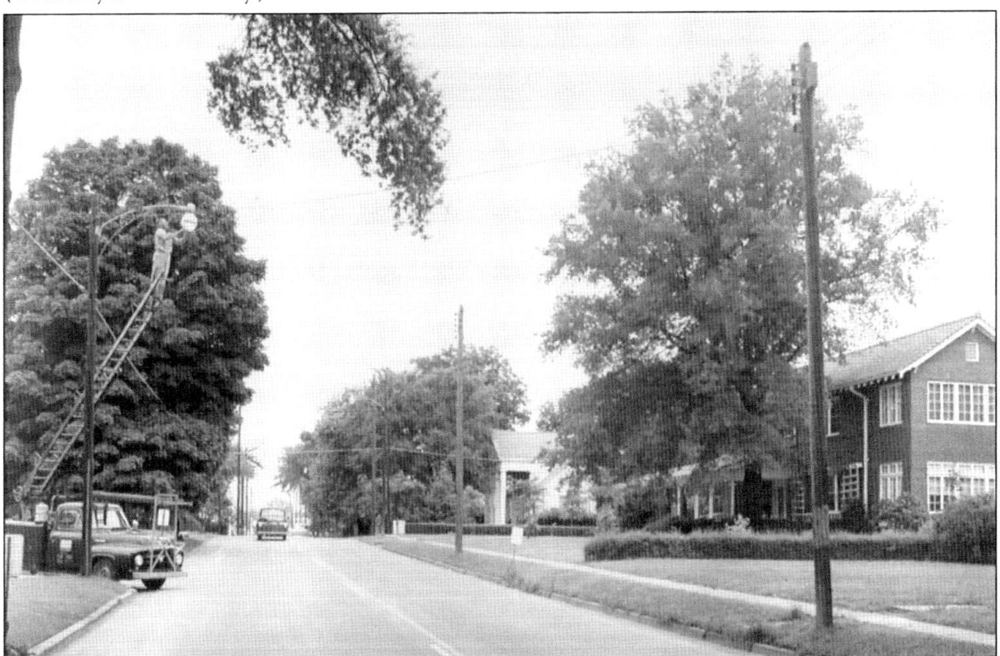

In this photograph from the mid-1950s, an unidentified lineman installs the first of new streetlights on Race Avenue (still much narrower than it is today). The homes on the right side of the image belonged to T.A. Watkins (foreground) and Dr. Porter Rodgers Sr. (background). (Courtesy SRCC.)

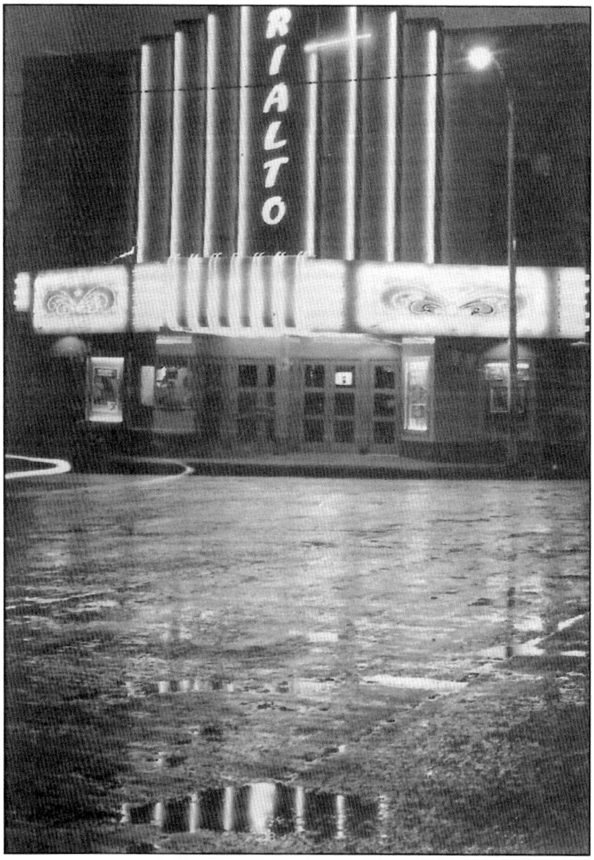

The Rialto Theater was built on the northeast corner of Race Avenue and Spring Street in 1923 and remains an operational movie theater today. K.K. (Deacon) King came to Searcy in 1937 and opened the Plaza Theatre in 1938. King acquired the Rialto in 1938 and combined it with the Plaza, creating the Commonwealth Searcy Theatre Corporation. After pleasing theatergoers for several years, the Rialto was closed. It was then restored and had a grand reopening on March 15, 1949. On the eve of the opening, a searchlight beam was visible to residents within a 20-mile radius of Searcy. The 10,000,000-candlepower searchlight and a generator were brought to town on a truck. The Rialto had the largest neon sign in the county. The Dixie Drive-In Theater was also a part of Commonwealth Searcy Theatre Corporation for many years. (Both, courtesy Eloise Muncy.)

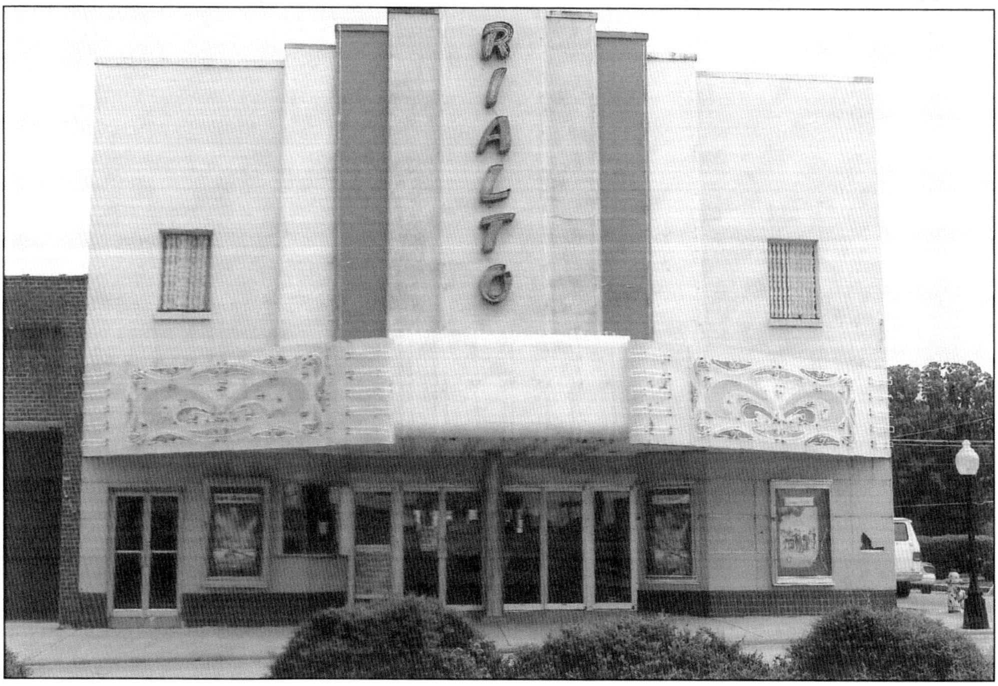

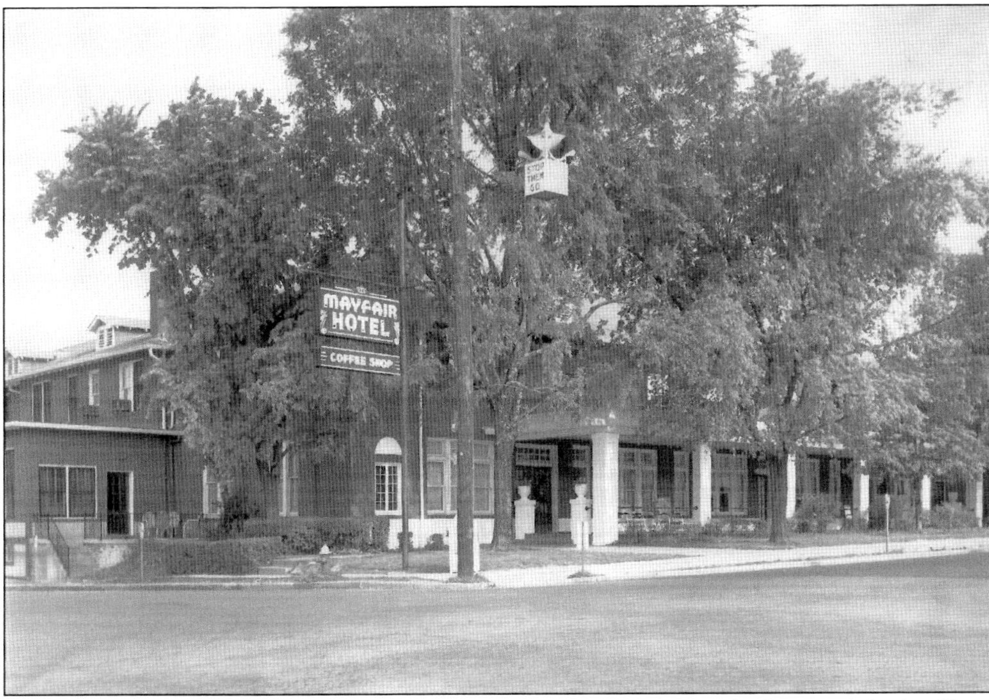

Erected on the site of the old Gill House on Spring Street in 1924, the historic Mayfair Hotel is 87 years old as of 2011. When Jack and Jawanda Pulliam purchased this built-to-last hotel in the center of town in 1986, they became the third owners of one of the South's grand old ladies. Searcy's Nick D'Auteil and R.H. and May Dale Branch were the previous owners. The Spanish Revival–style hotel was listed in the National Register of Historic Places in 1990. Jawanda Pulliam now owns and manages the hotel as a multiple-family dwelling for 36 occupants. (Courtesy Jawanda Pulliam.)

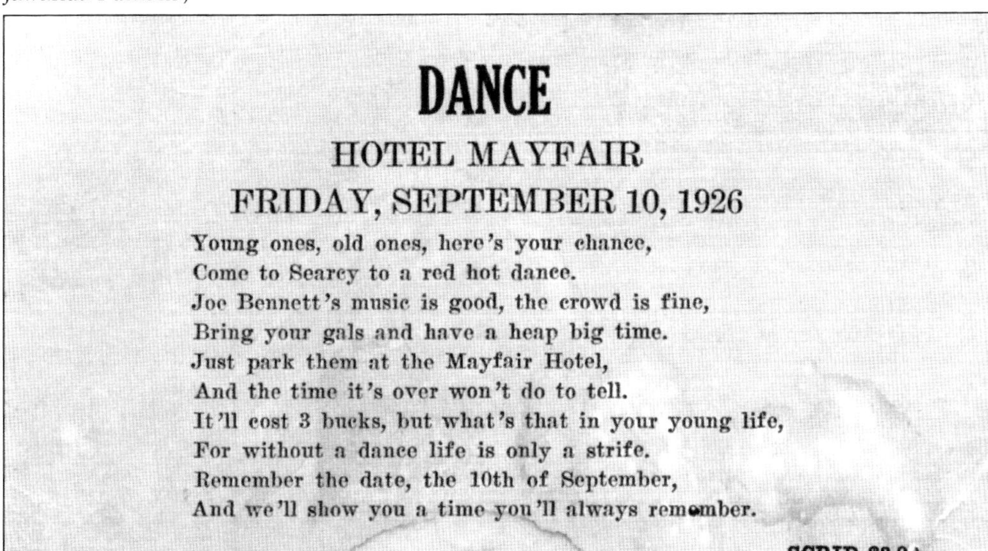

DANCE

HOTEL MAYFAIR

FRIDAY, SEPTEMBER 10, 1926

Young ones, old ones, here's your chance,
Come to Searcy to a red hot dance.
Joe Bennett's music is good, the crowd is fine,
Bring your gals and have a heap big time.
Just park them at the Mayfair Hotel,
And the time it's over won't do to tell.
It'll cost 3 bucks, but what's that in your young life,
For without a dance life is only a strife.
Remember the date, the 10th of September,
And we'll show you a time you'll always remember.

SCRIP $3.00

This is an invitation to a dance at the Mayfair Hotel. The reason for the name reversal on the invitation is unknown. (Courtesy Nancy Williams Showalter.)

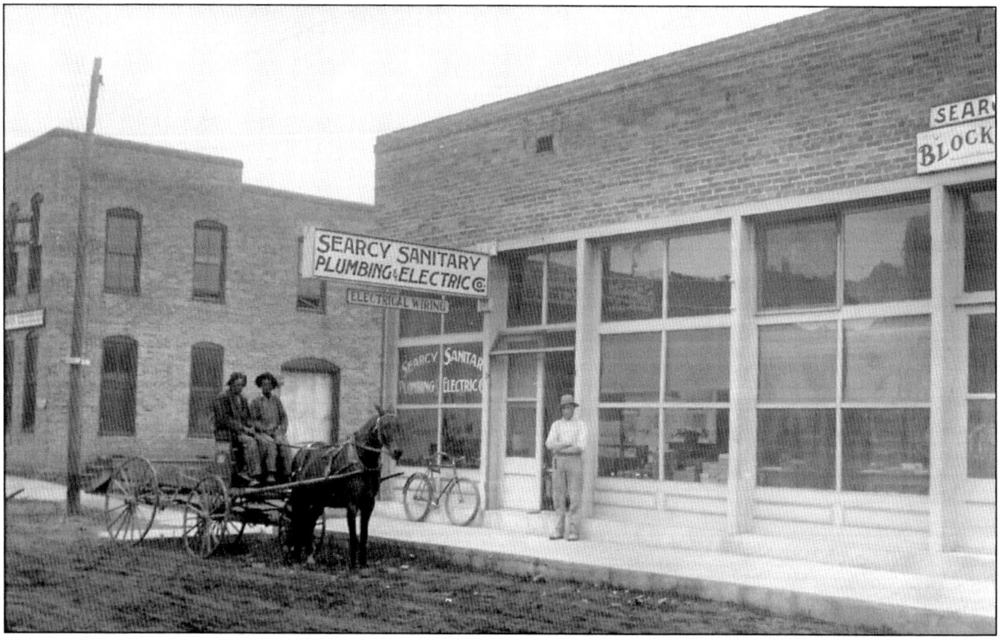

Searcy Sanitary Plumbing & Electric Company occupied the corner of Market and Spruce Streets in the early 1900s. It was located near the Black Cat Cafe. In this undated postcard image, the sidewalks have been paved, but the streets are still dirt. The building on the left side of the photograph is still standing and in good condition. The back of the postcard reads that it was given to Roger Williams by Mrs. O.C. Wakenight. (Courtesy Nancy Williams Showalter.)

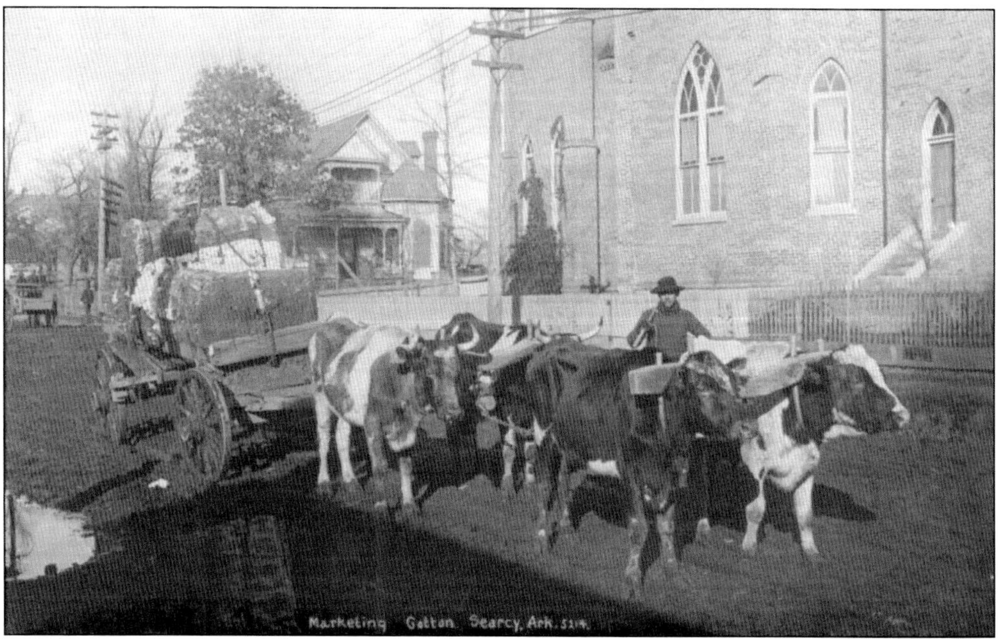

Cotton, often grown around stumps in partially cleared fields, grew well in the Searcy area in the early part of the 20th century. Farmers brought their crops to Searcy for ginning. The farmer in this early-1920s photograph drives a team of oxen down Main Street with his cotton bales. (Courtesy Shelly Keech.)

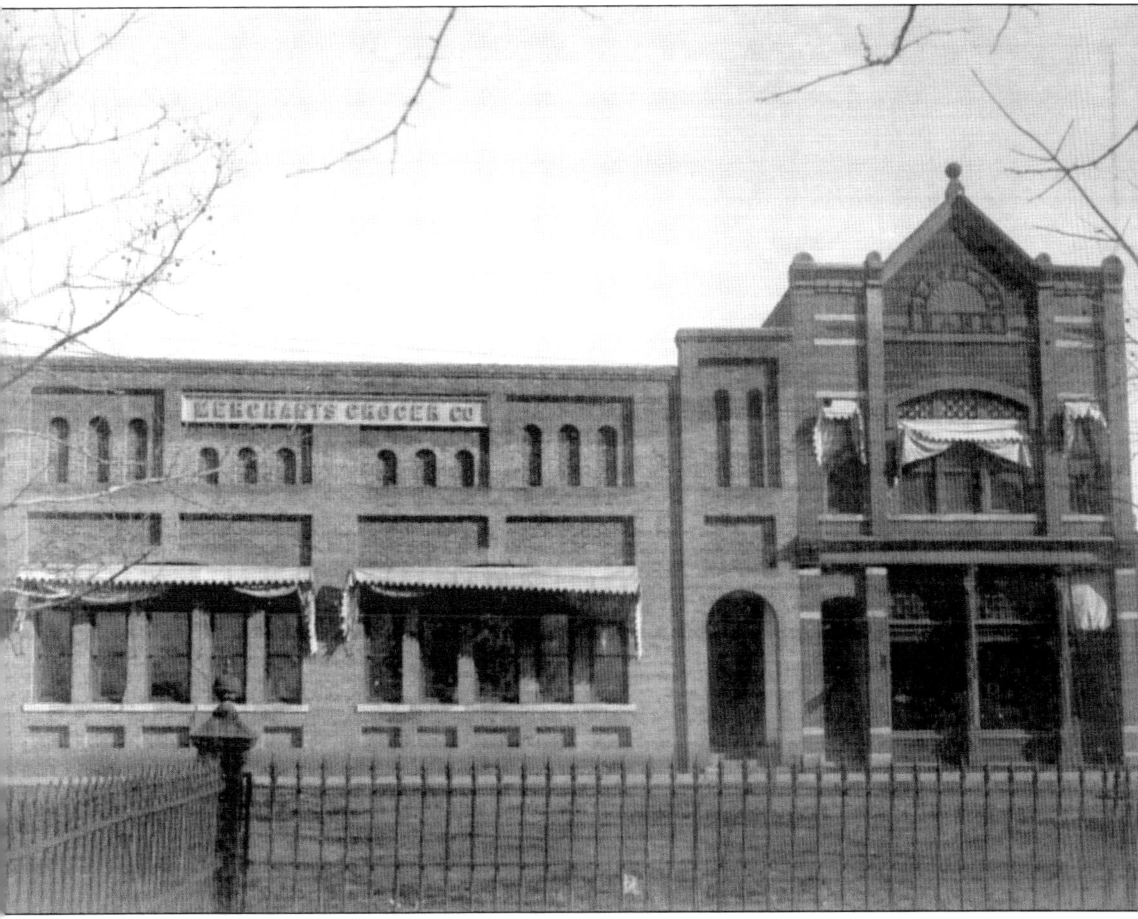

This is a photograph of the Merchants Grocer Company (MGC) and the People's Bank, which occupied the east side of the downtown square. The exact date of this photograph is unknown. The fence in the foreground surrounded the White County Courthouse. The People's Bank—founded on July 6, 1889—was a victim of the Great Depression, going out of business on September 30, 1931. Merchants Grocer Company was a wholesale grocer. The company had a bit of bad luck in 1908 or 1909, when it purchased some 18,000 cans of corn from the Ladoga Canning Company of Indianapolis. When the first cans were opened, it was discovered the entire lot was spoiled, and the grocery company had to buy replacement corn at a higher price. Merchants Grocer Company refused shipment, and the Ladoga Canning Company refused to replace the corn or refund the purchase price. MGC was forced to store the corn in its Little Rock warehouse when it was unable to find a buyer for it, and the company sued Ladoga. The case went to the Arkansas Supreme Court and was reversed and remanded back to the lower court for trial. The outcome of the case was not recorded by the legal system. The Charles F. Penzel Grocery Company on East Markham Street in Little Rock eventually bought the spoiled corn. (Courtesy WCHS.)

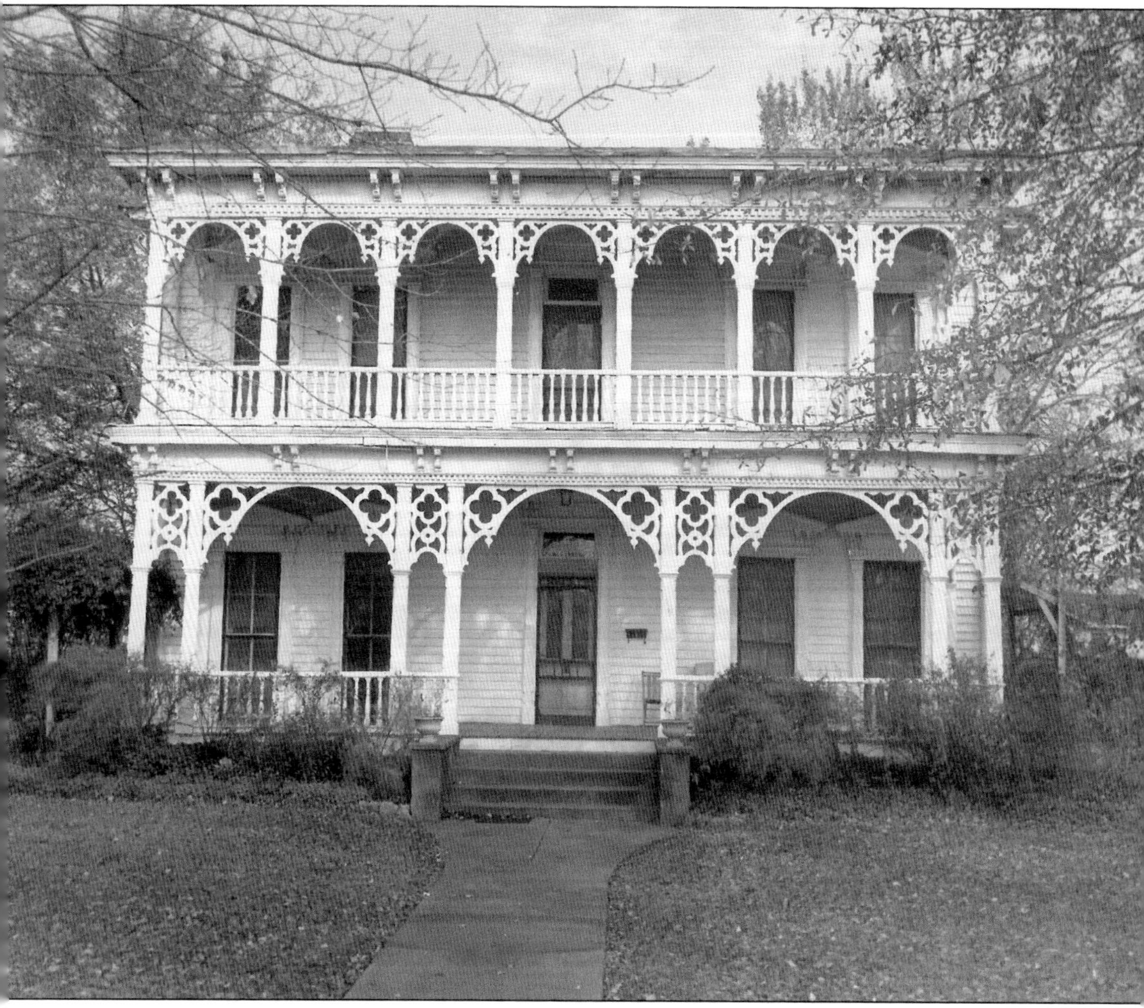

The two original rooms of this house were built in 1858. Capt. Benjamin Clayton Black purchased it following the surrender of his Confederate troops in Searcy and his marriage to Rosamond Jones. Black purchased the entire block in 1866 and completed a renovation of the house in 1874. The Black family had 11 children; they were the only people to ever live in this house. Lorena, the last surviving sibling, died here in 1979 at the age of 101. The home was purchased by Dr. Porter Rodgers Jr. and his wife, Carol, in 1980 and remodeled under the watchful eye of the Arkansas Historic Preservation Program. Since 1999, it has been home to the Searcy Art Gallery. In 2011, the Rodgers family deeded it to the City of Searcy. (Courtesy John Baker Photography.)

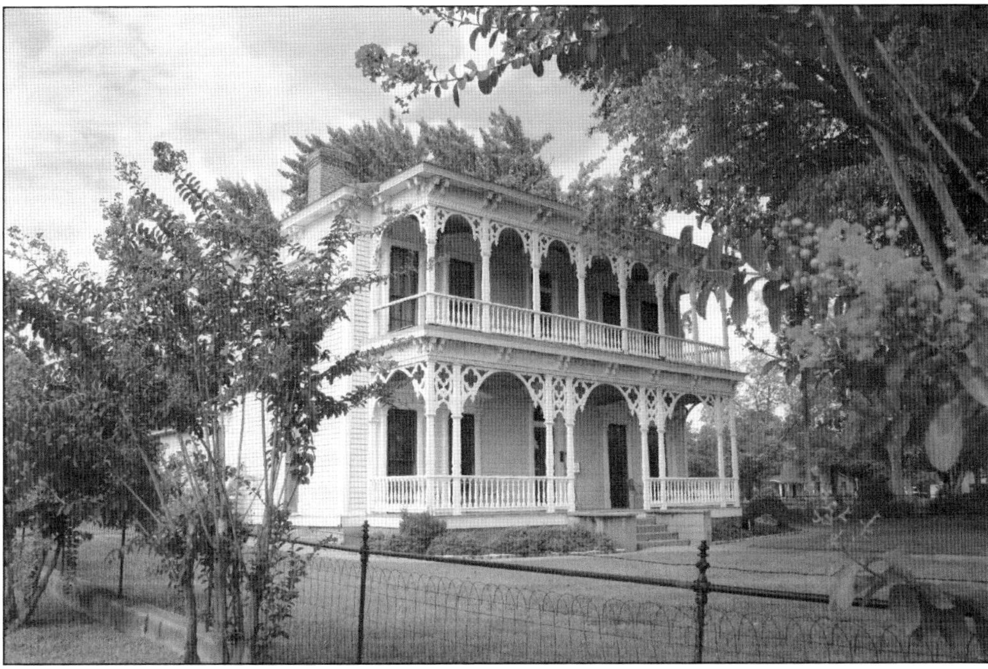

The Searcy Art Gallery is located on the corner of East Race and Locust Streets. This lovely gallery features period furnishings, including furniture from the original owner, and works of artists from all over Arkansas. (Courtesy Kenneth Mills.)

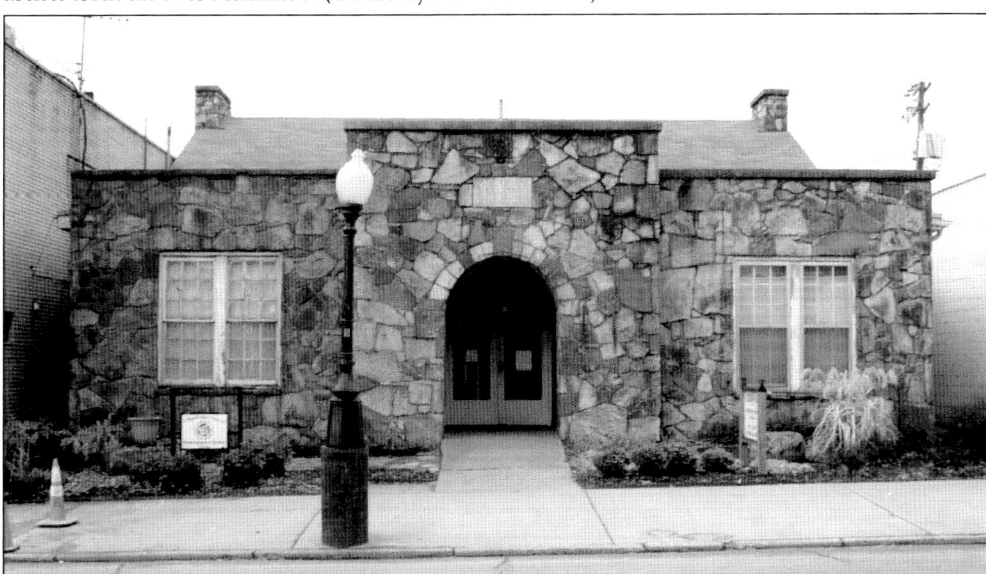

Searcy's Armstrong-Caldwell Post No. 106 of the American Legion was organized in January 1920 when Hubert Smith Sr. called for World War I veterans to unite and apply for a charter. Thirty members regularly met inside the White County Courthouse until their ranks expanded sufficiently to build the American Legion Hut on the north side of the square. Smith was elected the first commander, Clyde Allison the first adjutant, and A.S. (Sid) Faulk the first historian. (Courtesy Carolyn Boyles.)

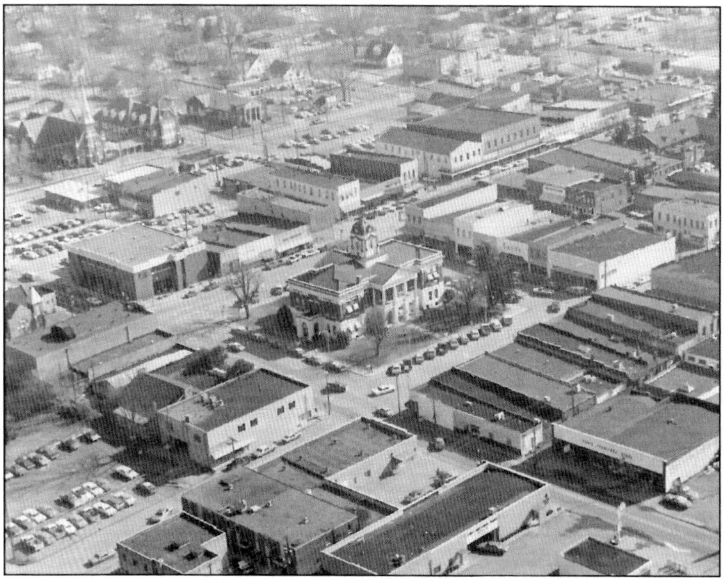

In this aerial photograph of downtown Searcy, the stately old White County Courthouse is in the center. In recent years, many commercial establishments have moved toward the state highway, which bypasses downtown, but the center of town remains an active area with shops and offices surrounding the courthouse square. (Courtesy Eloise Muncy.)

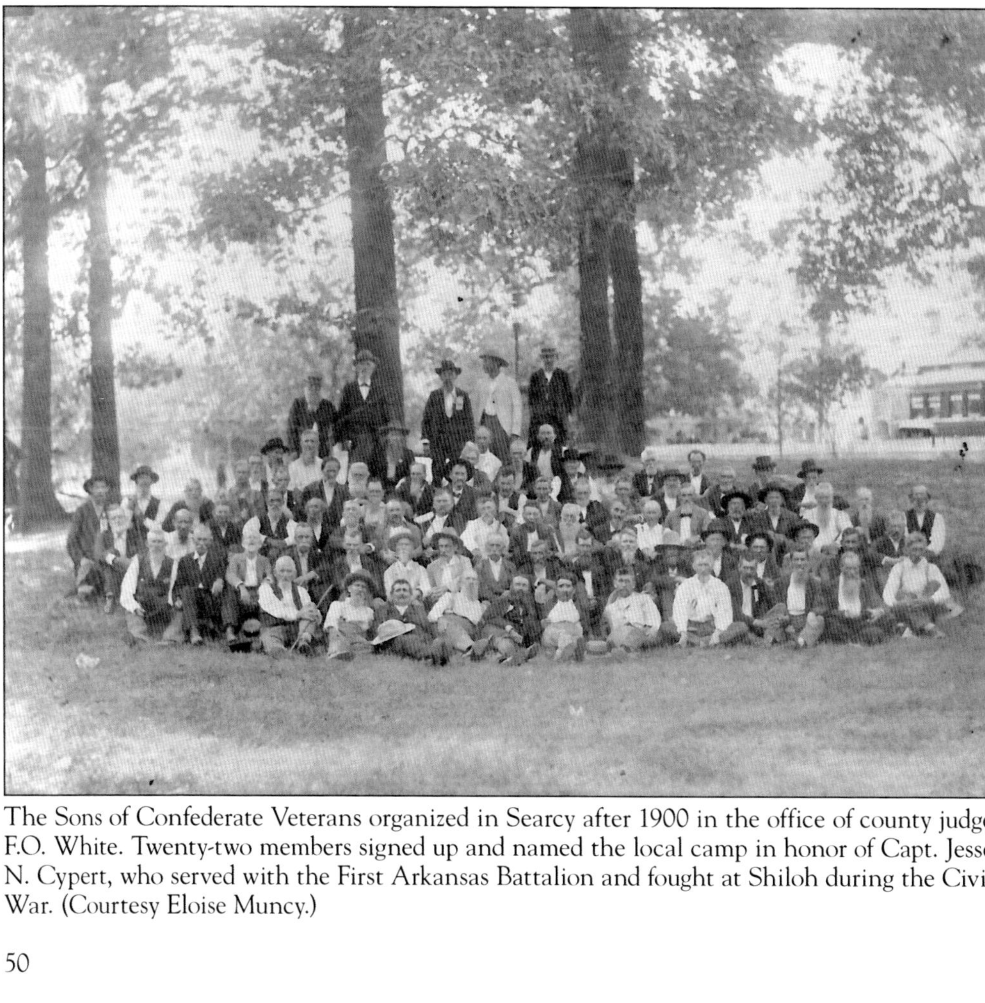

The Sons of Confederate Veterans organized in Searcy after 1900 in the office of county judge F.O. White. Twenty-two members signed up and named the local camp in honor of Capt. Jesse N. Cypert, who served with the First Arkansas Battalion and fought at Shiloh during the Civil War. (Courtesy Eloise Muncy.)

At a Confederate reunion in Spring Park in 1917, the group, accompanied by a band, marched to the courthouse square to unveil the monument. The monument was erected by public subscription. (Courtesy Carolyn Boyles.)

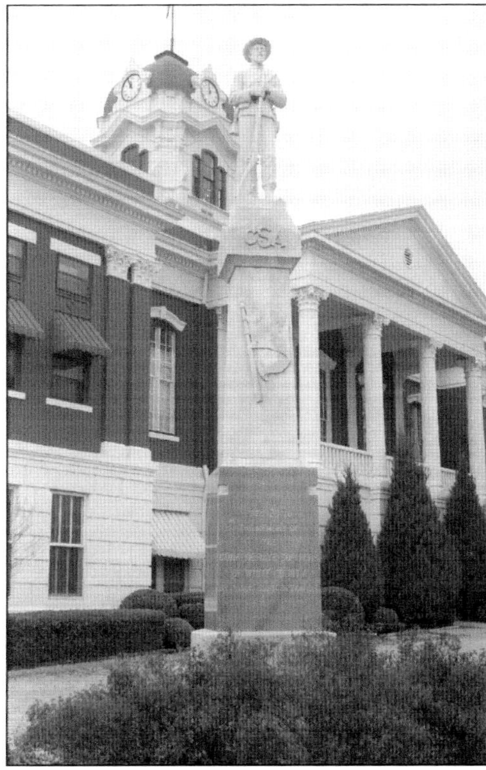

This is a current view of the south side of the square, showing Arch Street. Looking east, from right to left, Stotts Drug Store is in the center, John Baker Photography is on the right, and Quattlebaum Music is seen on the far left. (Courtesy Carolyn Boyles.)

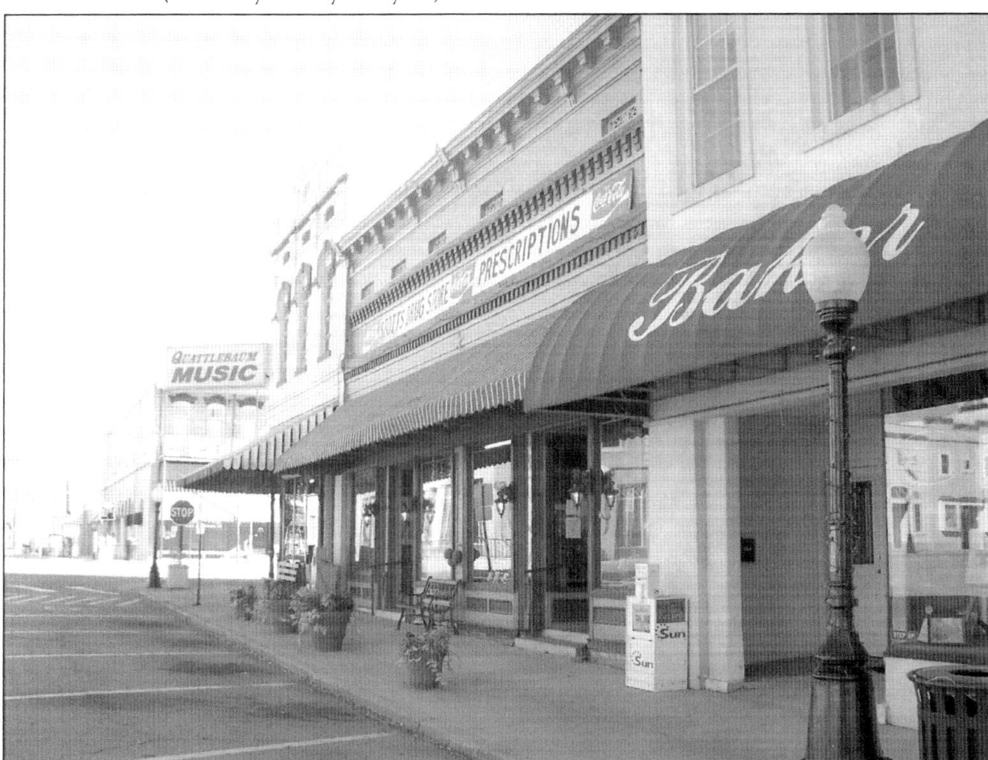

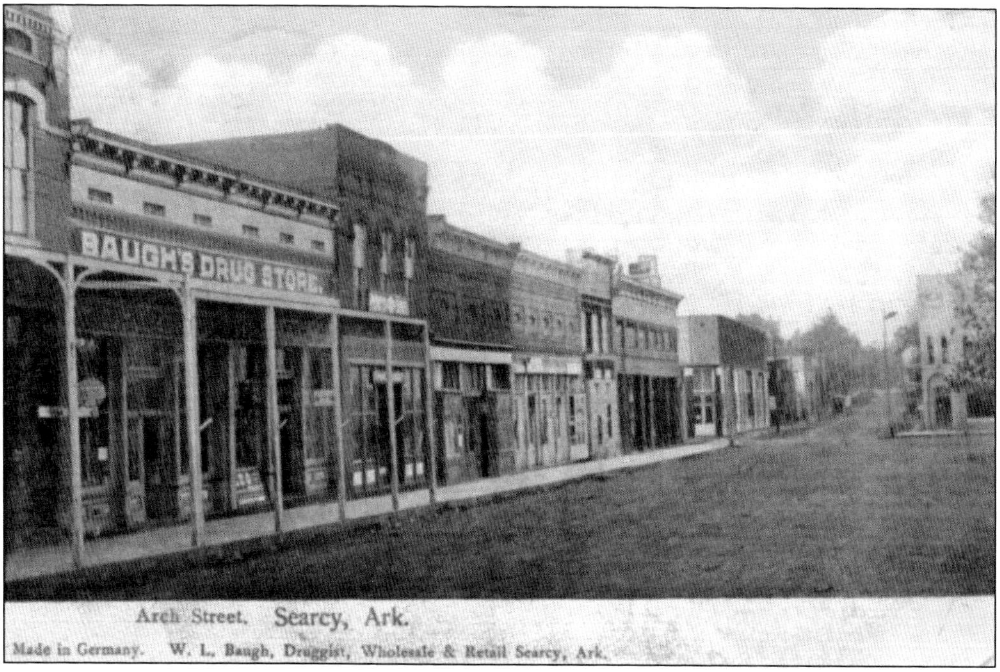

Before 1899, if a person in Searcy wanted to make a long-distance call, the Emmett Snipes Drug Store was the place to go. After 1899, the W.L. Baugh Drug Store offered the only long-distance service. (Courtesy Shelly Keech.)

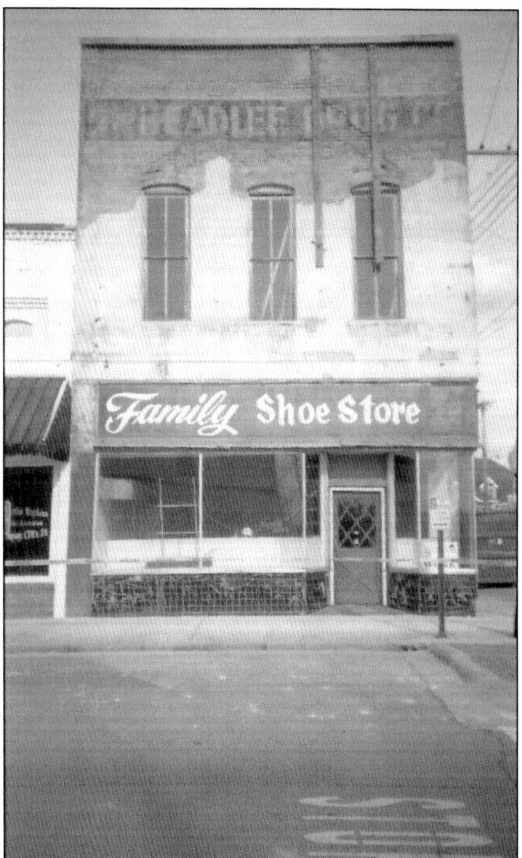

This is a later photograph of the building that housed the Headlee Drug Store on the corner of Spring and Market Streets. The Family Shoe Store occupied the building for many years; it closed in 2005. (Courtesy Leon and Sherry Person.)

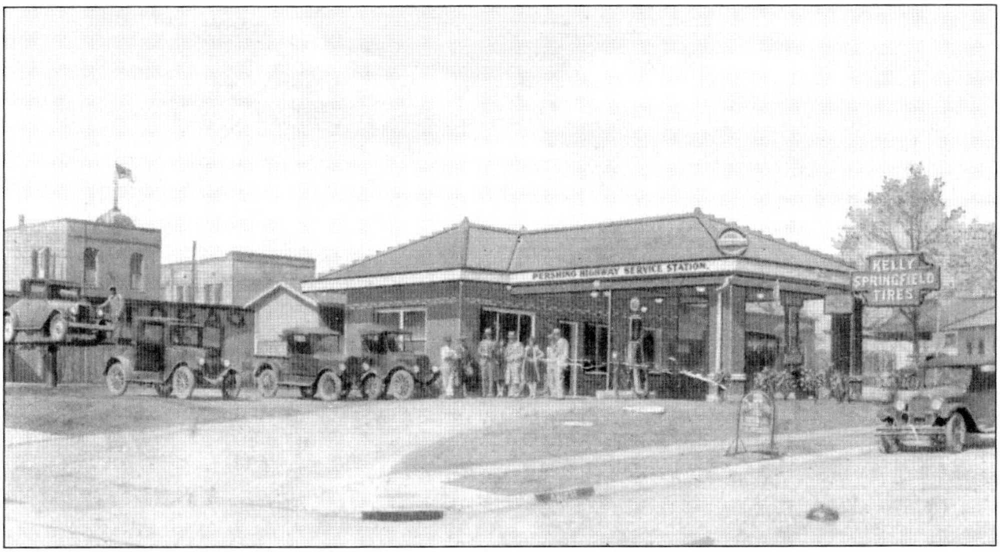

This c. 1930 image shows the first stand-alone gas station in Searcy. The Pershing Highway Service Station, owned and operated by Sinclair Lightle, was located on Main Street, across from the First Methodist Church. The gas station sold Texaco gasoline and Kelly Springfield tires. (Courtesy Nancy Williams Showalter.)

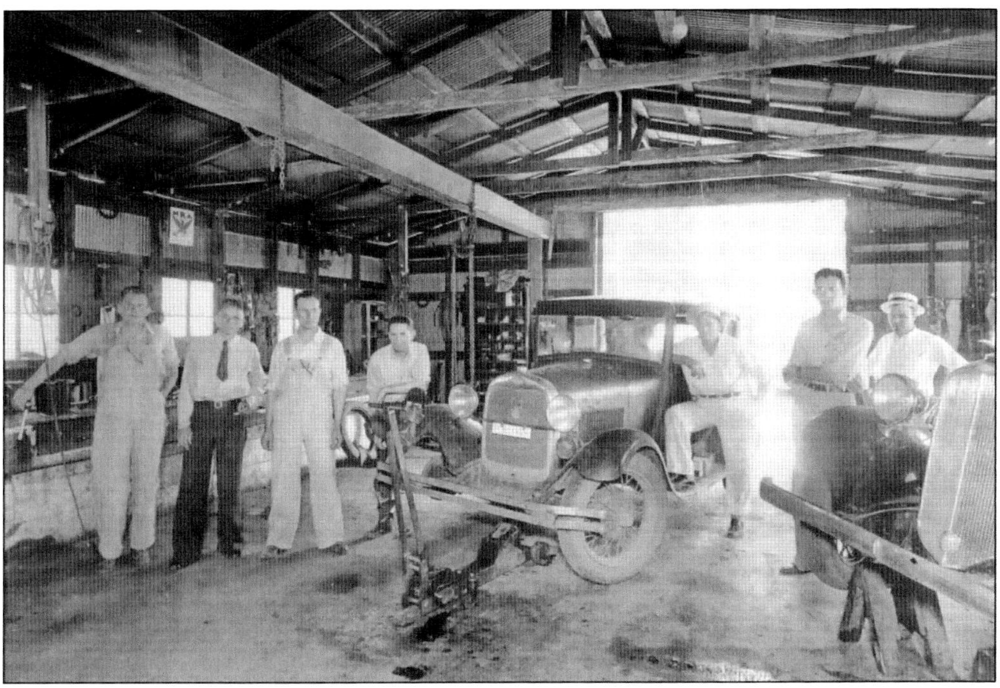

In the 1930s, Simon Person had a garage behind the Pershing Highway Service Station on Arch Street. Pictured here are, from left to right, Person, Obe Martindale, Paul Person, Sinclair ("Puny") Lightle, unidentified, Guy Knox, and Clarence Maness. (Courtesy Leon and Sherry Person.)

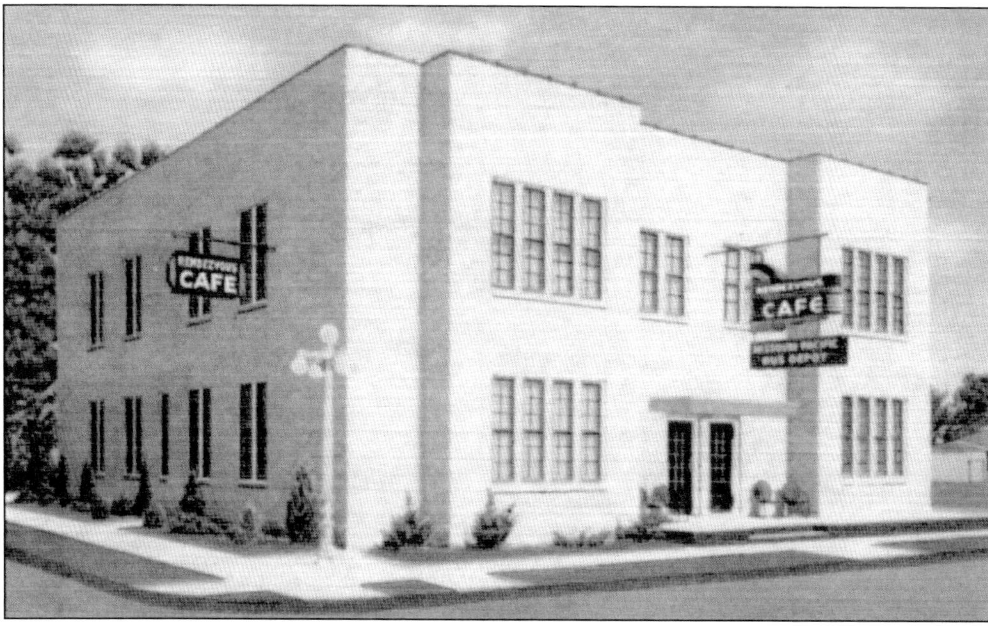

E.C. Robertson and his wife, Betty, opened the Rendezvous Cafe in 1932 on Main and Center Streets, where the First Presbyterian Church once stood. Through the years, the café became one of Arkansas's finest dining establishments. In 1961, the Rendezvous Cafe was honored as a 20-year member of the Duncan Hines family by the Duncan Hines Institute in Ithaca, New York. (Courtesy Shelly Keech.)

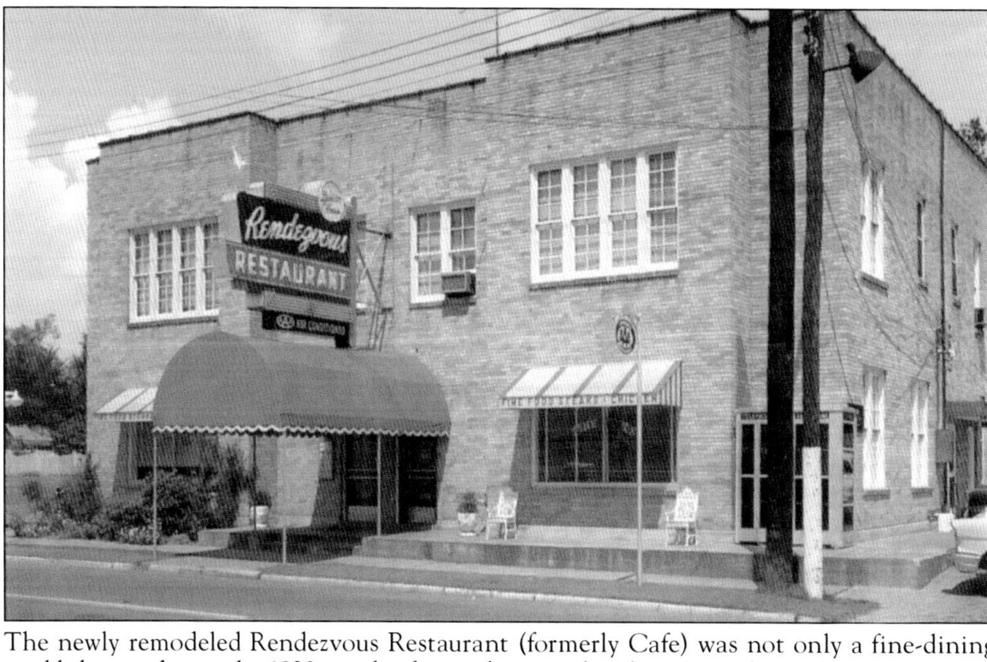

The newly remodeled Rendezvous Restaurant (formerly Cafe) was not only a fine-dining establishment during the 1930s, it also featured various bands on Saturday nights and served as the Missouri Pacific bus line depot. The new restaurant had its formal reopening on August 9, 1945, the day the atomic bomb was dropped on Nagasaki, Japan. The Missouri Pacific Band furnished entertainment, and new banquet halls were opened upstairs. (Courtesy Shelly Keech.)

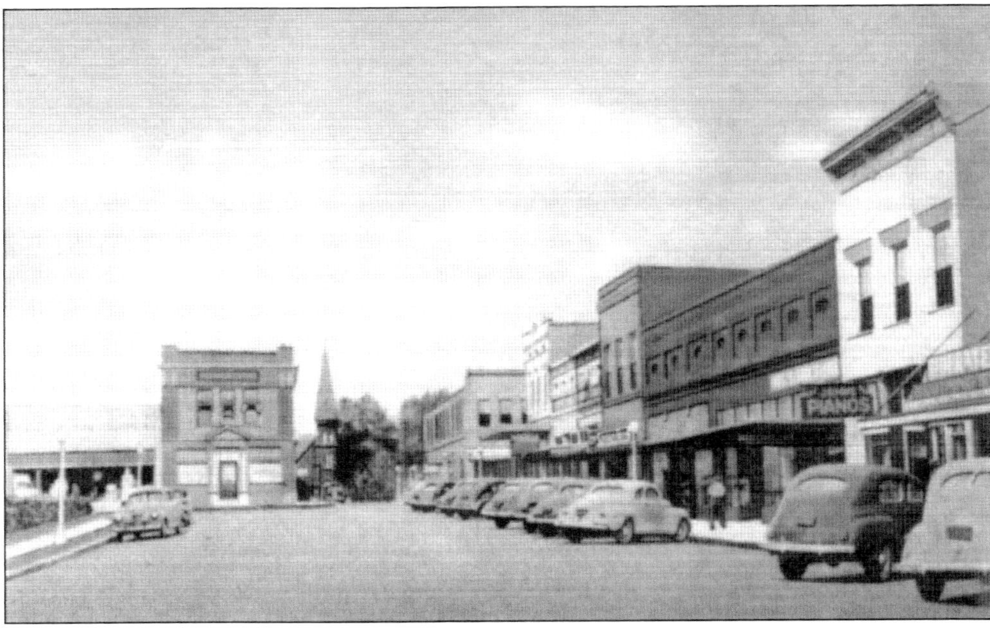

Looking east, this c. 1940 postcard shows West Arch Street. John Dee Pope's piano store is on the right. Security Bank is now located in the center rear building. The First Methodist Church is on Main Street, at the end of West Arch Street. (Courtesy Leon and Sherry Person.)

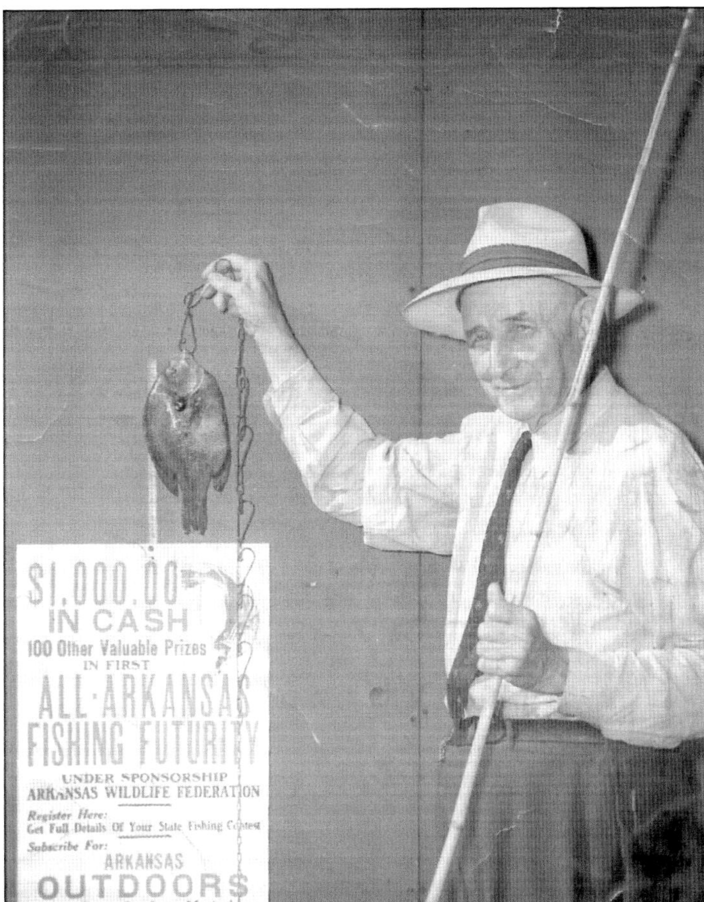

John Dee Pope opened a piano store in 1889, and on November 27, 1934, at age 73, unloaded a 500-pound piano by himself. This feat got Pope in the *Arkansas Gazette* and in Ripley's *Believe It or Not!* Pope was a good fisherman too, but, perhaps, not the winner of this contest. (Courtesy Nancy Williams Showalter.)

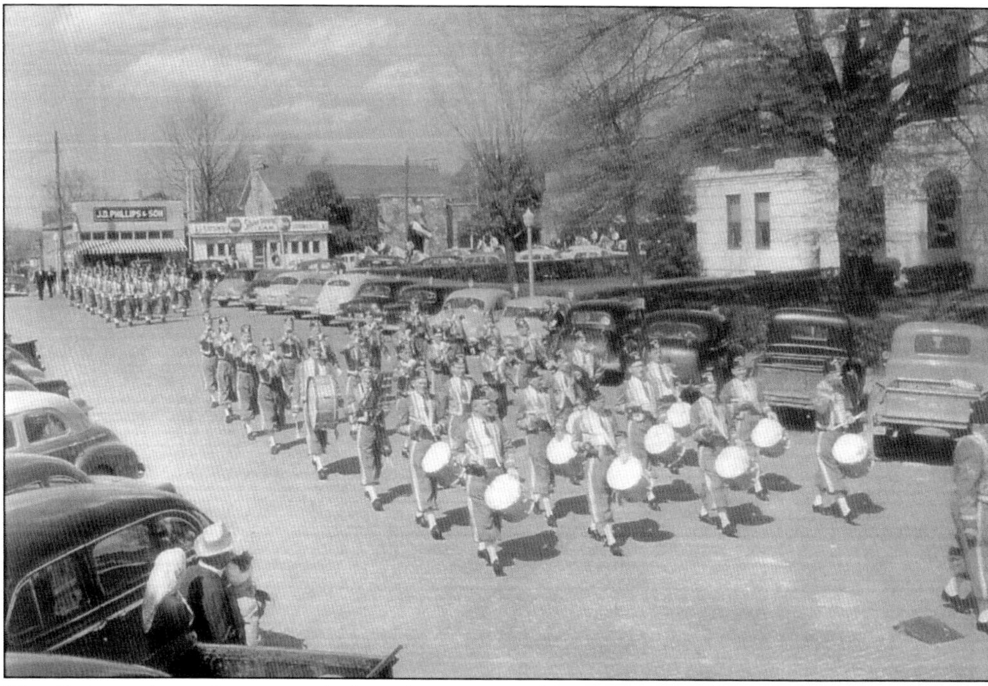

The Shriners drew a large crowd when they came to Searcy for a grand parade through downtown around 1940. (Courtesy Leon and Sherry Person.)

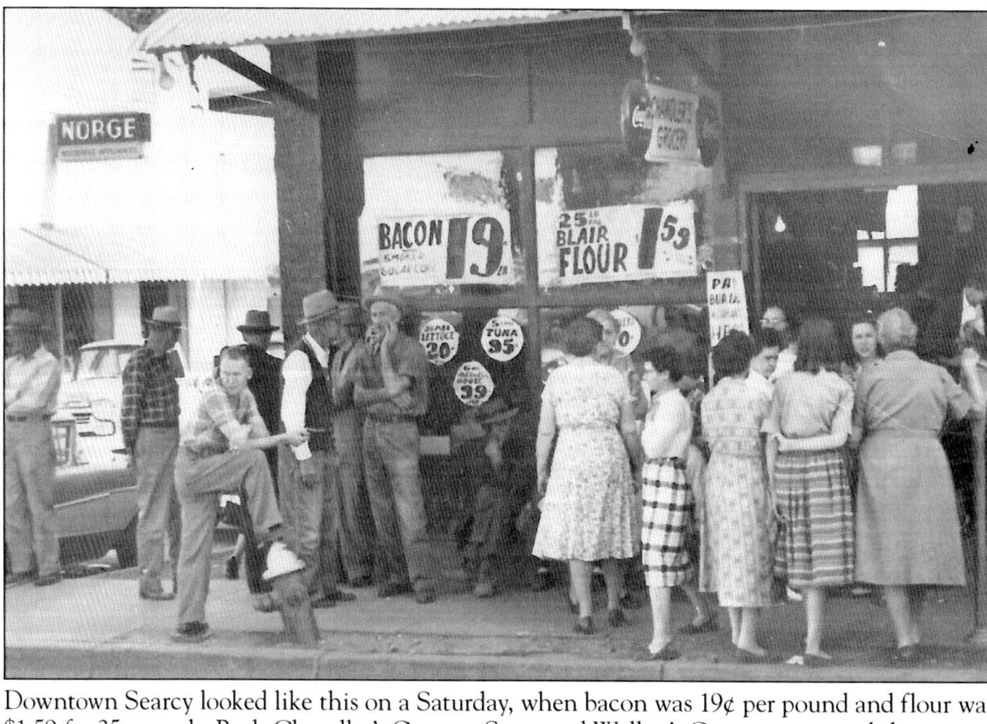

Downtown Searcy looked like this on a Saturday, when bacon was 19¢ per pound and flour was $1.59 for 25 pounds. Both Chandler's Grocery Store and Walker's Grocery occupied this corner of Market and Spruce Streets at one time or another during the 1940s. The stores were across the street from the current location of the Underground Coffee Shop. (Courtesy Eloise Muncy.)

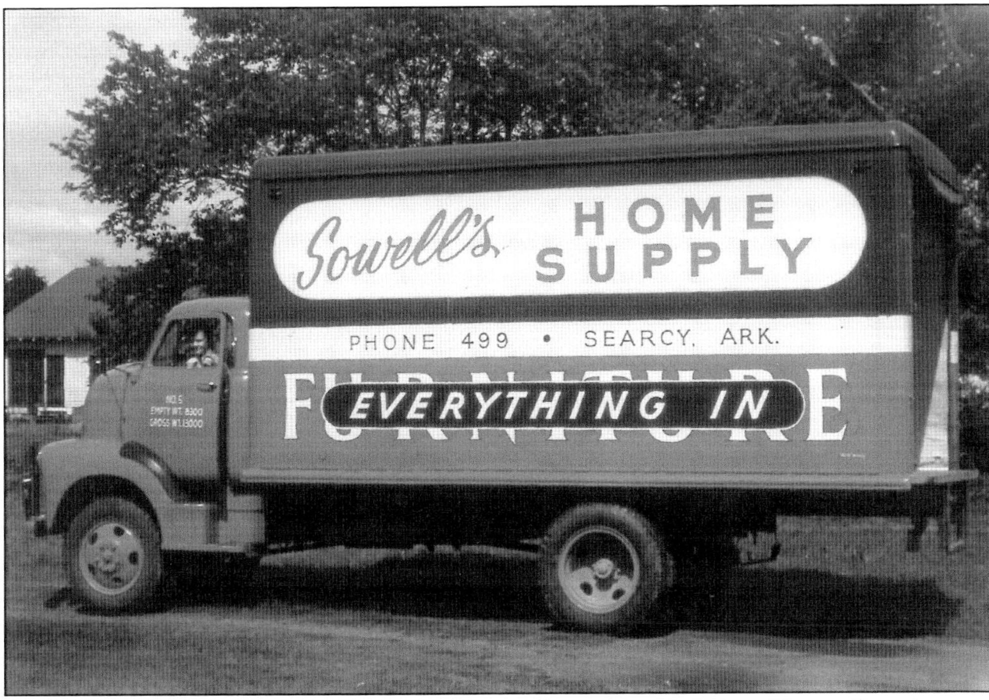

John and Lora Sowell opened Sowell's Home Supply store in 1945. Sowell's is still in the same downtown location on Arch Street. In 2009, the family enterprise observed its 64th year in business. Betty Sowell Mote and Nancy Sowell Hatfield, daughters of the original owners, now operate the business. (Courtesy Leon and Sherry Person.)

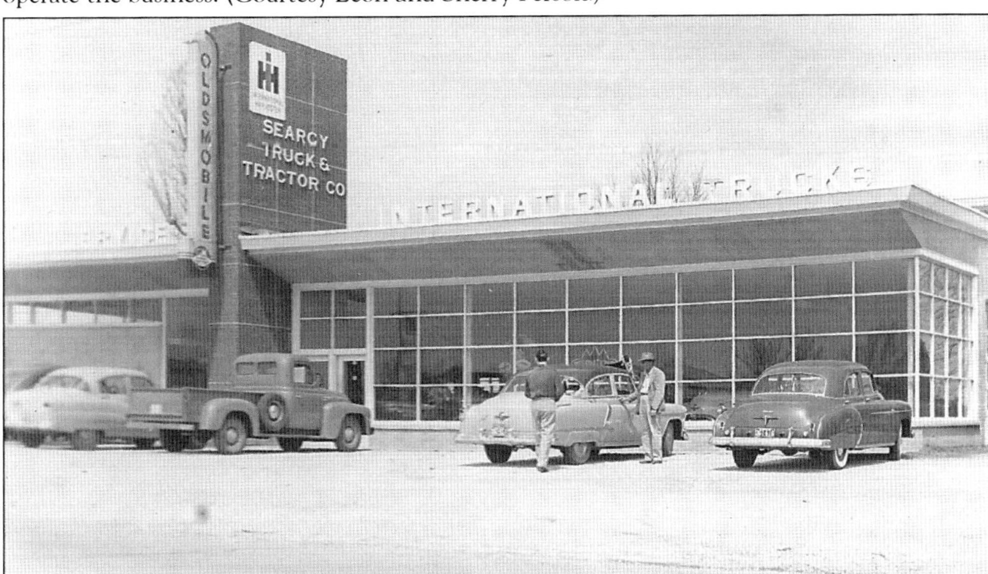

The Searcy Truck & Tractor Company's Motor Truck Division moved into its new building at 1500 East Race Avenue in 1947 and held an open house on May 14 of that year. Sam Lanier was shop foreman, and Hubert Coward and Redus Gentry were mechanics. Conley Bolding managed the parts department, and James Aclin was general manager and co-owner with his father, Cal Aclin. (Courtesy SRCC.)

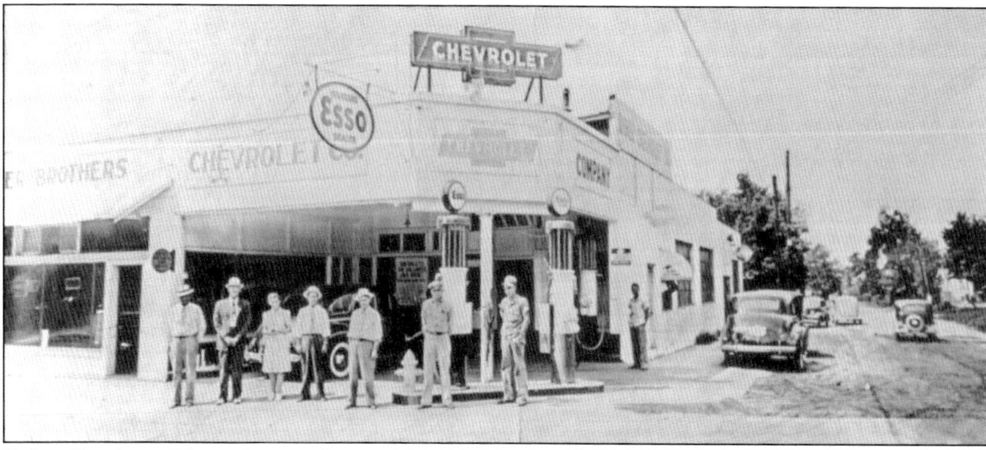

Baker Brothers Chevrolet was located on the corner of Race Avenue and Spruce Street in the 1940s. Race Avenue was paved at the time, but Spruce Street was still dirt. Standing in front of the business are, from left to right, Otis Hunt, Truman Baker, Johnnie Forrest, Herman Baker, Mac Spriggs, Lloyd Baker, and Pierce Maddox. Hattie Mae Maddox, who turned 94 in 2011, said her husband started working in 1940 for $10 per week, and 10¢ was withheld each week for Social Security. Maddox continued working for the dealership, which became Truman Baker Chevrolet, until his retirement. Two Esso gasoline pumps stand out front. (Courtesy Hattie Mae Maddox.)

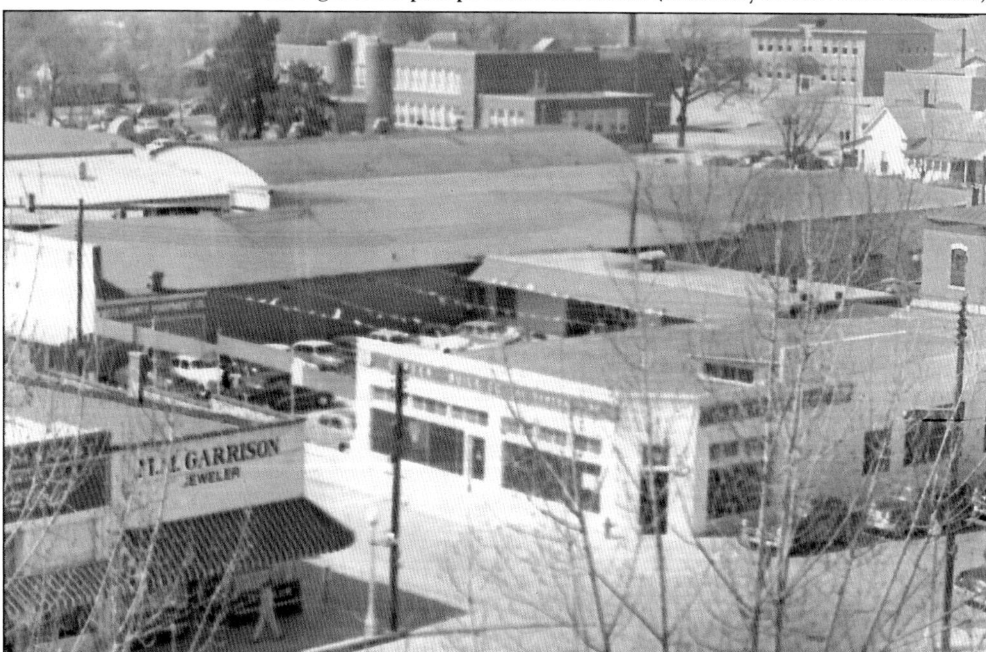

This is a view of the same building as in the photograph above. Baker Brothers Chevrolet occupied the building on the right, followed by Truman Baker Chevrolet, becoming Carder Motor Company and, finally, Carder Buick-Chevrolet before the building was torn down and Searcy Bank and Pyeatt Insurance built a new building in that location. Around 1940, M.M. (Doc) Garrison's Jewelry Store was on the opposite corner. Leslie Jewelry Store now occupies the building. Regions Bank is across from the jewelry store. A closer look reveals the high school in the background. (Courtesy SRCC.)

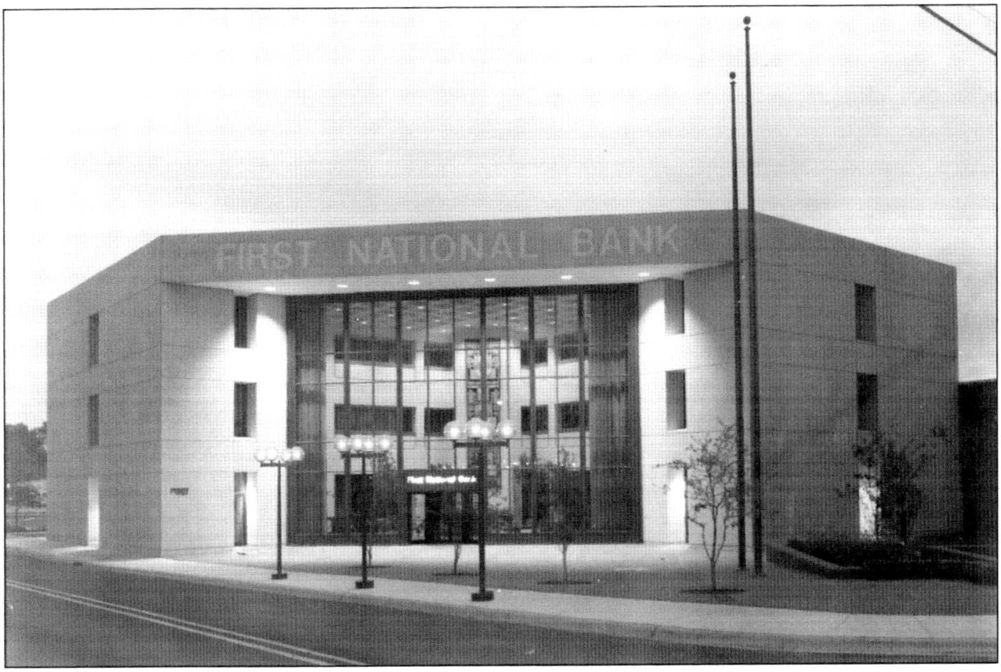

First National Bank moved into this building on the corner of Race Avenue and Spruce Street, the northwest corner of the courthouse square, in 1979. In 1998, the bank merged with Regions Bank. (Courtesy Regions Bank.)

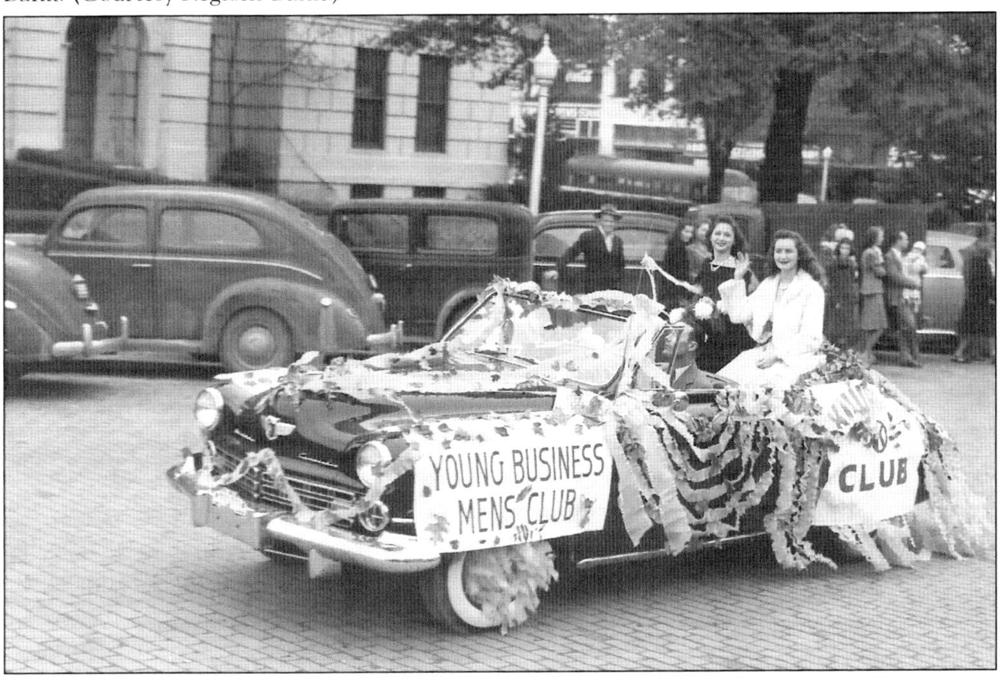

The Young Business Men's Club and the Kiwanis Club teamed up to decorate this float, which carried queen Tomile Abboud and an unidentified contestant in the Fall Festival Parade in 1947. The driver of the car is unidentified. Arch Street, as well as other streets around the courthouse, was constructed of beautiful brickwork at the time. (Courtesy SRCC.)

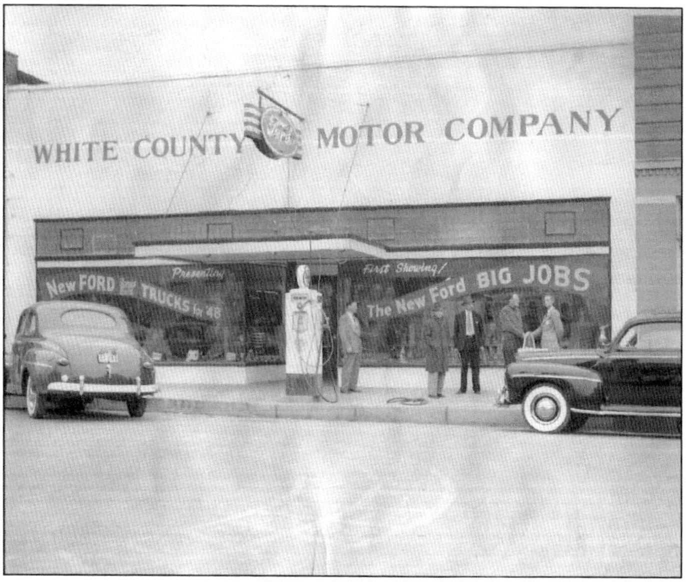

The White County Motor Company was on the east side of the courthouse square. In 1948, (from left to right) Palmer Webb, Louie Horn, unidentified, Joe Tom O'Guin, and John "Whitey" Whitescarver gathered on Spring Street to see the new Fords. Whitescarver bought the dealership from John McElwee in 1944. A gas pump stood on the sidewalk out front, and the service garage was located behind the dealership. (Courtesy Duke Webb and Hallie Sanford.)

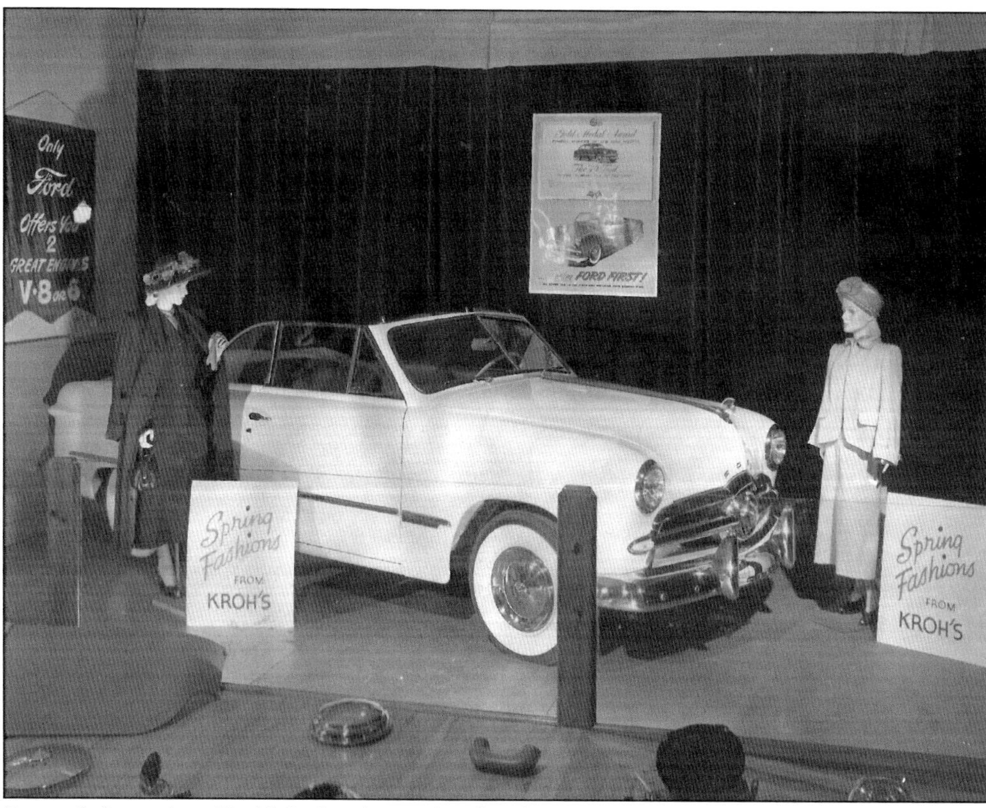

Spring fashions from Kroh's Ladies Apparel, a shop located on Spring Street, were displayed along with the new 1949 Ford. Kroh's was located just south of the old J.C. Penney location, close to the Mayfair Hotel at 102–104 North Spring Street. By 1959, Searcy Fabric Center occupied the space at 102 North Spring Street. (Courtesy Duke Webb and Hallie Sanford.)

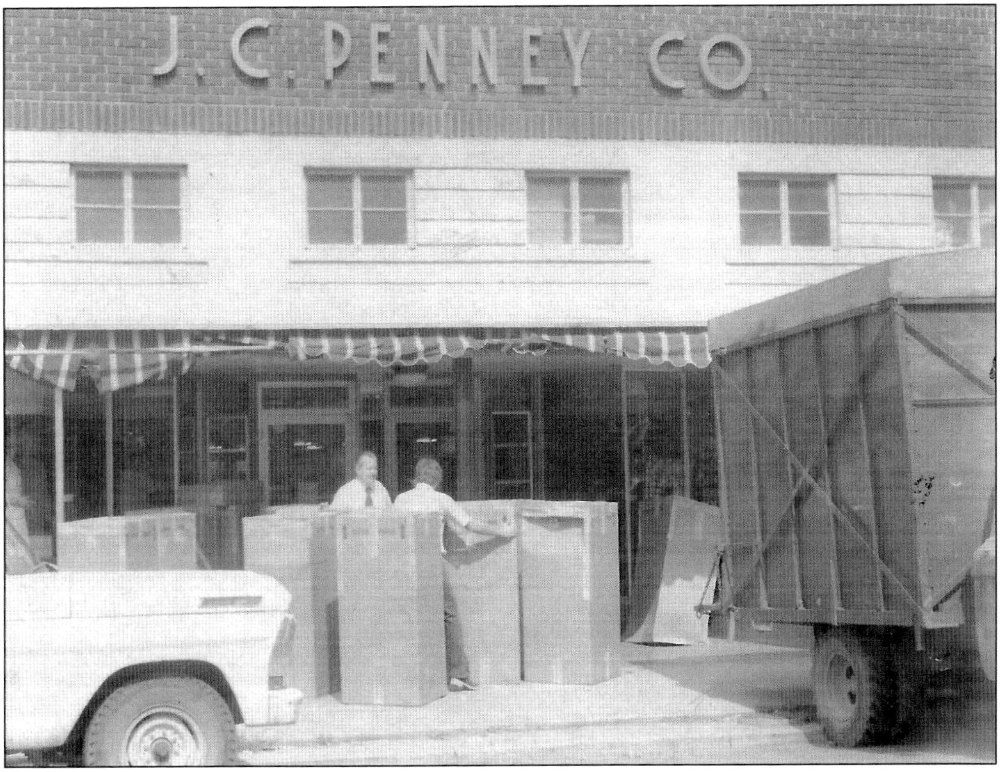

In this 1950s photograph, unidentified men unload women's coats from a delivery truck in front of the J.C. Penney store on Spring Street. (Courtesy Herb and Mitzie Bacon.)

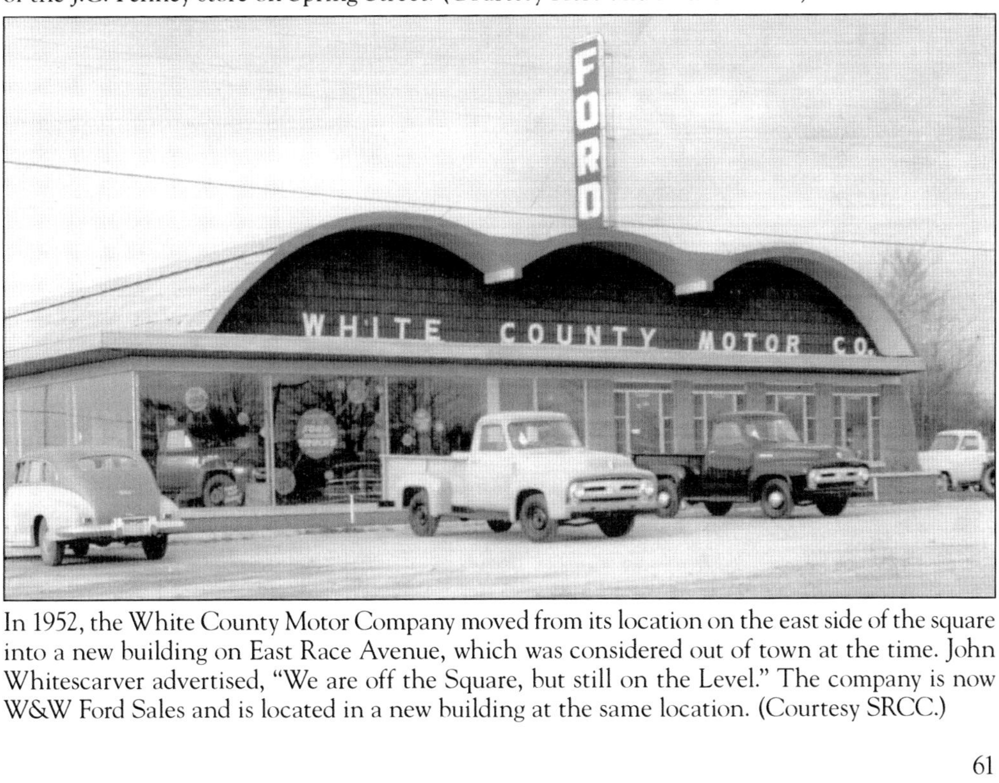

In 1952, the White County Motor Company moved from its location on the east side of the square into a new building on East Race Avenue, which was considered out of town at the time. John Whitescarver advertised, "We are off the Square, but still on the Level." The company is now W&W Ford Sales and is located in a new building at the same location. (Courtesy SRCC.)

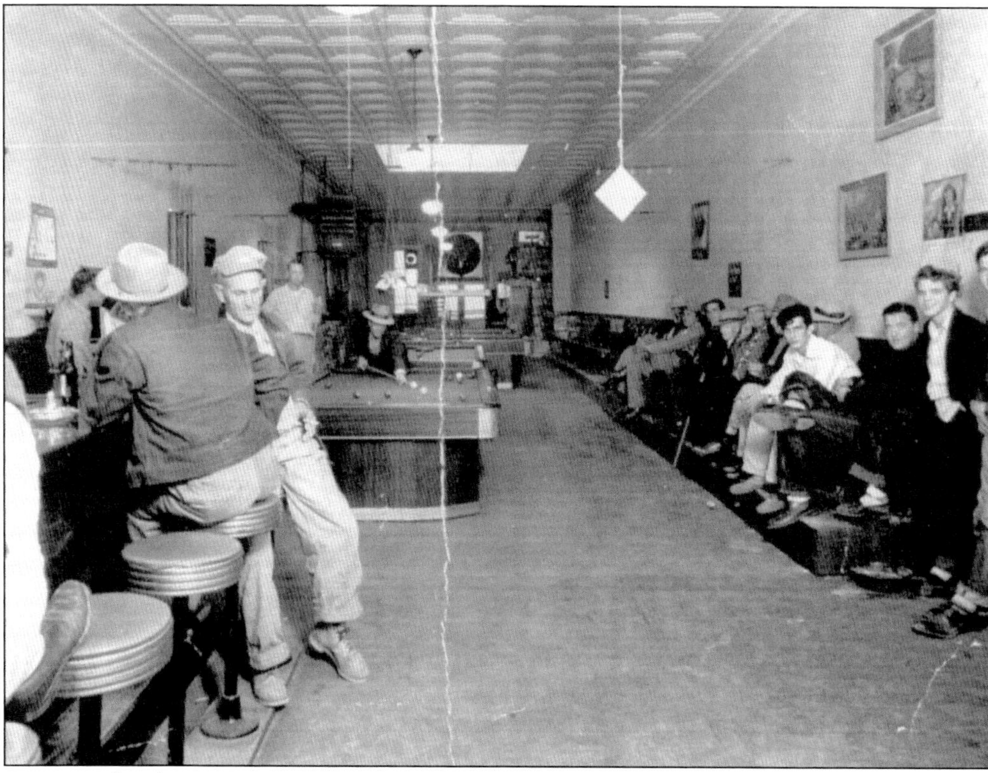

Pastime Billiards was a popular gathering place for the men of Searcy in the 1950s. It was located on Spruce Street, on the west side of the courthouse, and was owned by Tommy Killough. (Courtesy Nancy Williams Showalter.)

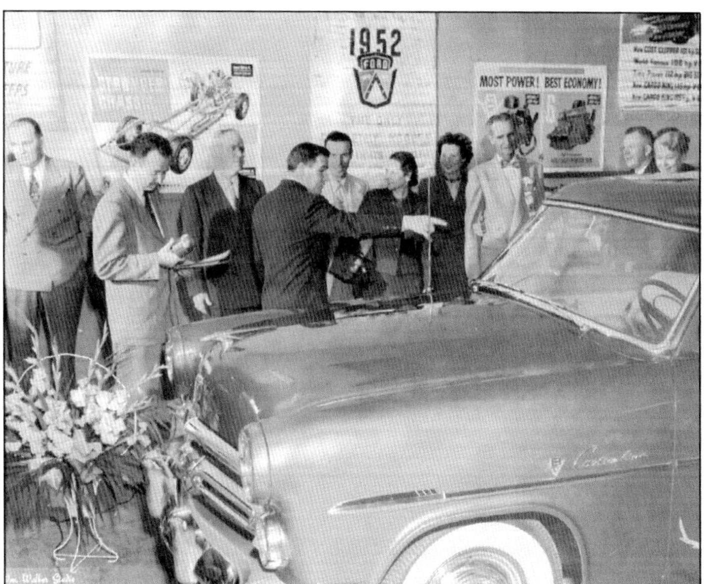

This group admiring the new Ford automobile in downtown Searcy includes, from left to right, Jim James, Johnny Argo (from radio station KWCK), A.C. Webb, Palmer Webb, George Bell, Alice Lynn Bell, Gretchen Whitescarver, I.J. Whitescarver, Loyal V. Norman, and ? Norman. (Courtesy Duke Webb and Hallie Sanford.)

Seen here decorating a large cedar tree on the courthouse square in preparation for the Christmas holidays in 1952 are, from left to right, Wayne Morris, John Sanford, unidentified, and Troy Wright. (Courtesy John Baker Photography.)

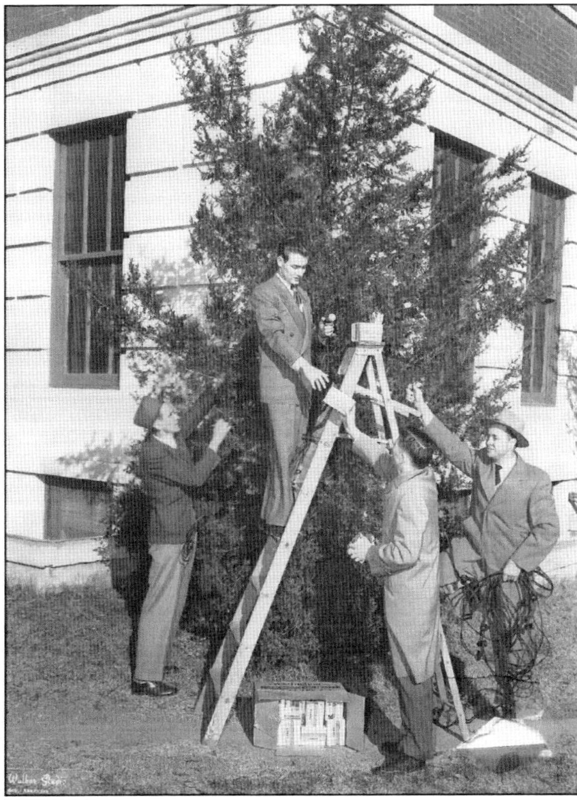

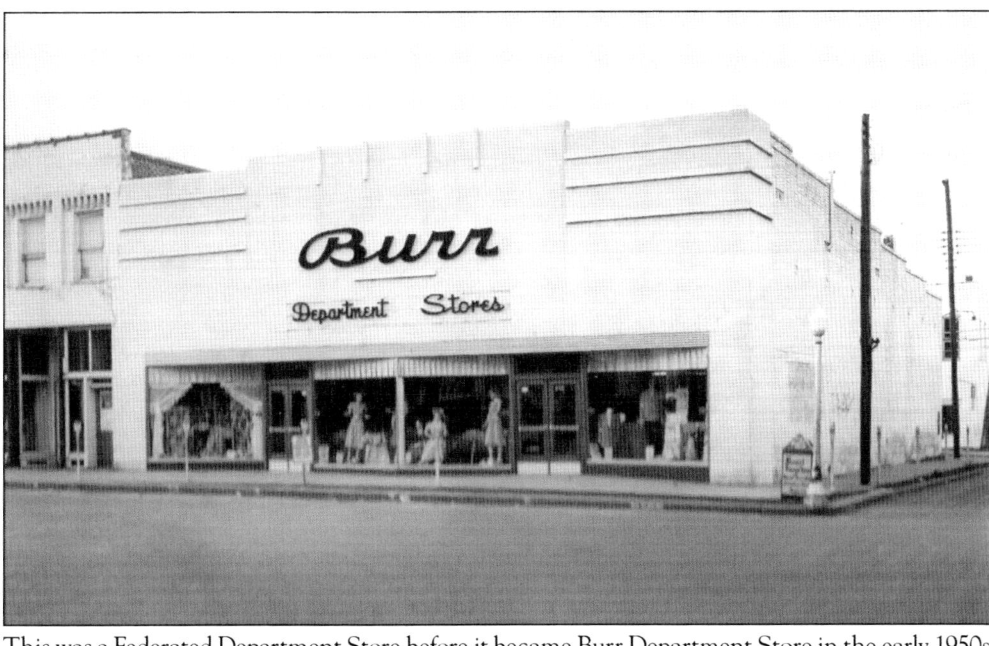

This was a Federated Department Store before it became Burr Department Store in the early 1950s, when it was remodeled and given the new name. The Searcy Chamber of Commerce featured this photograph in a scrapbook that was entered in a state competition for the years 1952 and 1953. (Courtesy Main Street Searcy.)

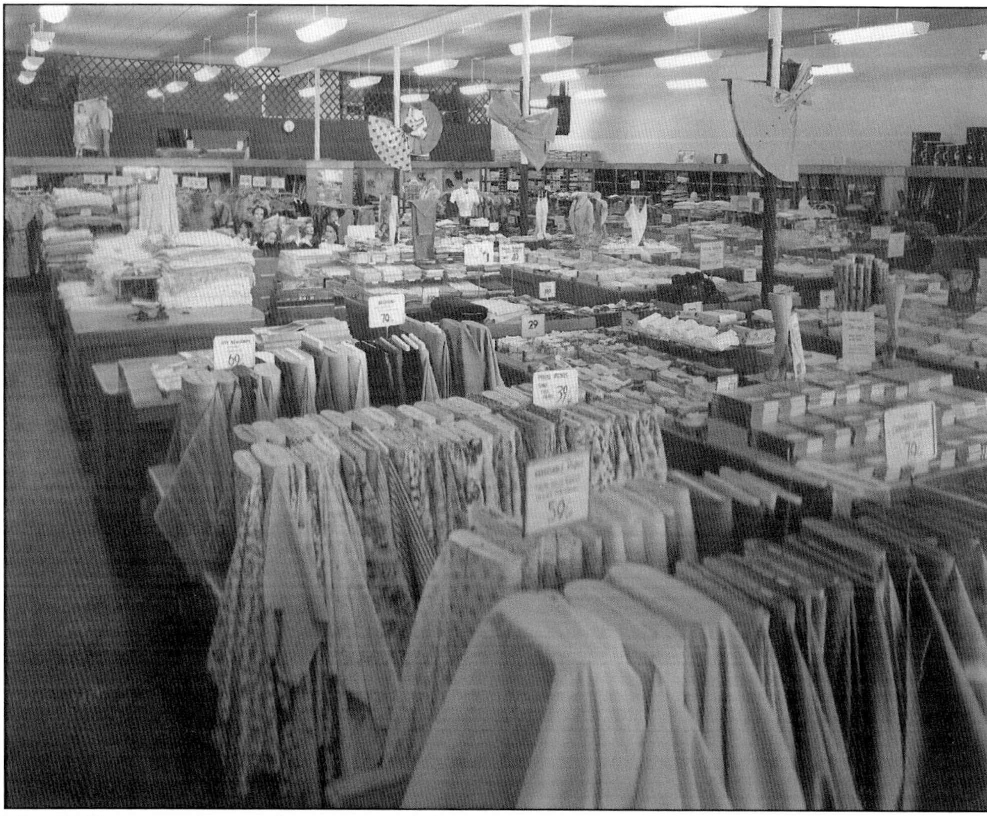

This 1950s image depicts the interior of the Burr Department Store. The fabric cost less than a dollar per yard. The store was located on the corner of Spruce and Arch Streets, on the south side of the square. An Anthony's Store later occupied this location. (Courtesy Main Street Searcy.)

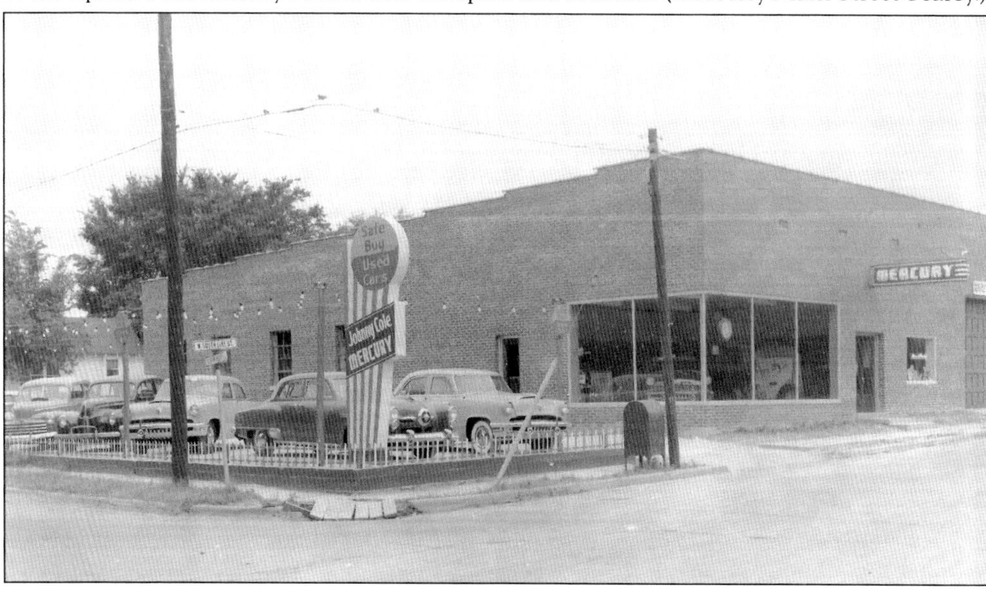

In 1952, Johnny Cole Mercury was located on West South Line (now Woodruff Street) and South Spring Streets, across from Spring Park. (Courtesy Steve Barger.)

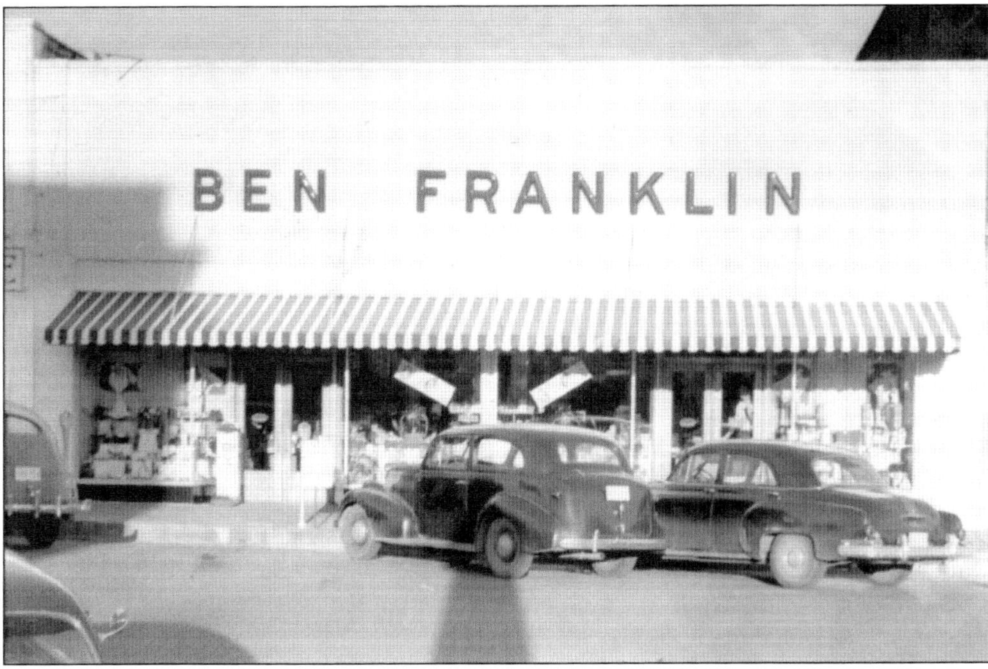

In 1952, White County Motor Company, which had been in this building on the east side of the square, moved to East Race Avenue, beyond Gin Creek. The Ben Franklin store took over the dealership's former location. The gas pump that stood in front of the automobile dealership had been removed by the time this photograph was taken. (Courtesy SRCC.)

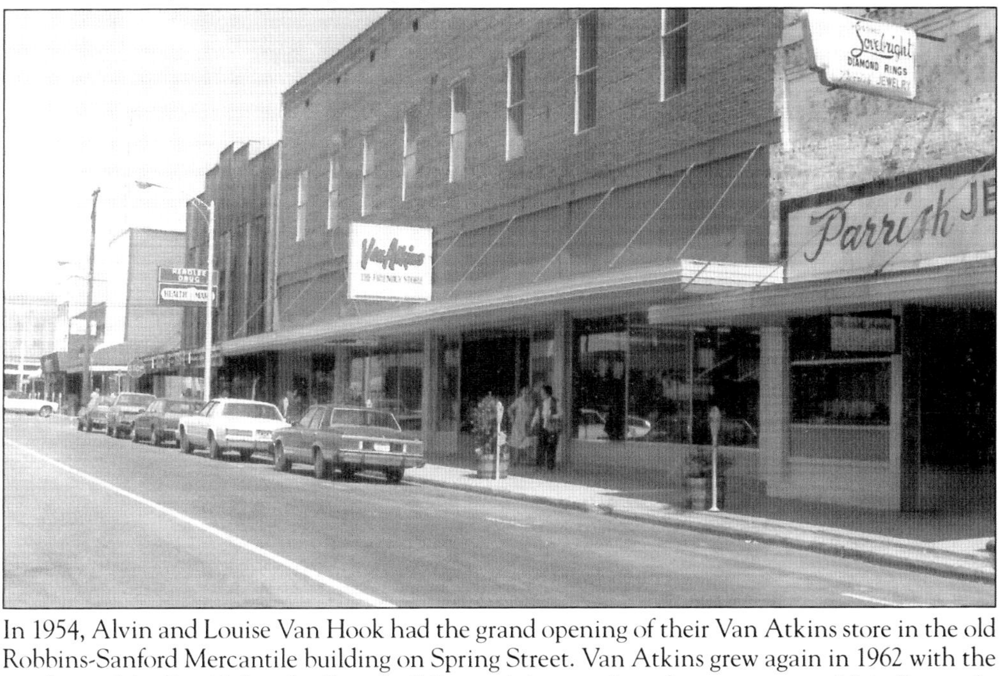

In 1954, Alvin and Louise Van Hook had the grand opening of their Van Atkins store in the old Robbins-Sanford Mercantile building on Spring Street. Van Atkins grew again in 1962 with the purchase of the Parrish Jewelry Store building and the opening of an entrance on Main Street. At that time, they also remodeled and added a jewelry department. For 44 years, Van Atkins was a major store in the downtown shopping area until it closed in 1998. (Courtesy Ron Van Hook.)

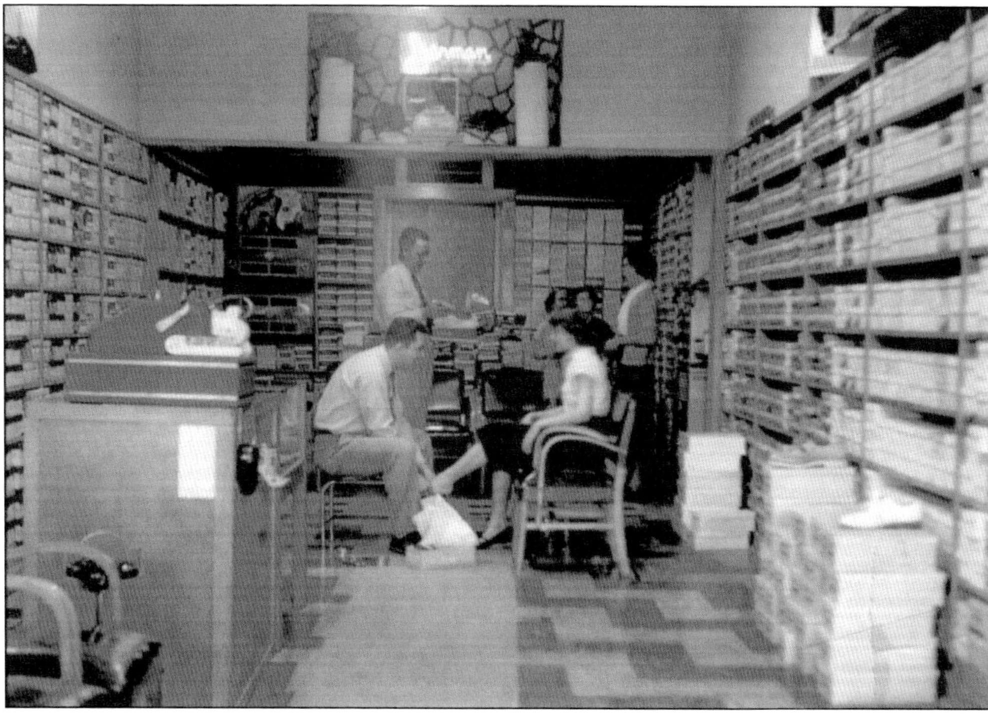

Women are assisted by male sales clerks while trying on shoes at the Family Shoe Store in the 1950s. (Courtesy SRCC.)

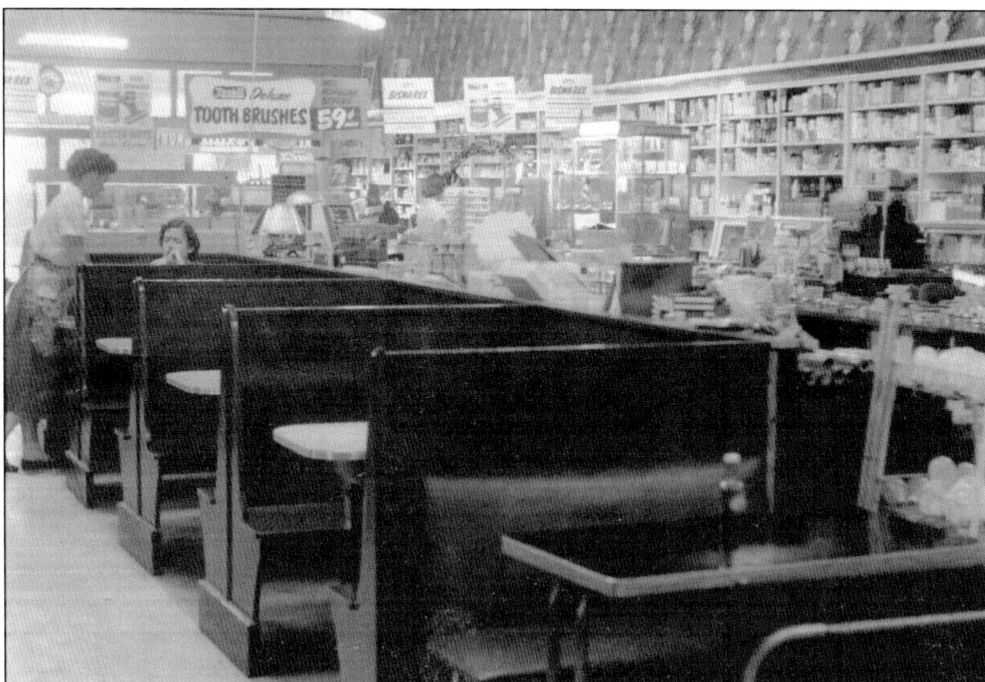

A woman ponders her food order while a waitress stands by inside the Headlee Drug Store during the 1950s. (Courtesy SRCC.)

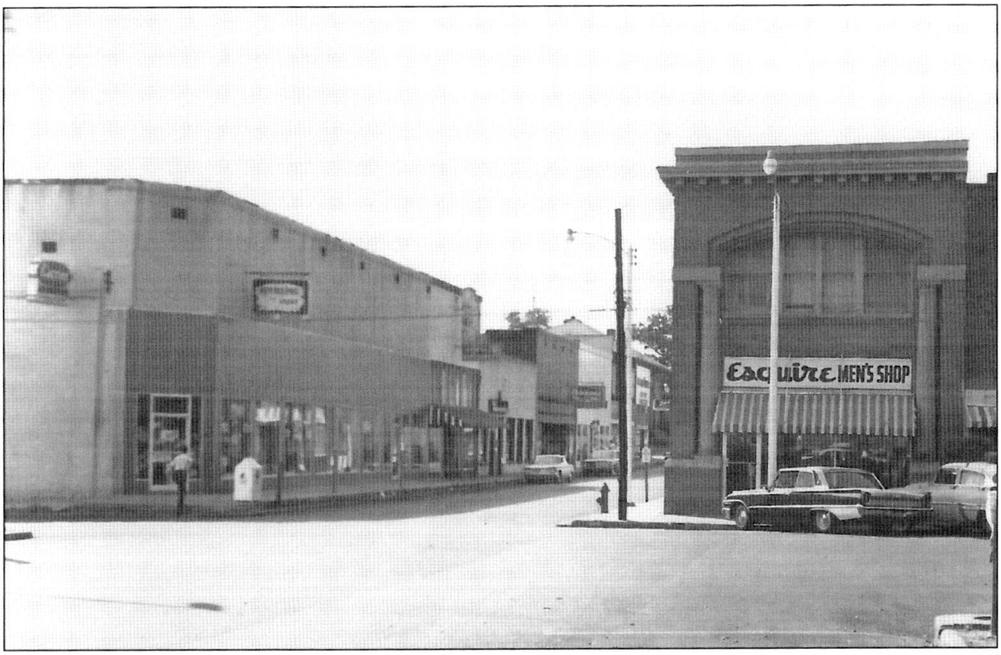

Esquire Men's Shop was located on the corner of Arch and Spruce Streets in the 1960s. Frank Headlee Jr. owned and operated the store. (Courtesy Eloise Muncy.)

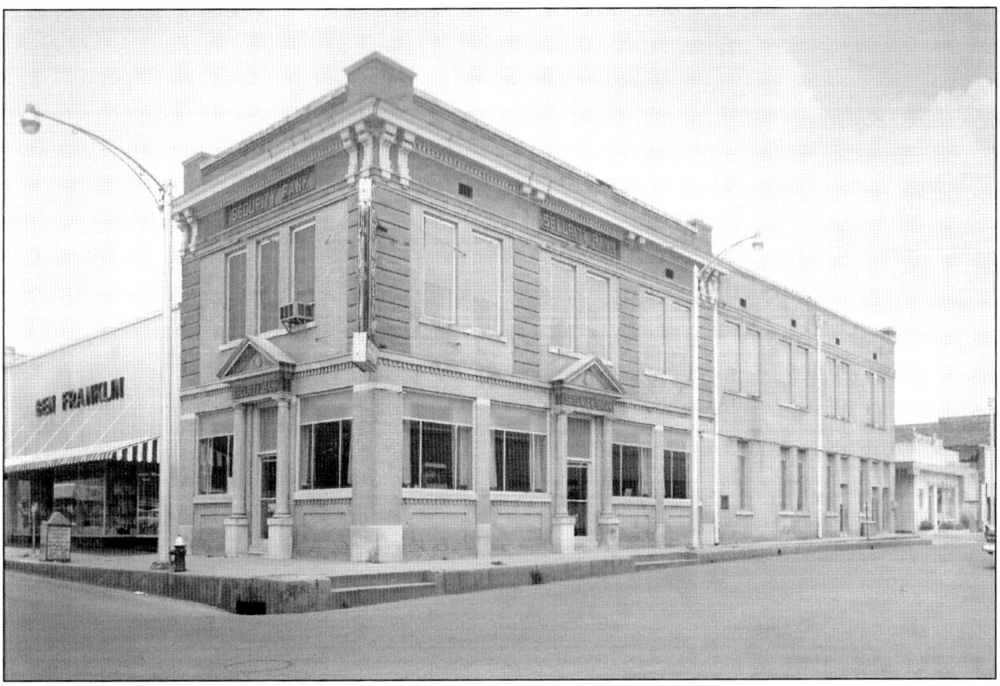

In the 1950s, First Security Bank occupied the corner of Spring and Arch Streets, next door to the Ben Franklin store. During the 1960s, John Paul Capps's radio station KWCB broadcast from the corner of the building. The Van Heusen shirt company, which had a factory in neighboring Augusta, operated an outlet store in one of the buildings on the far right of this photograph. (Courtesy First Security Bank.)

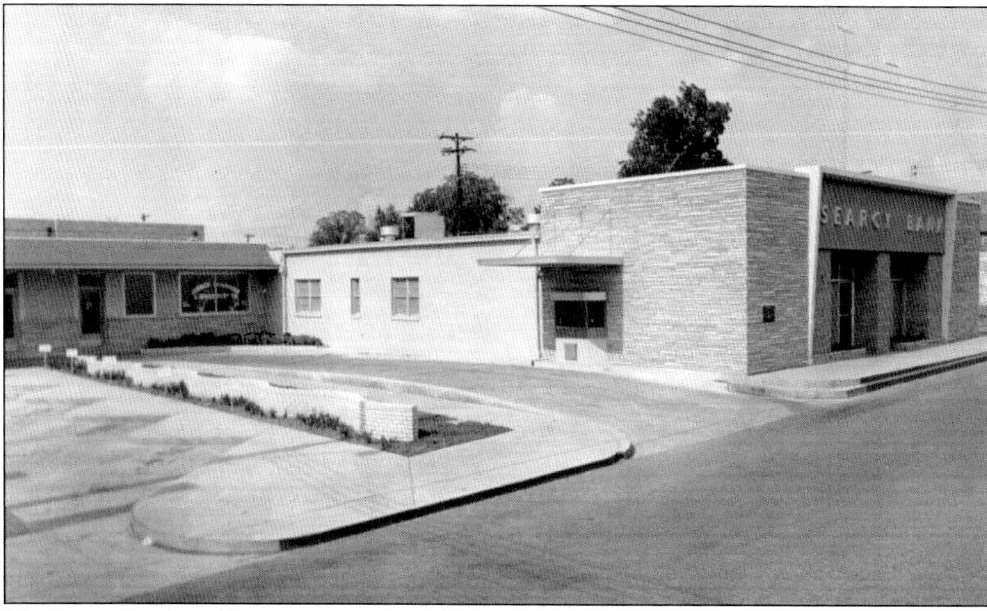

The Searcy Bank and Pyeatt Insurance and Investments both celebrated their 50th anniversaries while located in this new building in 1954. It was located on the corner of Race Avenue and Spruce Streets in the present-day location of Regions Bank. Officers and employees at the Searcy Bank in 1954 included Ewing Pyeatt, Marion Schwarz, Wayne Pyeatt, Phillip Pyeatt, Major Pickens, Modene Johnston, Joe Tom O'Guin, Paul King, Lela Duncan, Joyce King, Bobbie Loftin, Sylvia Tompkins, and Odie Dockens. (Courtesy Regions Bank and Phil Pyeatt.)

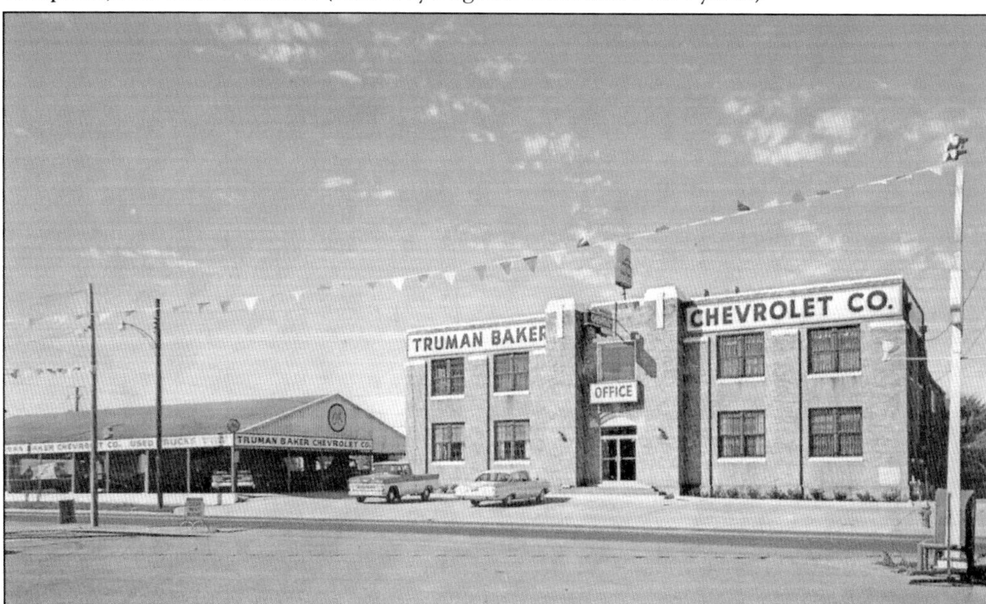

In 1958, Truman Baker Chevrolet moved to its third location—the old National Guard armory at 208–210 East Race Avenue. The back of this postcard says "Truman Baker Chevrolet has the Finest and Most Modern Parts and Service Departments in the Entire South." These buildings were demolished in 2005 to make way for a Walgreens. (Courtesy Nancy Williams Showalter.)

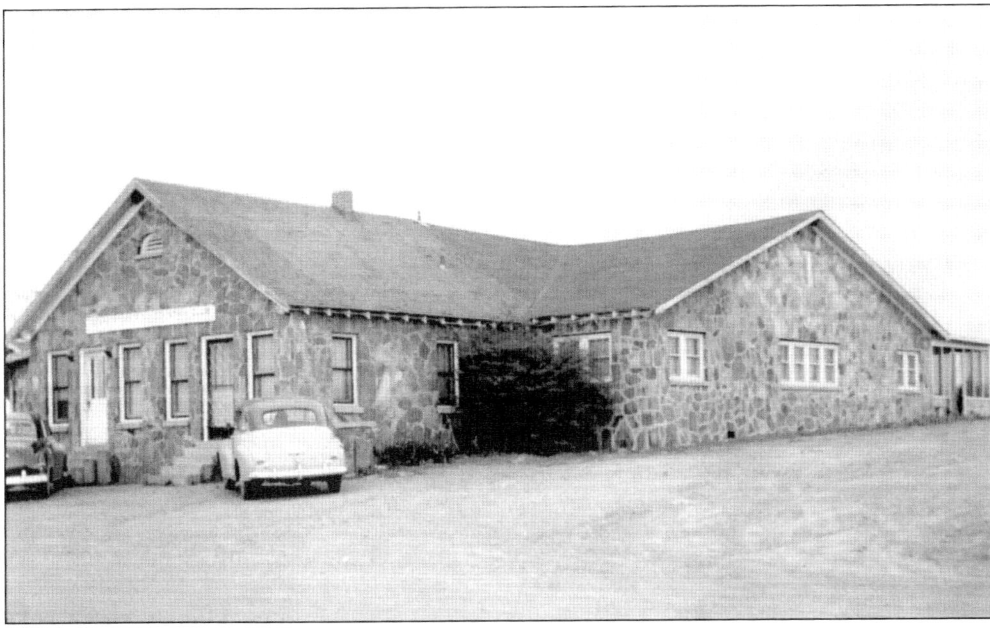

The first Searcy Country/Supper Club was located near the city limits on the east side of town where the White County Fair entrance on Davis Drive is today. It was a fieldstone building with a large dance floor. The club had a nine-hole golf course, with sand greens, located down the hill behind the club near the present-day Lightle Senior Center. (Courtesy SRCC.)

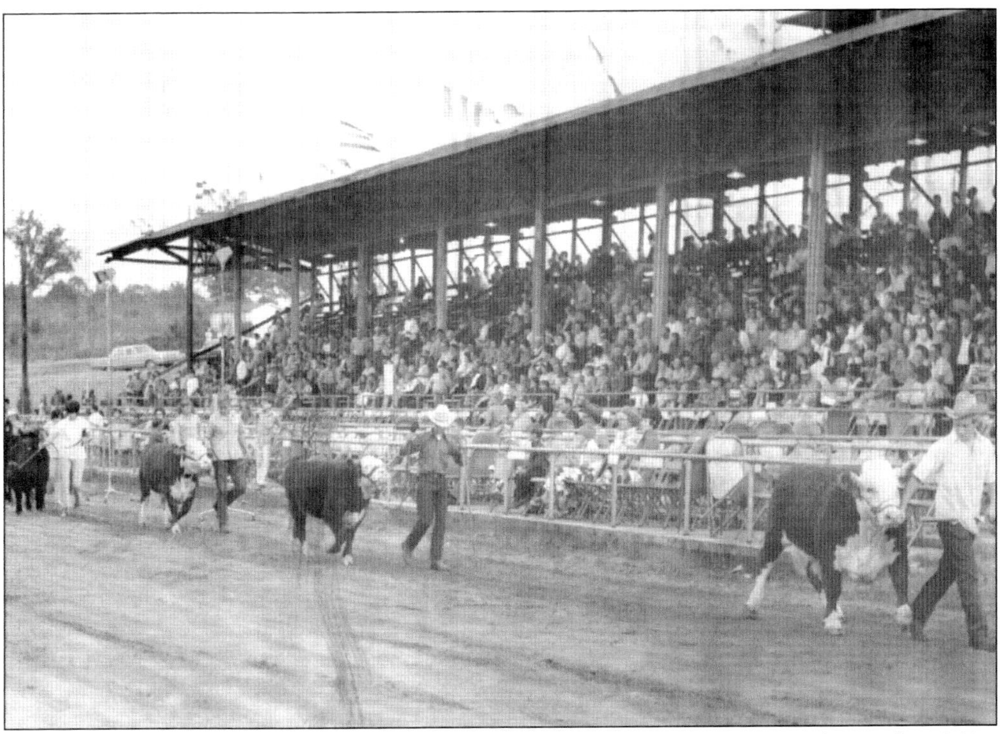

Cattle are led past the audience during the White County Fair in the early 1960s. (Courtesy SRCC.)

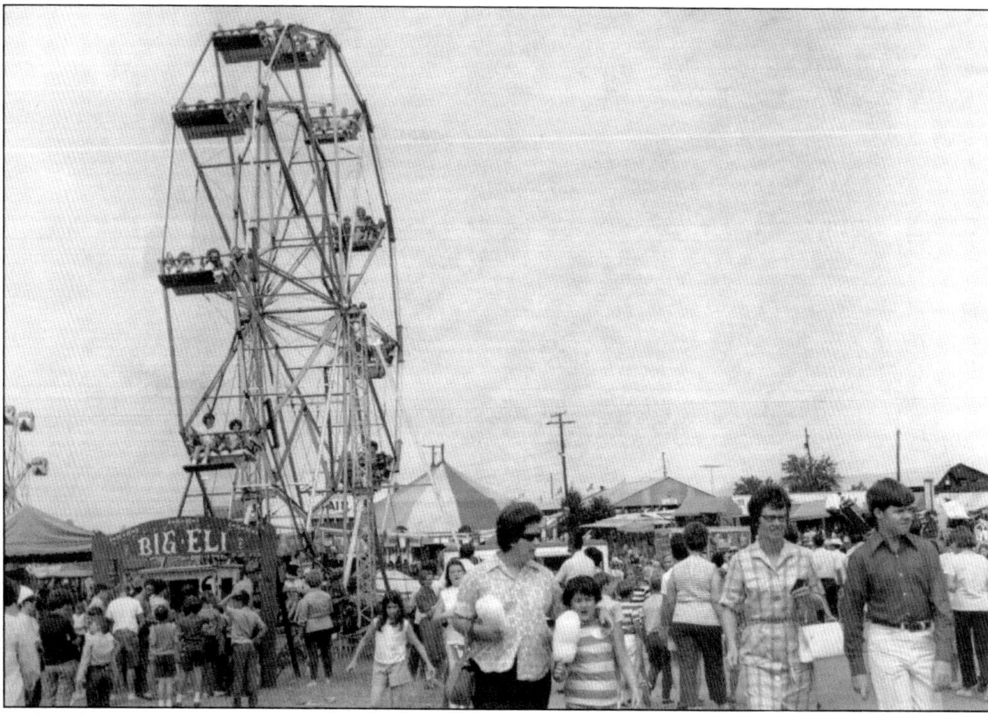

A family enjoys cotton candy at the fair. On August 19, 1993, the *Los Angeles Times* published a survey in its travel section. The article, written by a Mrs. Zook, said the White County Fair had been voted among the 10 best small county fairs in the United States. At that time, fairs still had blue-ribbon competitions in crafts, such as sewing, quilting, and canning. Pres. Bill Clinton learned about it and called the White County Fair office. He told Linda Benton, the secretary, about the newspaper article. It was Mrs. Benton's birthday, and she was thrilled not only to learn the news about the fair but also that President Clinton shared her birthday. Searcy resident, Irene Gray, was in Los Angeles at the time and brought the newspaper home to share the article. (Courtesy SRCC.)

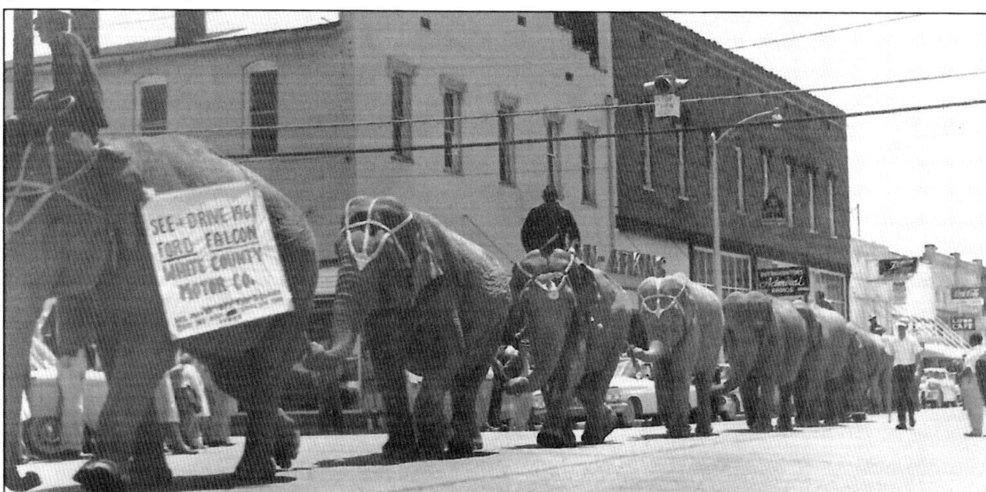

Elephants lead a parade through downtown Searcy in 1961. The lead elephant appears to be on its way to see the new Ford Falcon at White County Motor Company. (Courtesy Eloise Muncy.)

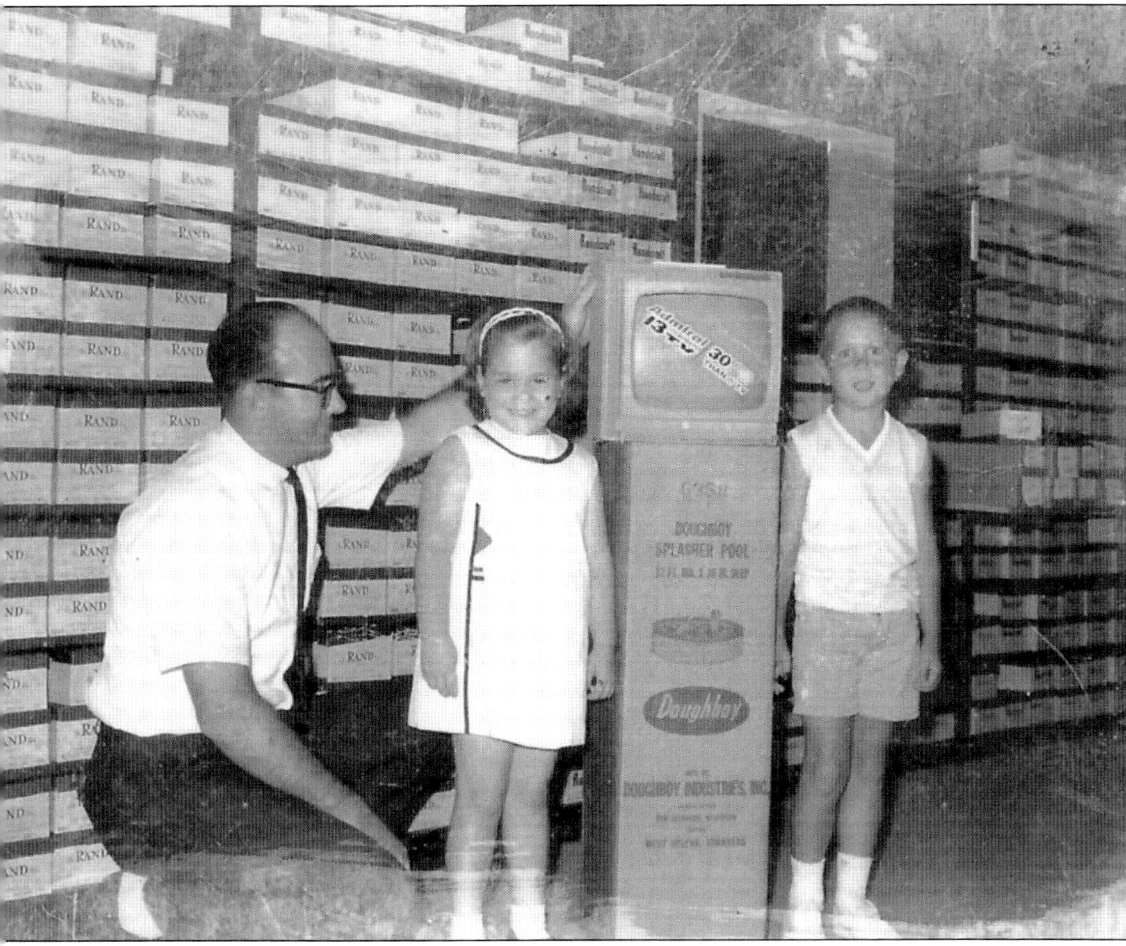

Dean Wallis (left) of Family Shoe Store, on the corner of Spring and Market Streets for many years, awarded prizes to contest winners Nancy Williams and David Pipkin in 1965. Poll Parrot Shoes held a national contest to name its mascot, and Family Shoe Store sponsored the local contest. The winning local entries were submitted in the national contest. Neither Williams nor Pipkin won the national contest, but as local winners, Williams received a television set and Pipkin got a plastic swimming pool. (Courtesy Nancy Williams Showalter.)

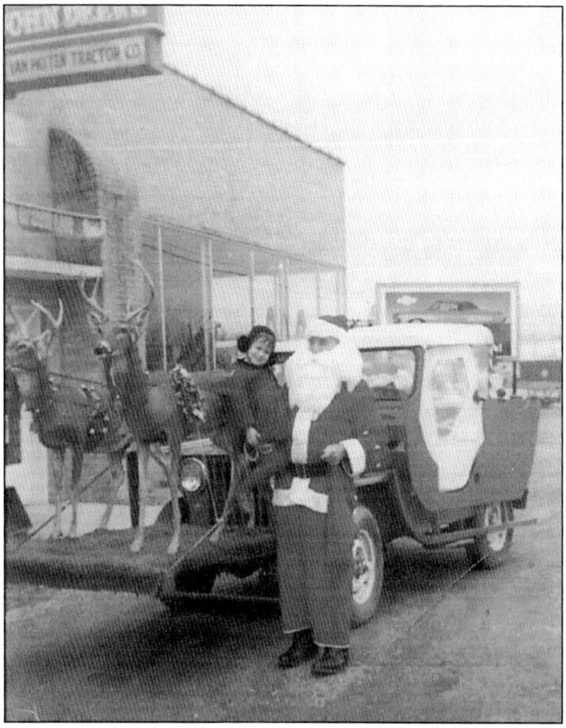

Herman and Hettivee Van Patten's daughter Suzanne, age three, poses with Santa Claus in 1968. Preacher Mullens played Santa in the Searcy area for many years. This photograph was taken in front of the Van Patten Tractor Company. In the background is a billboard for the year's new Chevrolet. (Courtesy Leon Van Patten.)

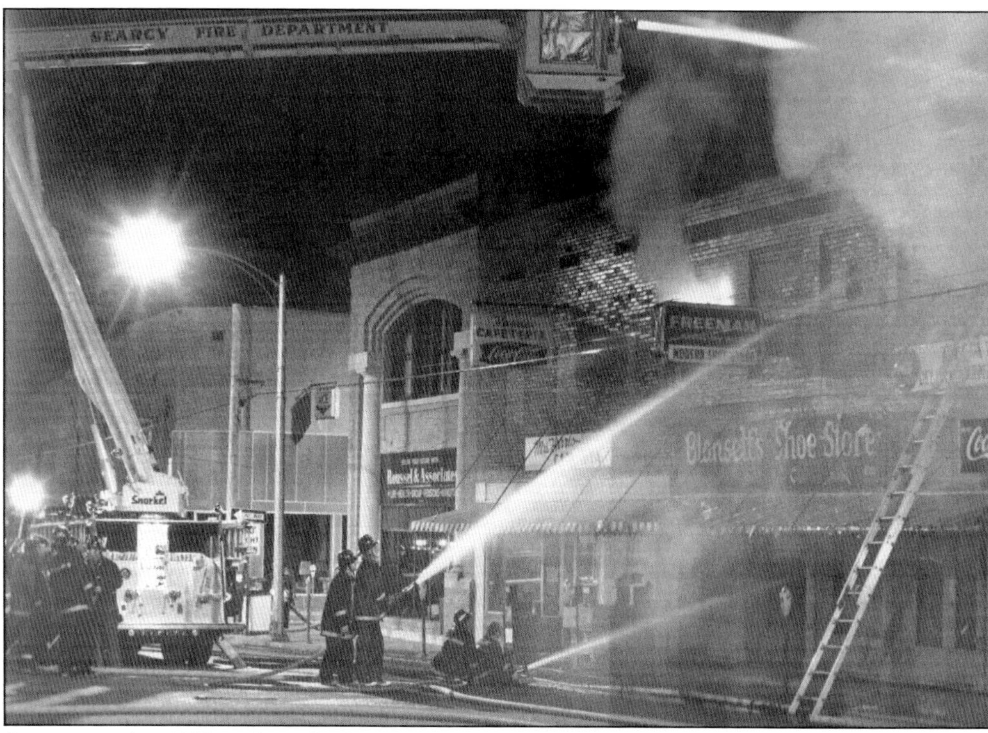

Sometime after 1975—when the Searcy Fire Department received its large fire truck—Blansett's Shoe Store and Mrs. Harris' Cafeteria, located across from the courthouse on Spruce Street, were damaged by fire during the night. (Courtesy Jack Wiseman.)

This is a picture of one of the two Esso stations located in Searcy during the 20th century. One was the Friendly Esso Station, and the other was 99 Esso. Friendly was at Spring Street and Pleasure Avenue; 99 Esso was across the street from the Rendezvous Cafe. (Courtesy SRCC.)

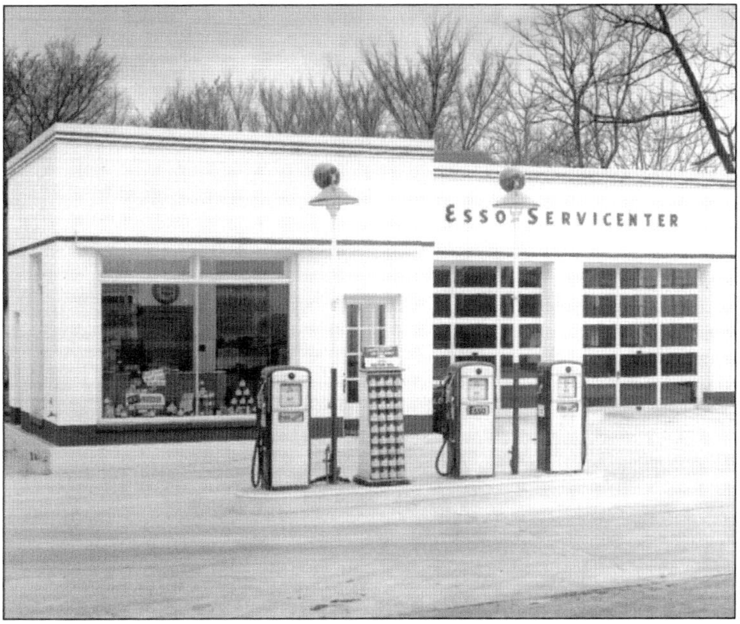

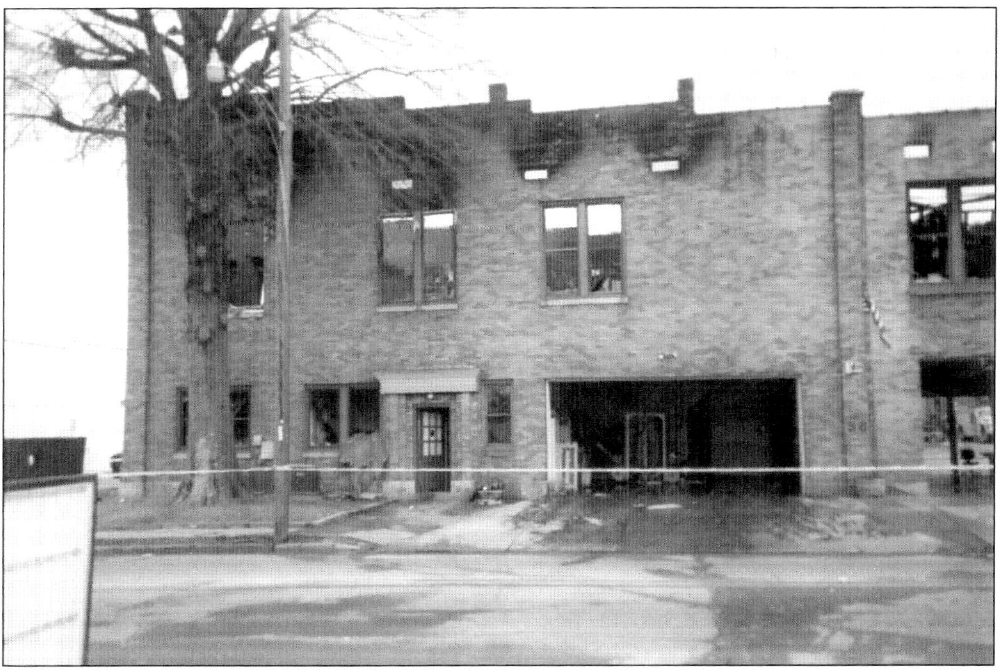

The building downtown that housed both the city court offices and the Searcy Fire Department suffered a fire in 2005. The fire started in the middle room, which was located above the garage entrance. Old wiring in the building caused the fire. The living quarters of the fire department were heavily damaged, but thankfully, no one was injured in the blaze. (Courtesy Leon and Sherry Person.)

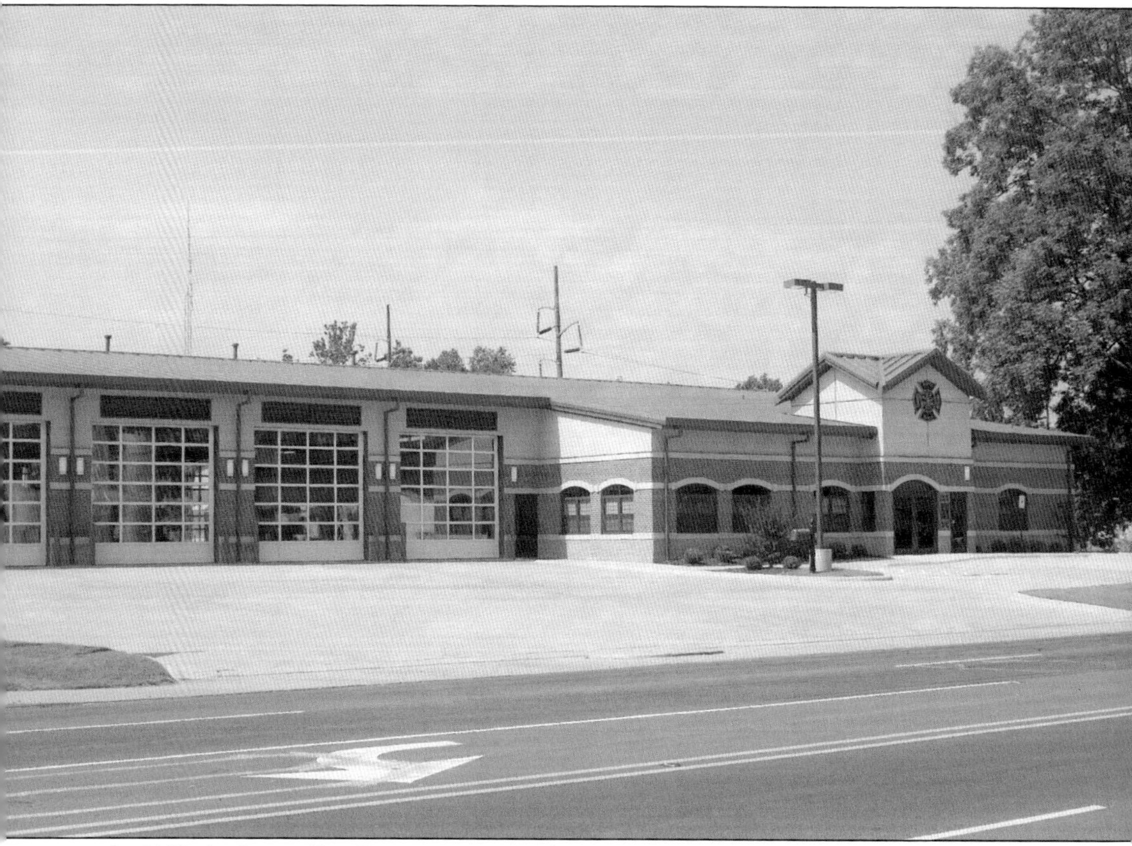

In 2007, the Searcy Fire Department moved into its new home on Beebe-Capps Expressway. This state-of-the-art facility was built with a combination of funds from the insurance settlement on the old fire station and a temporary nine-month special tax. (Courtesy Carolyn Boyles.)

Three

COMMUNITY

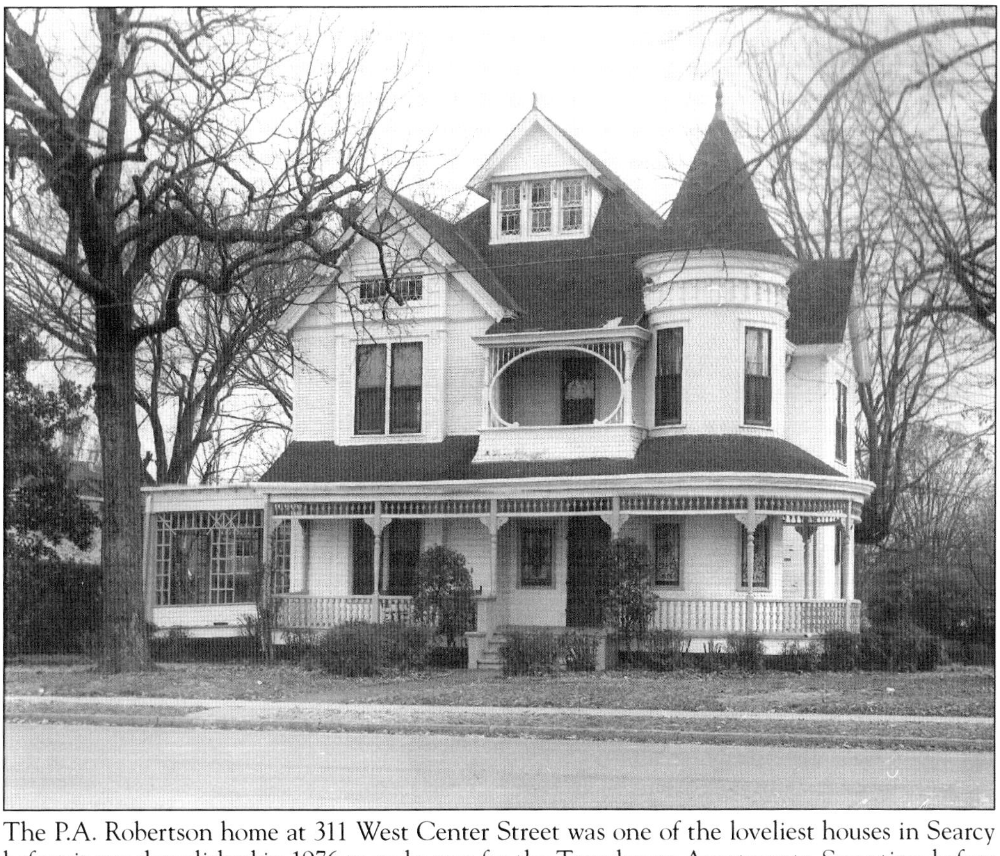

The P.A. Robertson home at 311 West Center Street was one of the loveliest houses in Searcy before it was demolished in 1976 to make way for the Townhouse Apartments. Sometime before 1900, Robertson constructed the two-story building on the southeast corner of the square for his drugstore, which is now Quattlebaum's Music. This house was built in a Queen Anne Victorian architectural style and was on the National Register of Historic Places. It had stained-glass windows. A group of Searcy residents formed a land company to raise funds to buy the house. Membership in the land company cost $1,000 per share. Sadly, the land company failed to raise enough money, thus, the house and land were sold at public auction. The house was 78 years old when it was torn down. (Courtesy John Baker Photography.)

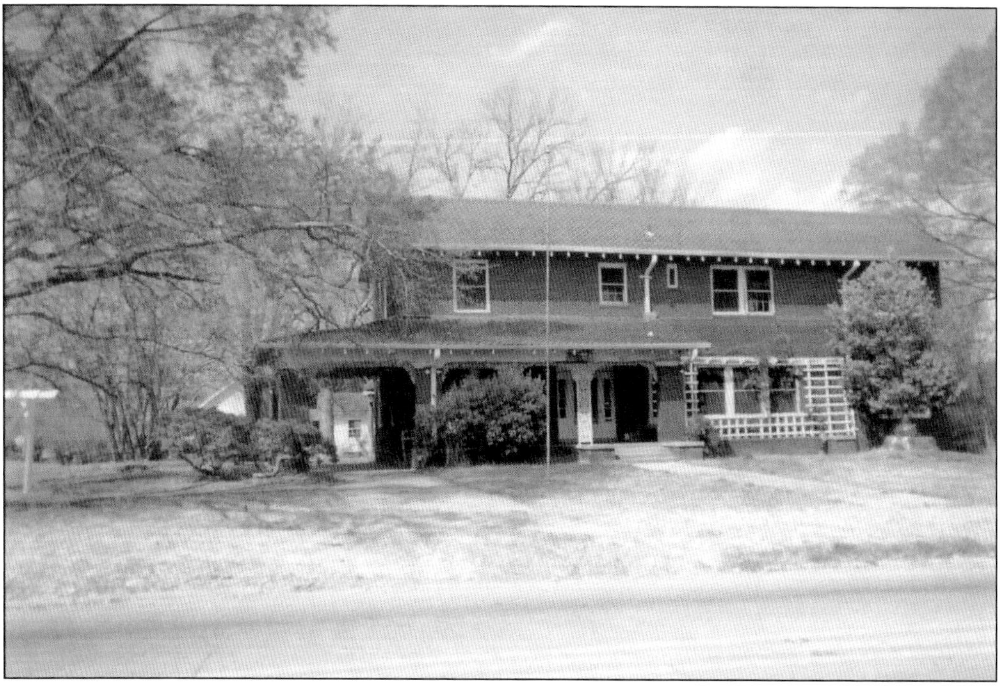

The Tom Watkins House on the corner of Oak Street and East Race Avenue was built in the 1920s. It is a Charles L. Thompson Craftsman design and is listed on the National Register of Historic Places. (Courtesy Leon and Sherry Person.)

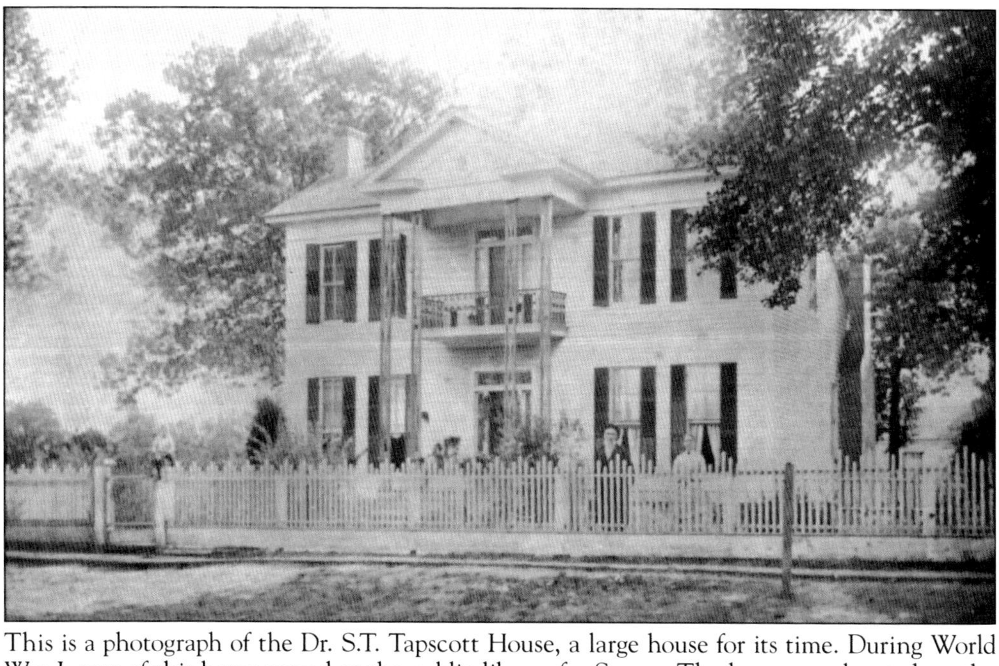

This is a photograph of the Dr. S.T. Tapscott House, a large house for its time. During World War I, part of this home served as the public library for Searcy. The house was located on the northwest corner of East Race Avenue and Main Street, where Highways 67 and 64 turned south and east before bypassing Searcy. First Security Bank's technology center and parking lot now occupy this corner. (Courtesy Eloise Muncy.)

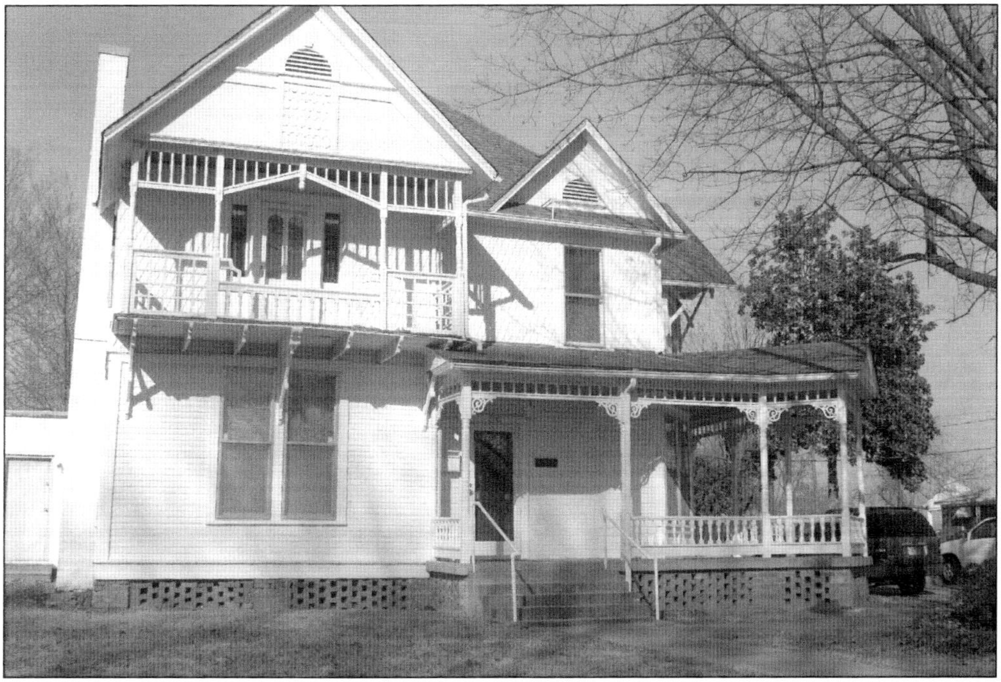

This picture shows the front of the Lattimer House, an 1895 Queen Anne Revival located at 308 East Market Street. It is now home to Strother-Wilbourn Title Company. (Courtesy Carolyn Boyles.)

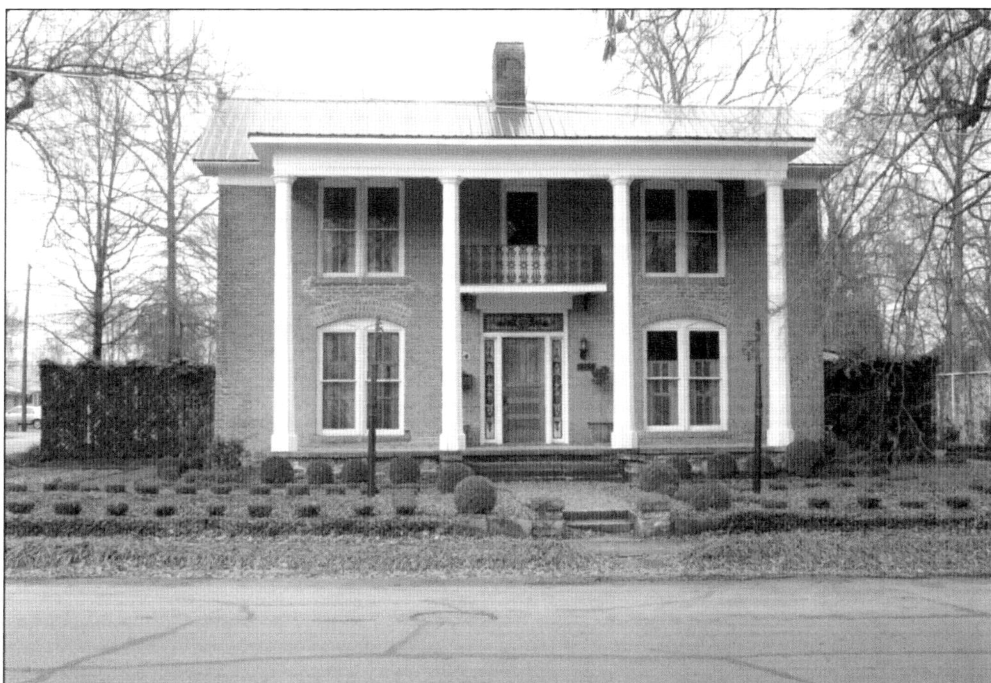

This is a photograph of the Paschall House at 400 East Center Street. It was built in 1890 in the brick "I" vernacular style. It is now a private residence. (Courtesy Carolyn Boyles.)

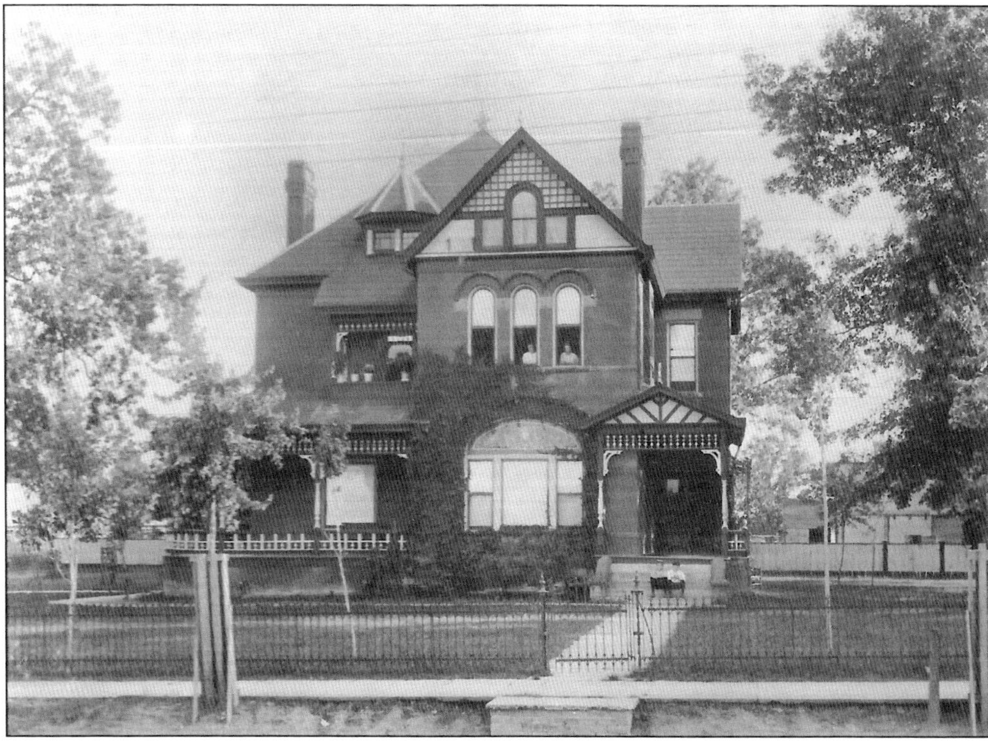

The Jim Skillern House, later known as the John Sanford home, was one of Searcy's most stately residences. It was located on West Arch Street. Old family records show the structure cost more than $5,000 when it was built in the 1800s. It was demolished for the construction of the West Side Church of Christ. The William Watkins home, which also served as the Searcy Male and Female Institute in 1893, is pictured below. Male students entered through one door, and females entered through a separate door. This was Searcy's first attempt at coeducation. (Both, courtesy Eloise Muncy.)

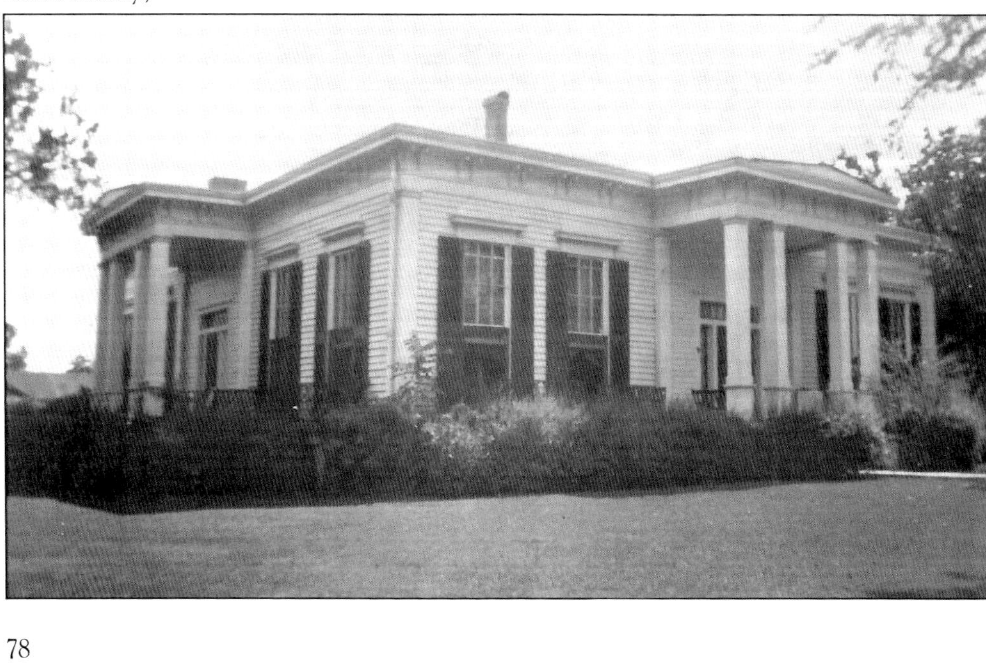

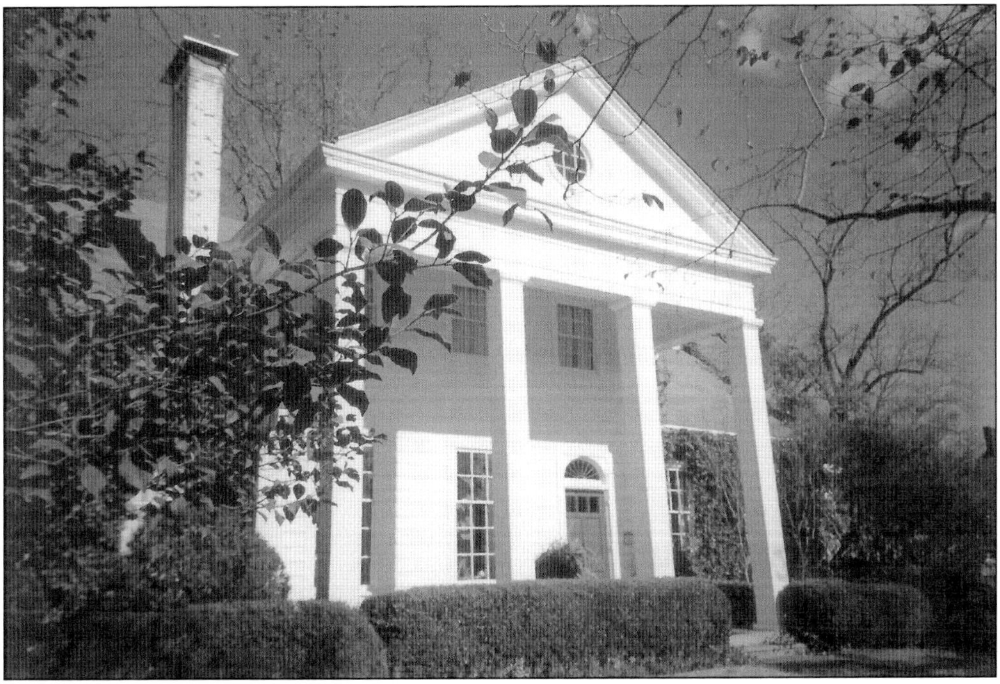

In the photograph above, Dr. Porter Rodgers Sr. and Fern Cowan Rodgers built their house on the corner of Oak Street and East Race Avenue in 1925. It was in the Colonial Revival style and listed on the National Register of Historic Places. The house was demolished at the request of Dr. Porter Rodgers Jr., who inherited it. The location is now a parklike setting next door to the Searcy Arts Gallery. Mary Neisbitt Jones's house, which had served as a hospital during the Civil War, was built on the land before the war but torn down to make room. Below is the E.A. Robbins home built in 1929 on the corner of West Center and North Gum Streets. Ivan Quattlebaum and his wife, Frances, bought this house in the 1960s and lived there for many years. (Both, courtesy Leon and Sherry Person.)

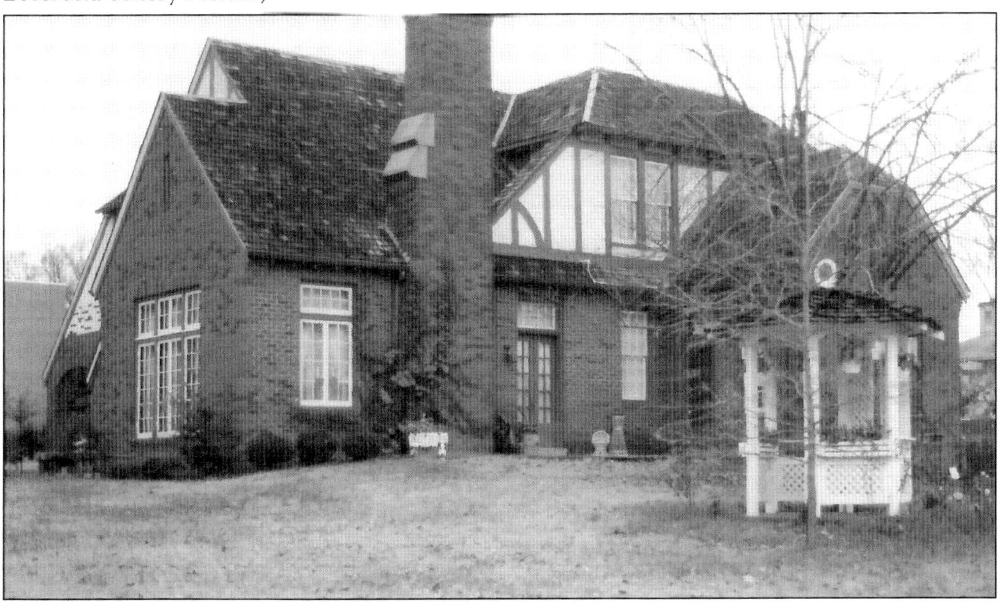

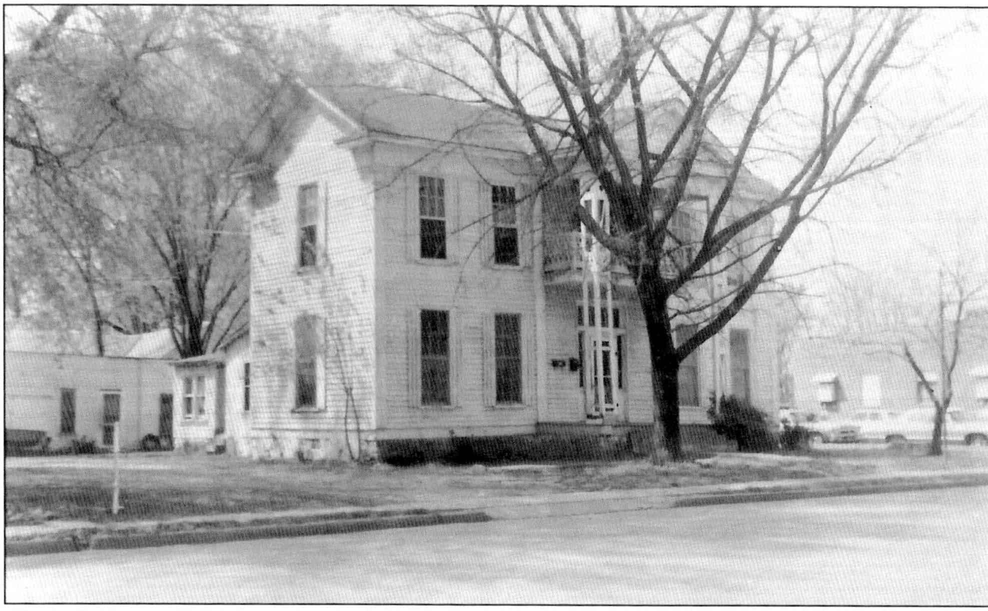

The Bob Rogers House was located on the corner of West Woodruff and South Spring Streets. The house faced Spring Park. This home, an 1879 Greek Revival I-style house, was listed on the National Register of Historic Places for many years. Simmons First National Bank now occupies this corner. (Courtesy Eloise Muncy.)

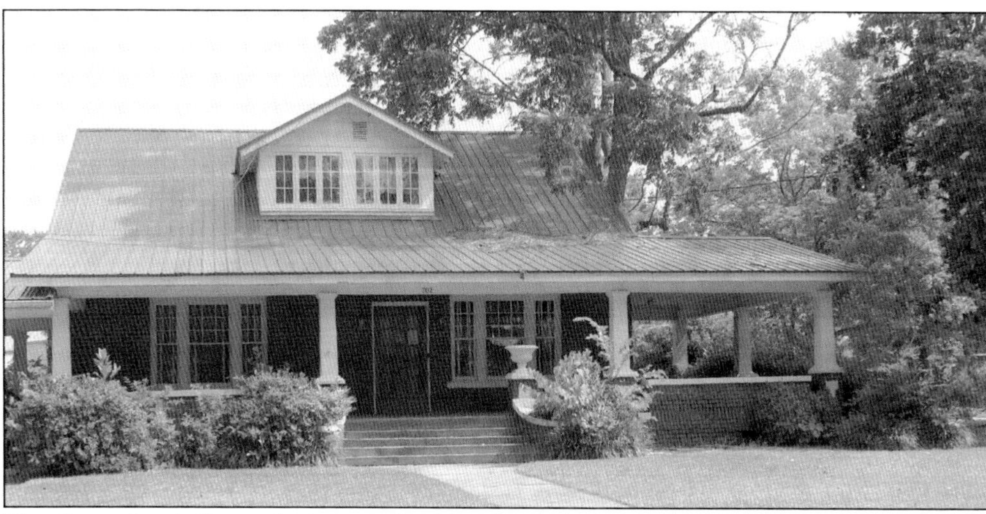

The Green Booth House, built around 1925, is located on the corner of South Pecan and West Center Streets. It was listed on the National Register of Historic Places in 1991. (Courtesy Carolyn Boyles.)

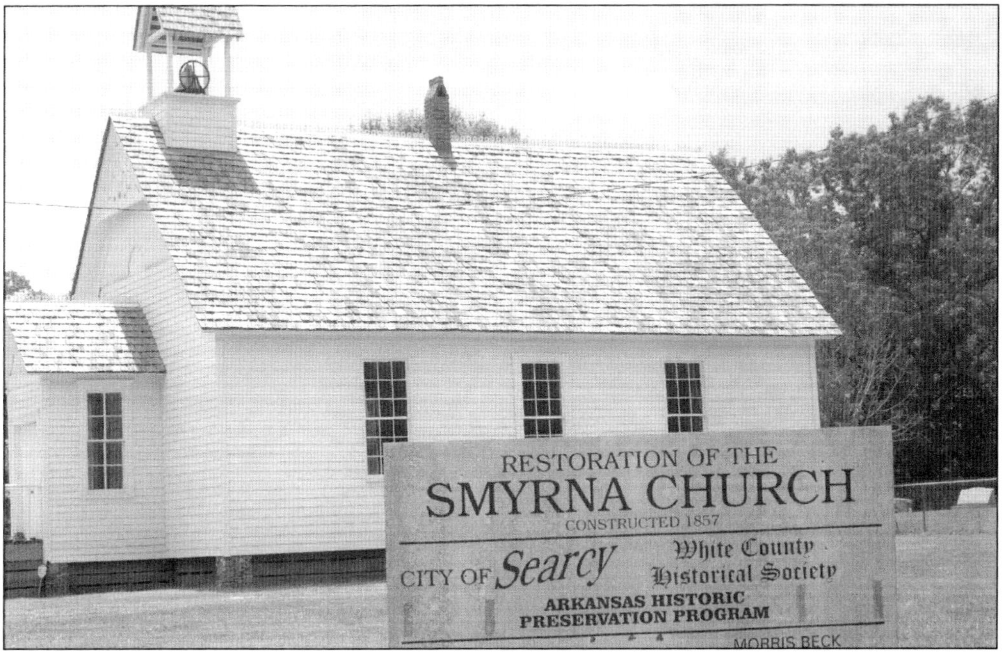

The Smyrna Church, completed in 1857, is the oldest documented church building in Arkansas. The cemetery behind the church has graves dating to the 1850s. After renovation by volunteers from the White County Historical Society and the Searcy Arts Council, and with the help of city employees, the church now looks like this. (Courtesy Carolyn Boyles.)

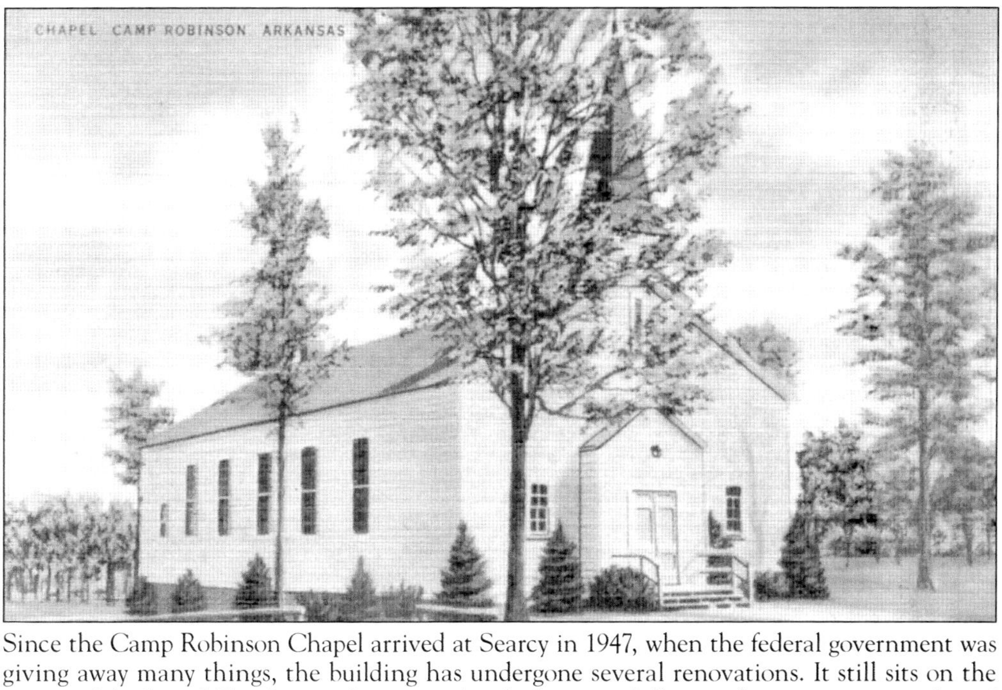

Since the Camp Robinson Chapel arrived at Searcy in 1947, when the federal government was giving away many things, the building has undergone several renovations. It still sits on the corner of Arch and Elm Streets downtown but looks quite different after renovations enlarged the building to include a fellowship hall, a kitchen, additional classrooms, offices, a library, and a fireside room. (Courtesy Margo Shoffner.)

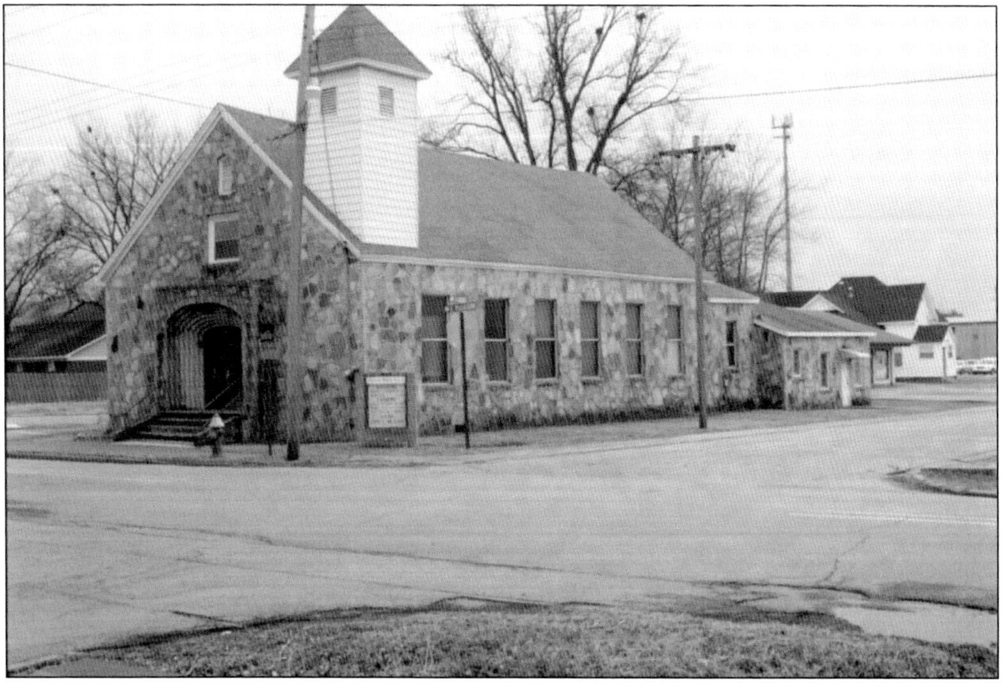

Bethlehem Baptist Church celebrated its 145th anniversary in 2011. Established in 1866 on the corner of Spring Street and Race Avenue, the church moved to its current location at 301 East Pleasure Avenue in 1872. After beginning at the East Pleasure Street location in a modest wood-frame building near the railroad tracks, fieldstone rock was added later. The church is home to one of the oldest black congregations in the city. (Courtesy Carolyn Boyles.)

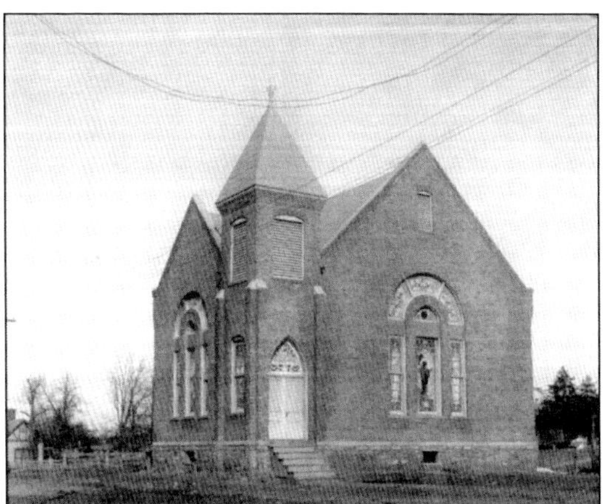

On July 16, 2000, the congregation of the Cumberland Presbyterian Church celebrated its 150th anniversary in Searcy. Alexander Stevenson and J.A. Wilson, ministers from Tennessee, founded the church. Searcy was a common stop on the circuit of traveling preachers during the mid-1800s. Today, the church has a small congregation but is still influential. Some of the original stained-glass windows were broken by the tornado that leveled nearby Judsonia, Arkansas, on March 21, 1952. They have since been replaced and are nearly indistinguishable from the originals. (Courtesy WCHS.)

In 1904, the Anti-Saloon Congress met in this First Presbyterian Church building, which was located on Main Street in Searcy at the time, in the future location of the Rendezvous Restaurant. First United Methodist Church now owns the old restaurant building. The First Presbyterian Church is currently located on the corner of Arch and Elm Streets. (Courtesy Leon and Sherry Person.)

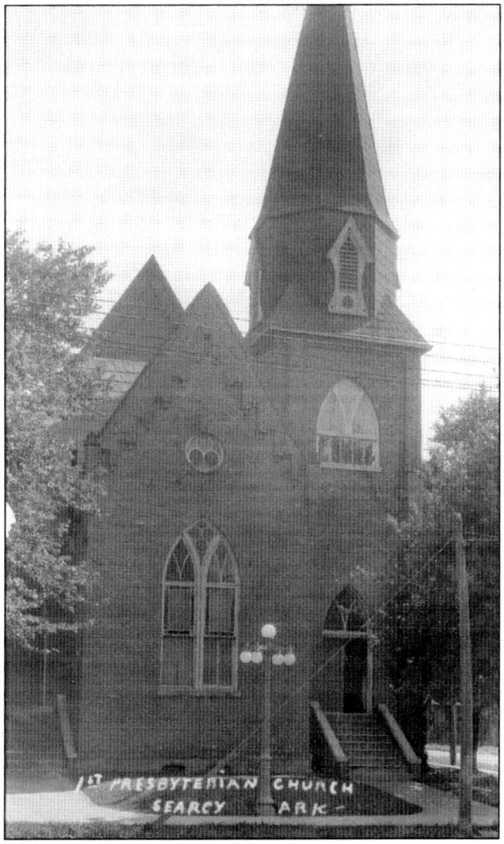

On May 16, 1892, the Sunday school class at the First Presbyterian Church sat for a photograph. Pictured here are, from left to right, (first row) Ada Cousan, Lida Chums, teacher ? Milliagan, Maud Miluer, and Kati Winsett; (second row) Fannie Faust, Lena Chambliss, Virginia Lightle, and Eula Enfrey. (Courtesy First Presbyterian Church.)

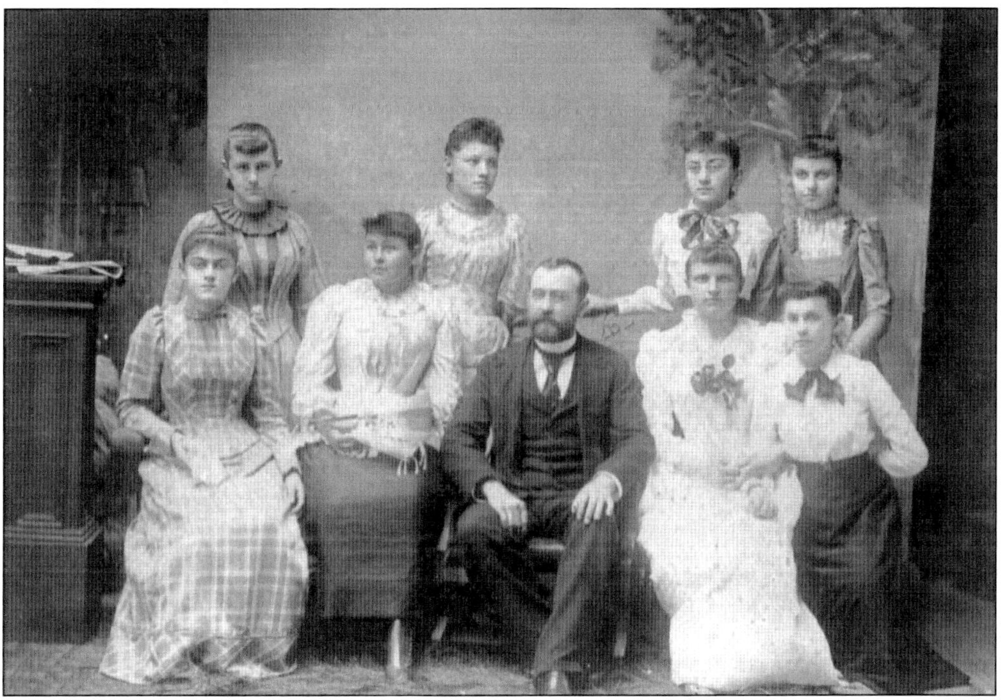

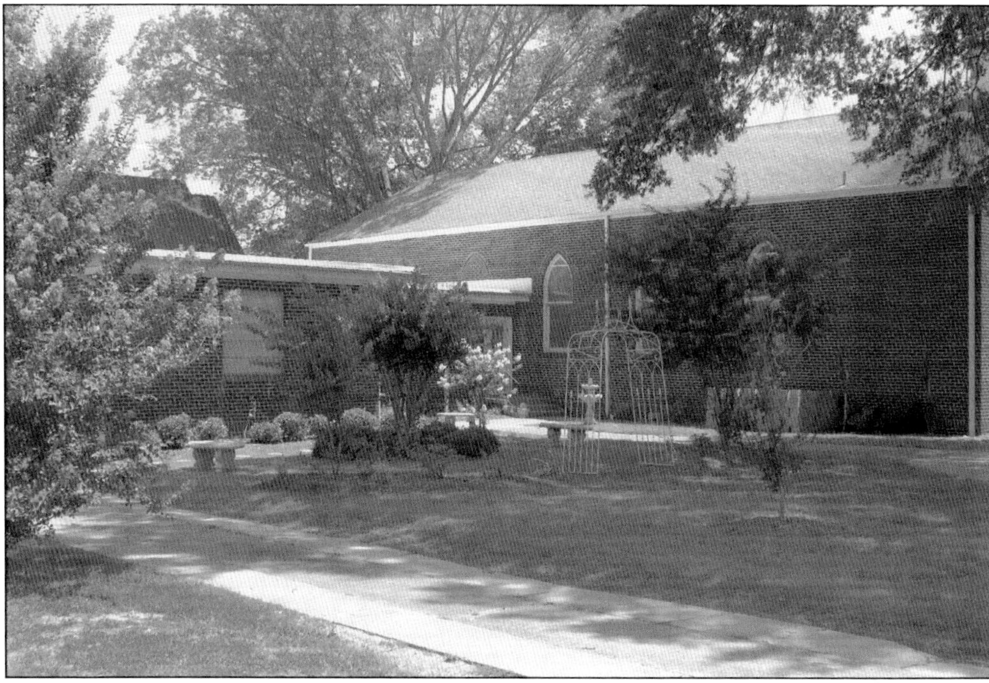

The Camp Robinson Chapel, originally located in North Little Rock, Arkansas, was moved to Searcy in 1947 and became the meetinghouse of the First Presbyterian Church. After being bricked, and following the addition of stained-glass windows, the building took on a new look and is now a lovely small church. (Courtesy Carolyn Boyles.)

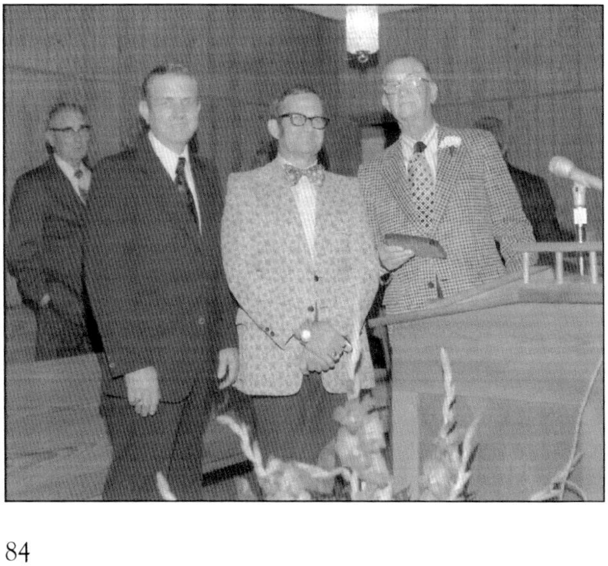

These men are taking part in the 1973 dedication service of the Honey Hill nondenominational church. They are Pierce Maddox, church councilman (left); Charles Lovell, builder (center); and Truman Baker, who provided the funding to build the church. Standing behind the three men is Jesse Beck. Witt Stephens of Little Rock wrote about Baker's generous memorial to his parents in the *Arkansas Democrat*'s "Sound Off!" column, saying "Honor Thy Mother and Thy Father—Truman Baker did." (Courtesy Hattie Mae Maddox.)

In 1867, George C. Watkins gave two lots on the corner of Pleasure Avenue and Main Street to the Trinity Episcopal Church to erect a building, but when the railroad was built nearby, the property was sold. Later, John Lightle, T.B. Paschall, W.C. Dugan, and John Hicks gave land at Arch and Elm Streets to the church. The Trinity Episcopal Church recently added a new building and a prayer garden. (Courtesy Carolyn Boyles.)

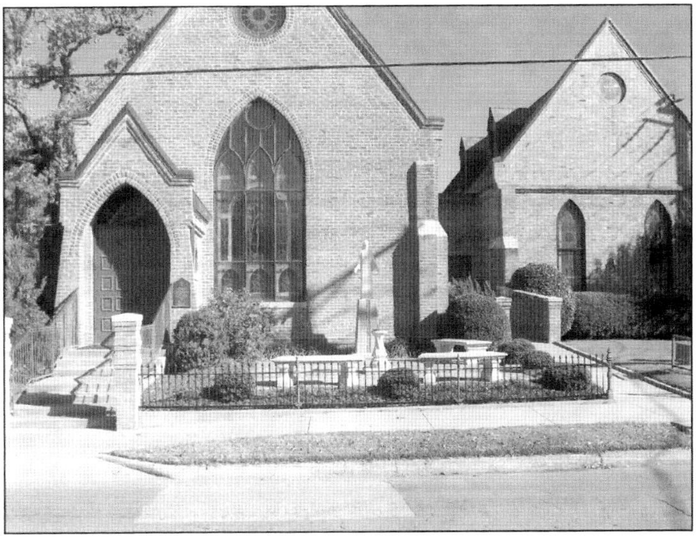

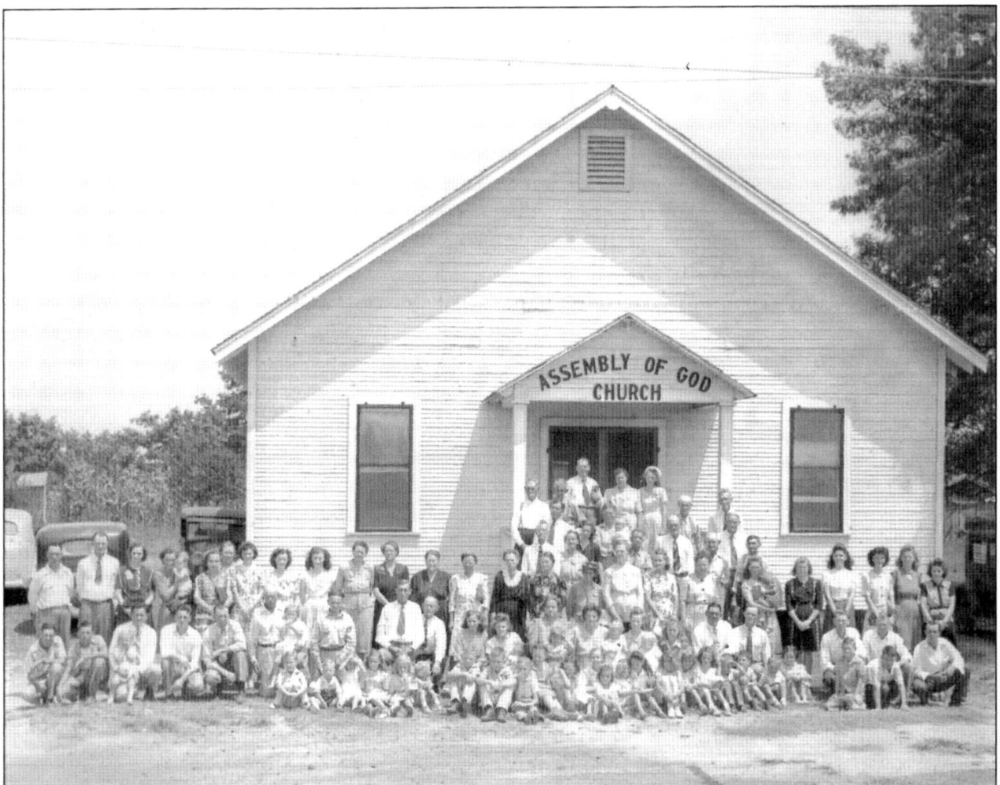

The congregation of the First Assembly of God Church constructed this building at 916 East Race Avenue in 1935. In May 1968, the church moved into its current building on Benton and Cloverdale Streets. (Courtesy Vernon Ables.)

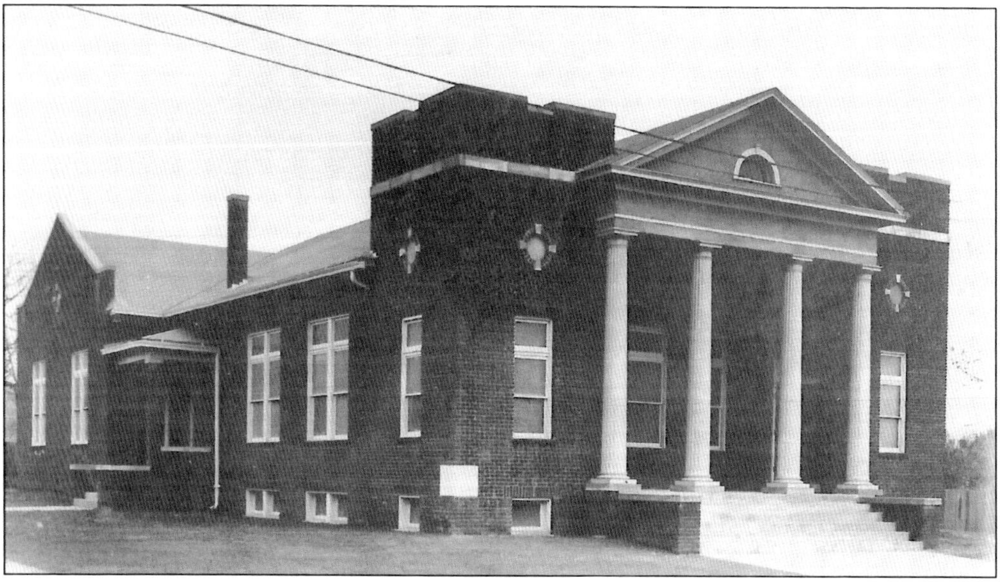

The First Christian Church of Searcy was organized in 1906. The 30 members purchased five lots across from the southeast corner of Spring Park on South Main Street with plans to build there, but they discontinued meeting in 1915. In 1920, the First Christian Church and the Church of Christ Disciples owned property on Main and Market Streets. Work began on this church building in 1925. The congregation's new church on Highway 31 was built in 1975. (Courtesy Eloise Muncy.)

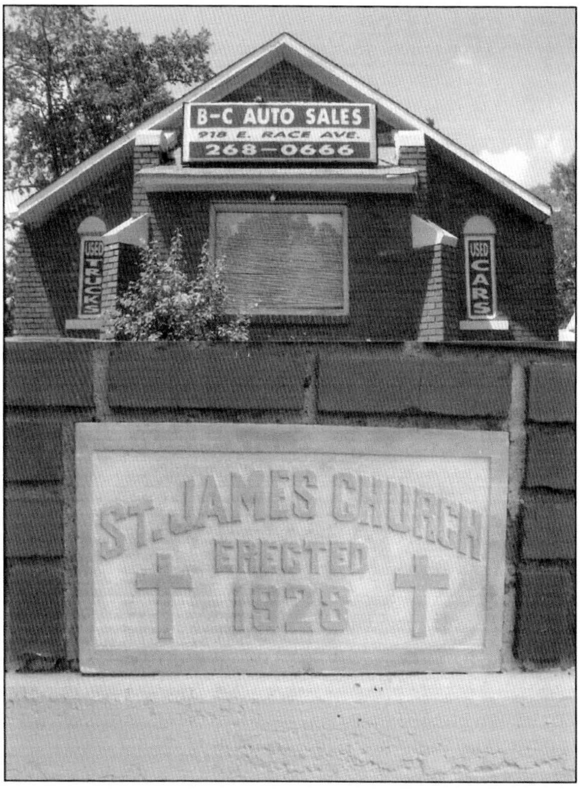

St. James Catholic Church was erected at 918 East Race Avenue in 1928. At the time, there were only two Catholics living in Searcy: John L. Wrape and his wife. Fr. Matthew Saettle, Order of St. Benedict (OSB), was instrumental in raising funds for Catholic churches to be built in Arkansas during the early part of the 20th century. In 1908, Father Saettle said Mass regularly at the Holy Redeemer Church in El Dorado, Arkansas, and in 1916, he oversaw construction of the Mission Church on Meek Street in Warren, Arkansas. St. James was the last church he was involved with building. The Catholic Church Extension Society also provided funding to build this church. The parishioners purchased 10 acres of land on Pioneer Road in 1960 and constructed a new, larger church building. This building is now the office of B-C Auto Sales. (Courtesy Mary Cook.)

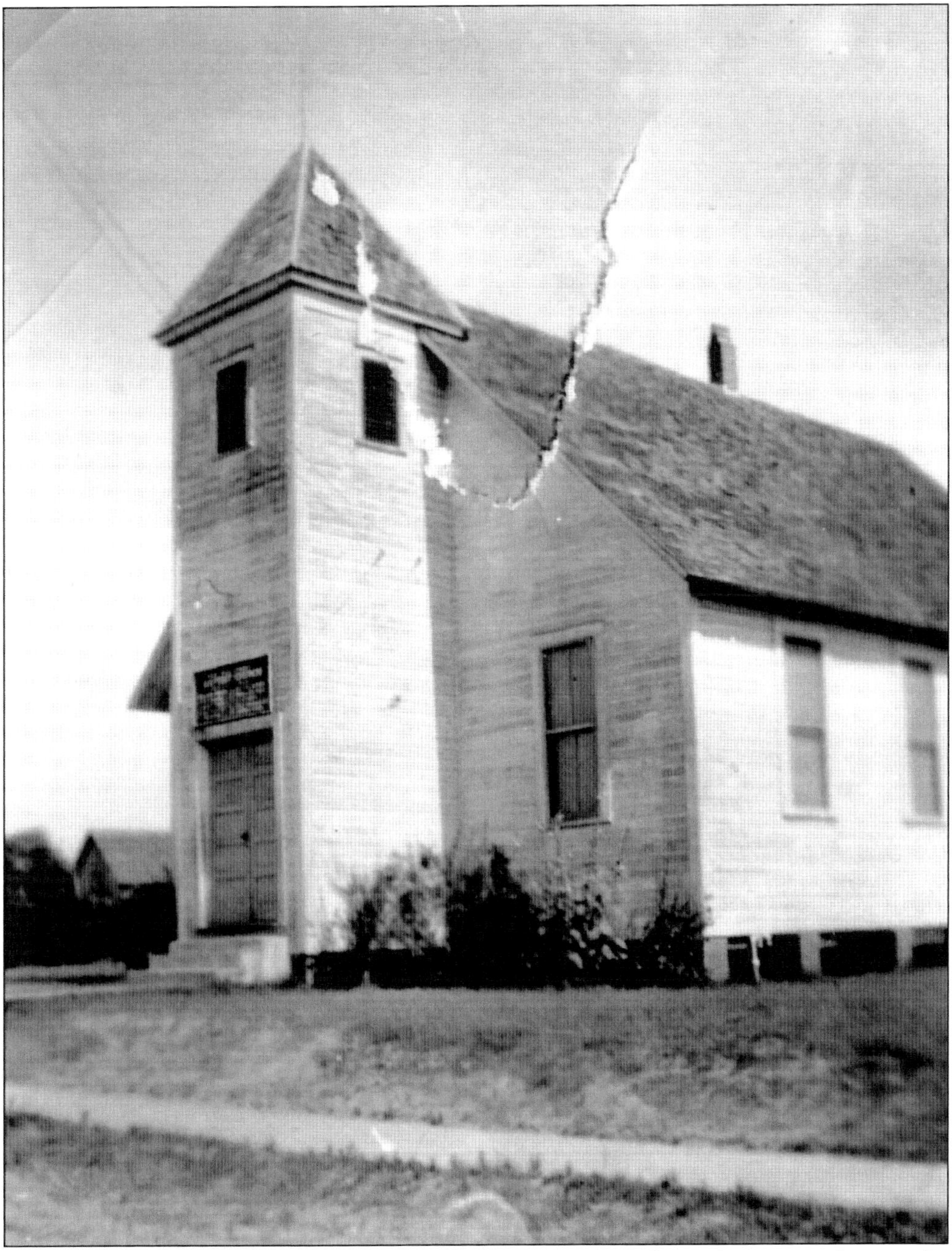

West Race Baptist Church was organized on June 6, 1921, with 18 charter members in the Cumberland Presbyterian Church building. In the fall of the same year, the church purchased a lot at 1006 West Race Avenue and constructed this building. The first pastor was G.L. Richardson. (Courtesy Eloise Muncy.)

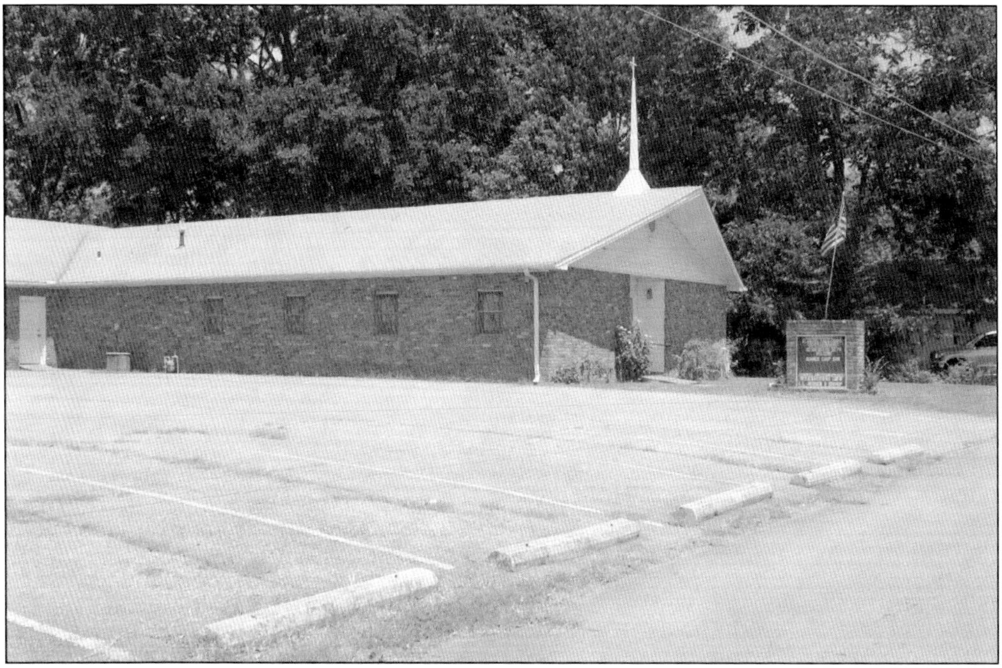

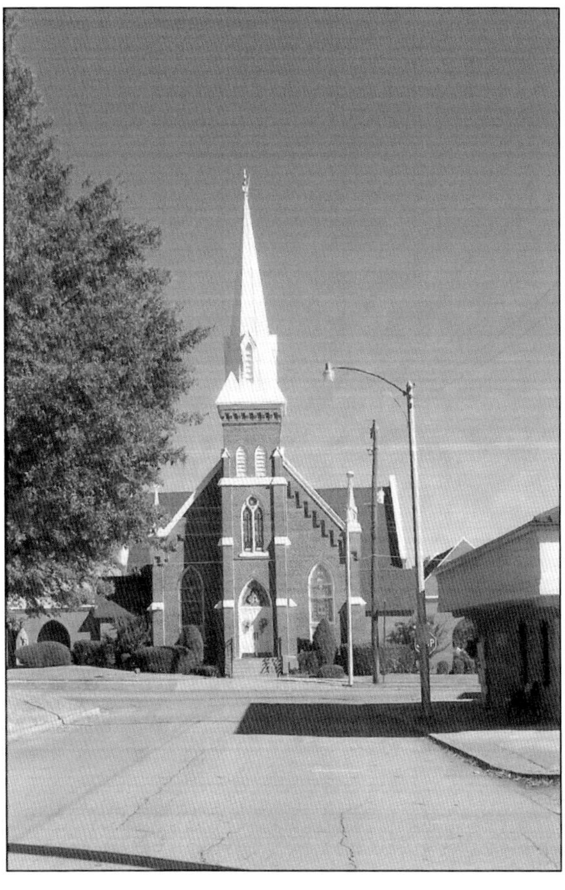

St. Mary Christian Methodist Episcopal Church, formerly located in this building at 601 Spring Street (now Beebe-Capps Expressway), is 122 years old and now located at 205 South Sowell Avenue. It traces its history back to a meeting of former slaves who joined together in Tennessee to experiment with creating a church for black people who wanted to leave an impression upon the thoughts of coming generations. (Courtesy Carolyn Boyles.)

The First United Methodist Church building was constructed in 1870. It is among the oldest continually used buildings in Arkansas. The congregation planned for the future in the design of this building, given that it seats 400 people even though the population of Searcy was only around 600 when it was constructed. This building replaced the original wooden frame church built in 1851. (Courtesy SRCC.)

In the 1940s, the First United Methodist Church expanded to build an education center. The two-story white house (right) on the corner of Main and Center Streets was demolished to make room for it. Note the Texaco service station across the street. The car at the curb is Jack Wiseman's 1935 Ford. (Courtesy First United Methodist Church.)

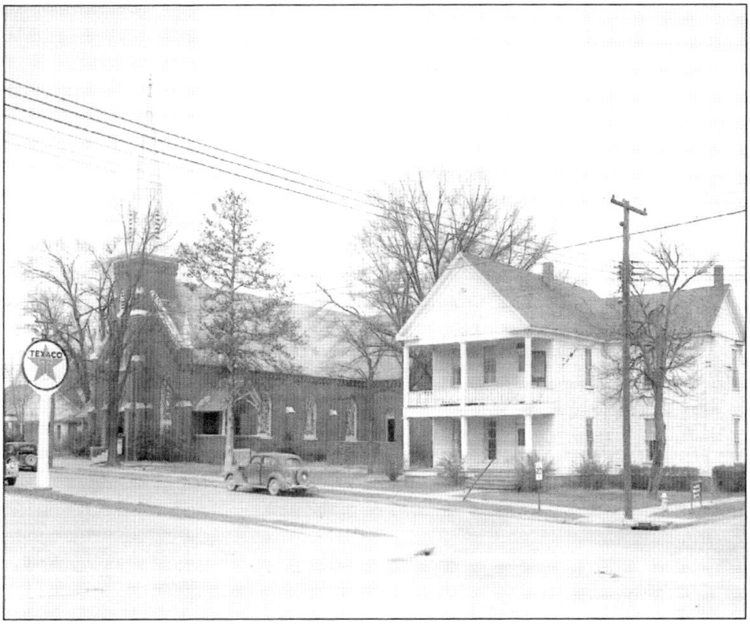

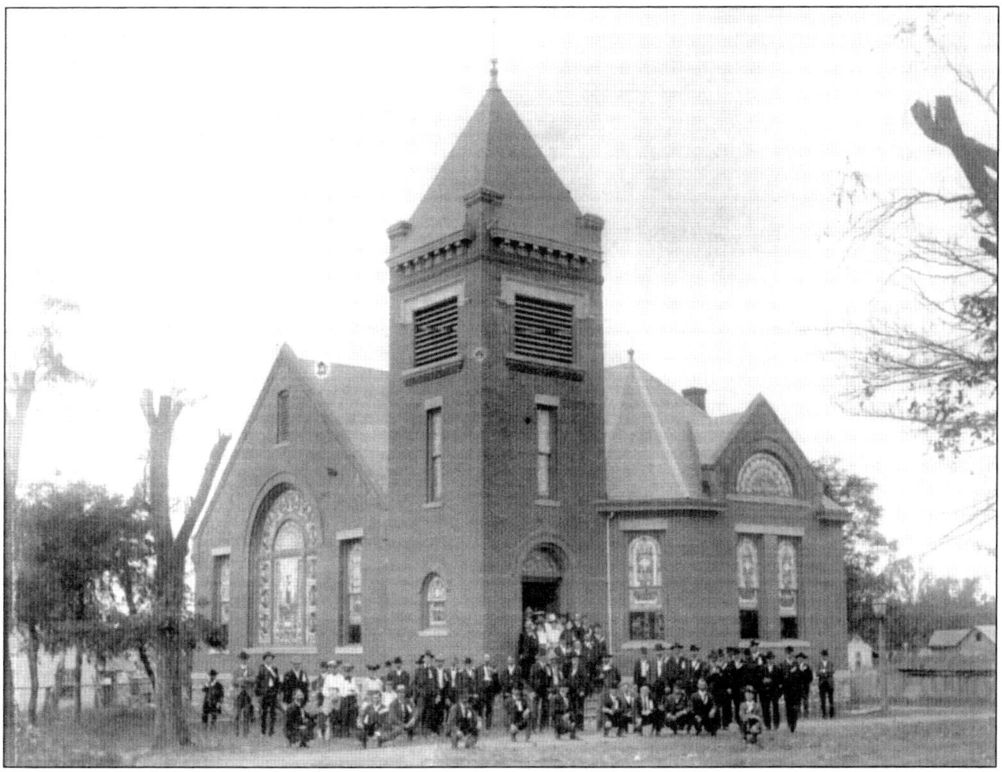

Gentry Memorial Baptist Church was built in 1901 on the site of the present-day First Baptist Church. It was called the Baptist Church in 1847, when members met in a log house. When this building was constructed on the corner of Spring and Center Streets, it was named in honor of Martin N. Gentry, whose sister Mary Gentry Welch gave a sizable donation to the building fund. (Courtesy Leon and Sherry Person.)

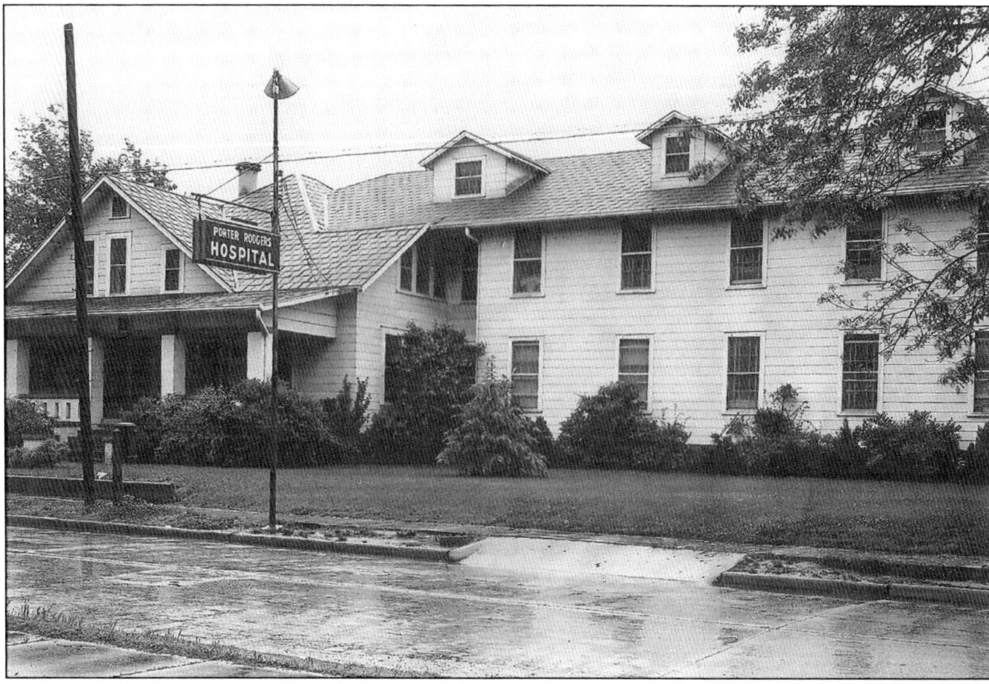

Dr. Porter Rodgers Sr. purchased the Wakenight Sanitarium in 1943, and it became part of the Porter Rodgers Hospital on Woodruff Street. Rodgers soon realized the need for more rooms and built an annex in 1947. With the addition of 50 rooms, the hospital's capacity increased to 70 patients. Dr. Hugh Edwards joined Rodgers in the practice of medicine and surgery. Dr. Frank Gosnell established his dentist office inside the hospital. (Courtesy SRCC.)

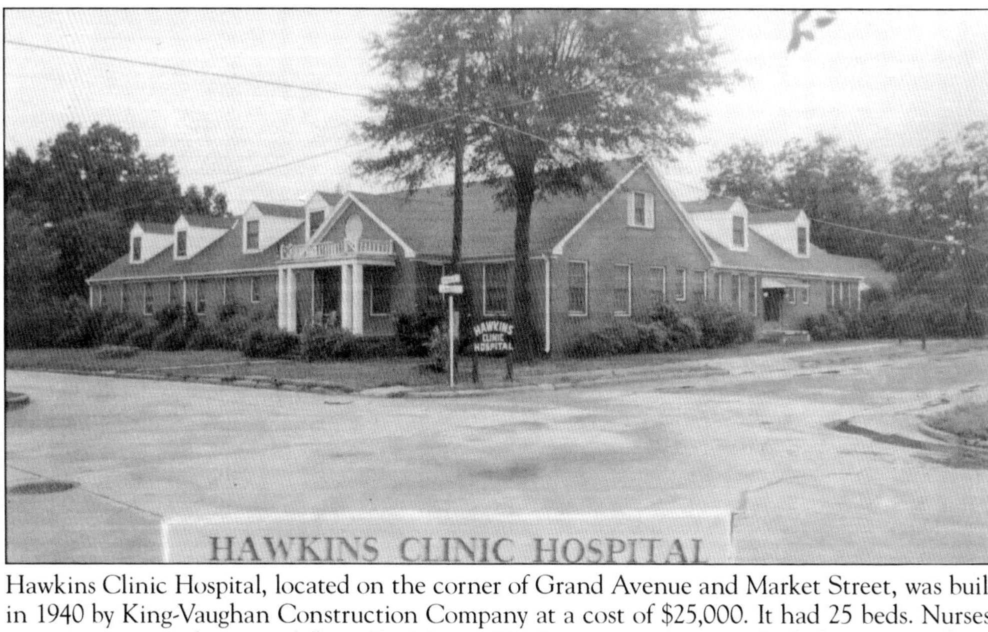

Hawkins Clinic Hospital, located on the corner of Grand Avenue and Market Street, was built in 1940 by King-Vaughan Construction Company at a cost of $25,000. It had 25 beds. Nurses' quarters were on the second floor. Dr. Martin Hawkins was a distinguished physician and was elected first president of the Arkansas chapter of the American College of Surgeons. (Courtesy Betty Robbins.)

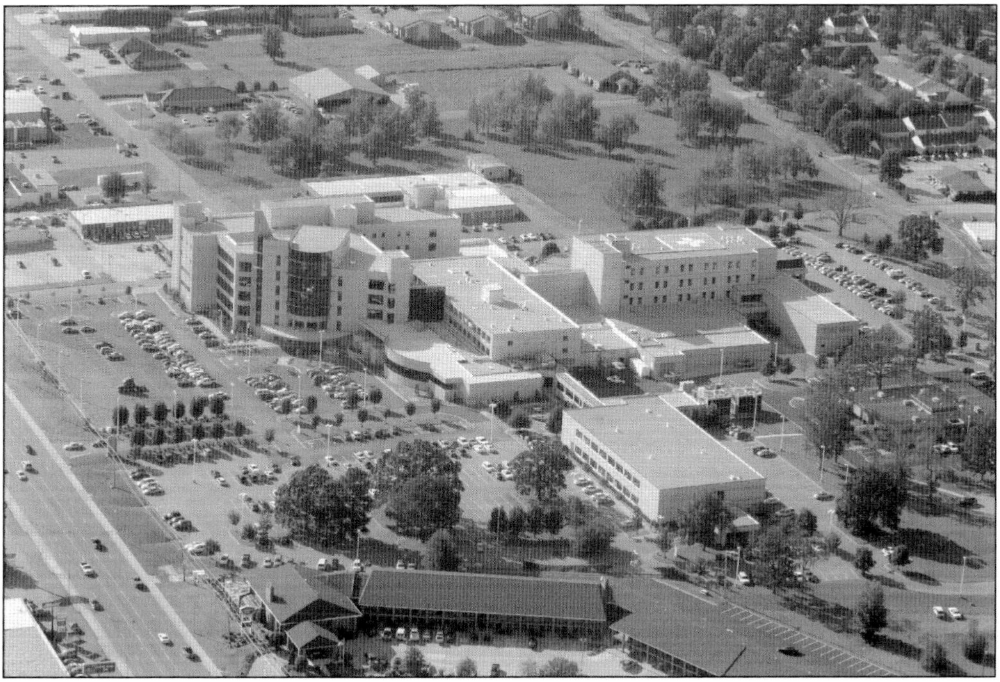

This is a 2011 aerial view of the White County Medical Center. It is a 501(c)(3) nonprofit organization and has built a Cancer Center of Excellence on Rogers Drive, near the south campus. White County Medical Center not only serves Searcy and White County but also the surrounding area. (Courtesy White County Medical Center.)

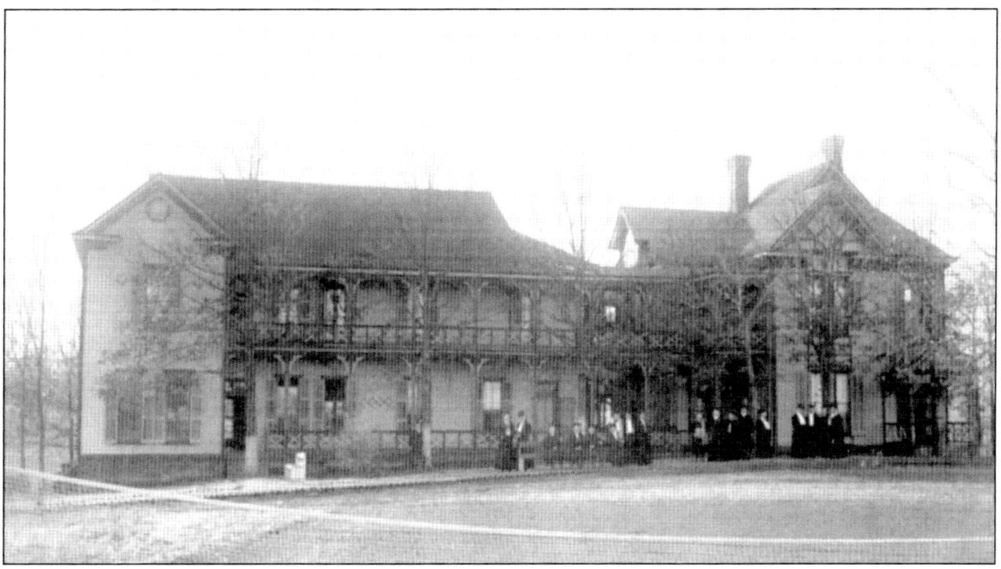

Before the Civil War, Searcy was home to Searcy Female Academy. It closed sometime before 1891, upon the founding of the Searcy Female Institute. The institute was not controlled by any particular religious denomination, but its students were required to attend church services. It was located at the north end of Second Street (now Apple Street). In 1907, the institute closed for unknown reasons, and the building was sold to Drs. J.M. Jelks, L.E. Moore Sr., and J.B. Grammer, who wanted to open a sanitarium. (Courtesy SRCC.)

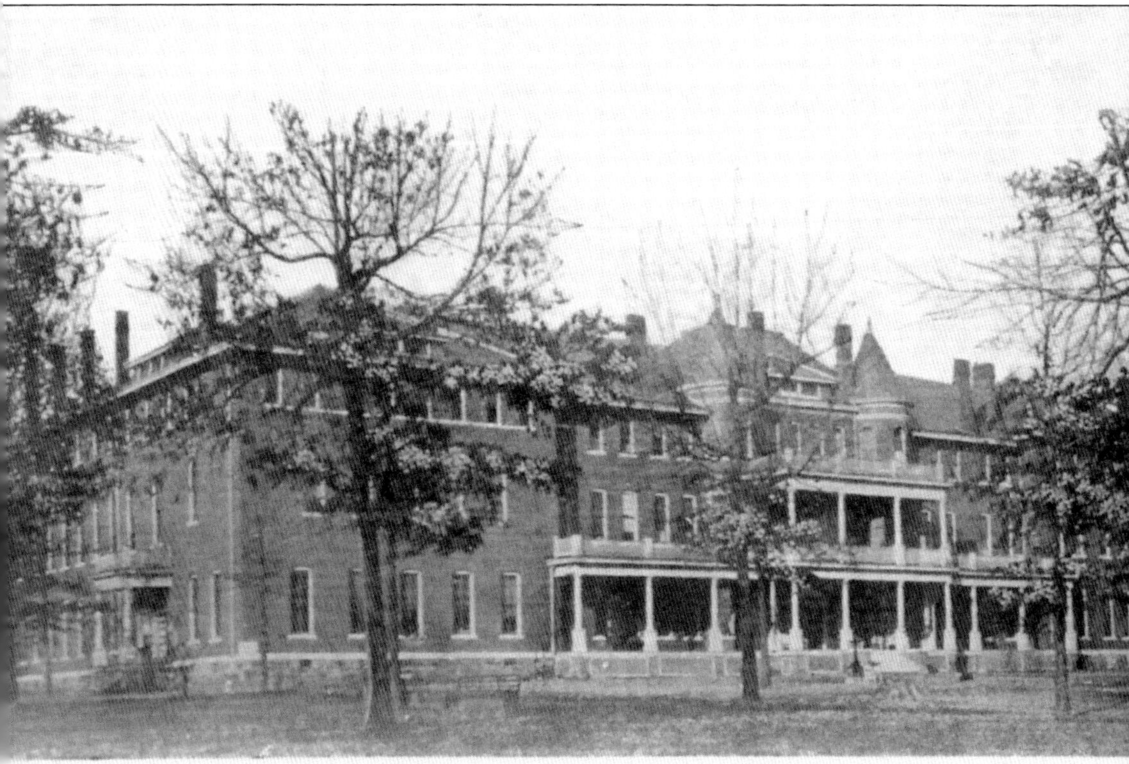

GALLOWAY FEMALE COLLEGE, SEARCY, ARK.

On April 11, 1889, approximately 2,000 people attended the laying of the cornerstone for a college to be "dedicated to the development of Christian womanhood in Arkansas." Brig. Gen. Dandridge McRae suggested that the name of the Methodist Episcopal Church bishop, G.B. Galloway, be given to the institution, and, thus, Galloway Female College was founded in Searcy. This building was destroyed by fire in 1898. (Courtesy Eloise Muncy.)

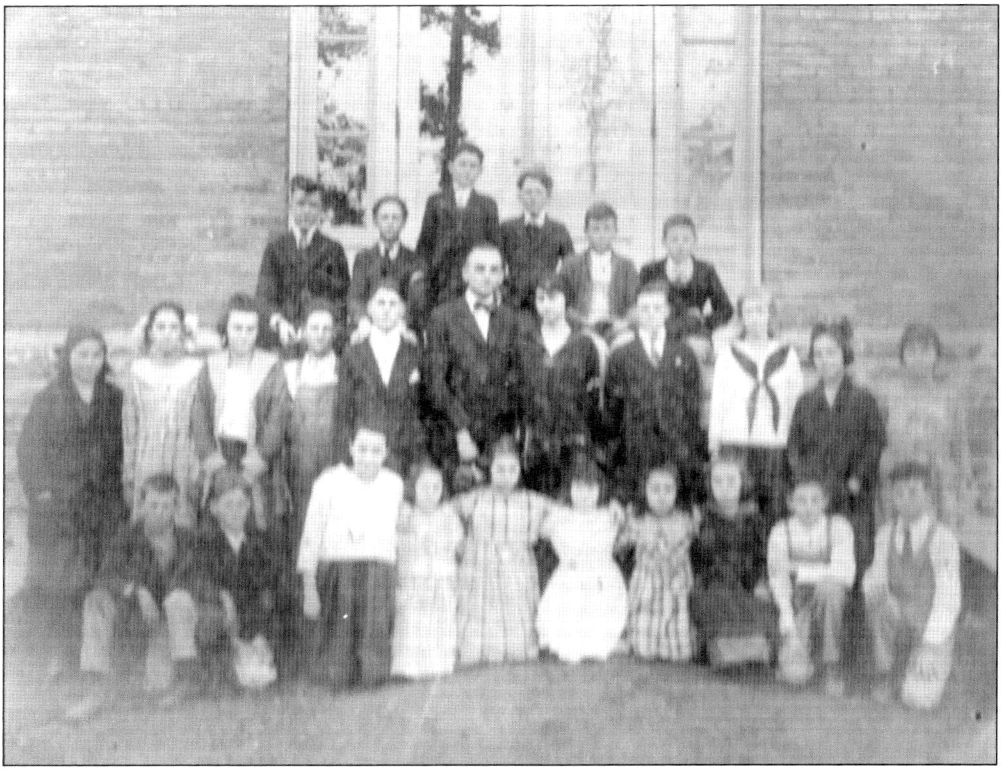

This photograph was a gift from Mrs. Willie May Walker Collison of Bald Knob, Arkansas, to L.O. Stotts in 1968. Mrs. Collison identified a Mrs. Woodard as the teacher of this group of children. Her husband, Fred Woodard, was superintendent of the public school in Searcy from 1918 through 1921. (Courtesy Nancy Williams Showalter.)

This is an aerial view of the Morris School for Boys, a Catholic boarding school operated by the Brothers of the Poor of St. Francis. It was located on the site of the old Armstrong Springs. When the school built a gym in 1927, it had the distinction of having the only school gym in White County. Searcy High School built its first gym in 1929. (Courtesy John Baker Photography.)

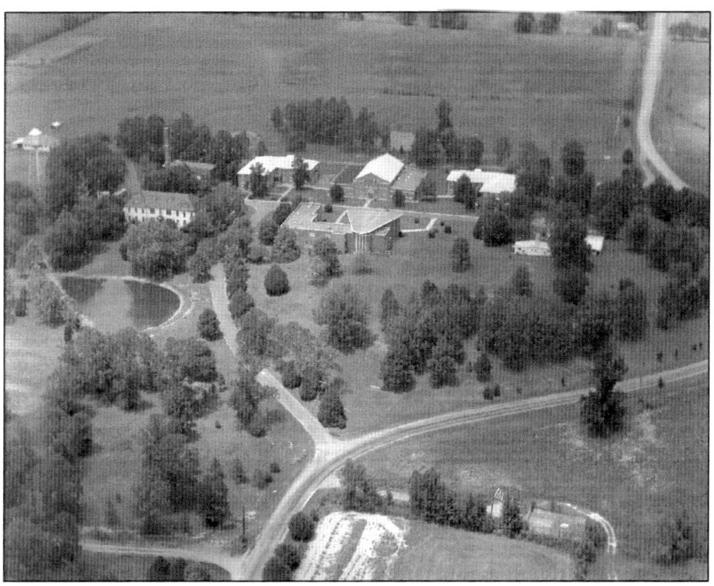

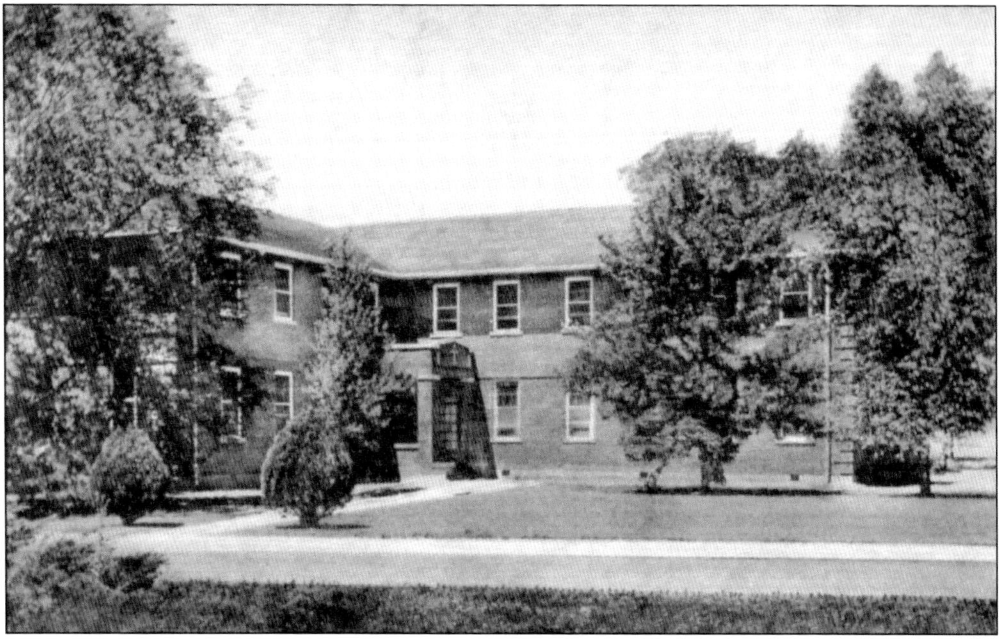

This is one of the buildings at Morris School for Boys in the early 20th century. The kitchen and dining room were downstairs, and the dormitory rooms were upstairs. The Brothers at the school were known for their cooking and were said to make "the best rolls you ever put in your mouth." The school closed in 1993, and the last of the Brothers supposedly left the area around 2000. (Courtesy Leon and Sherry Person.)

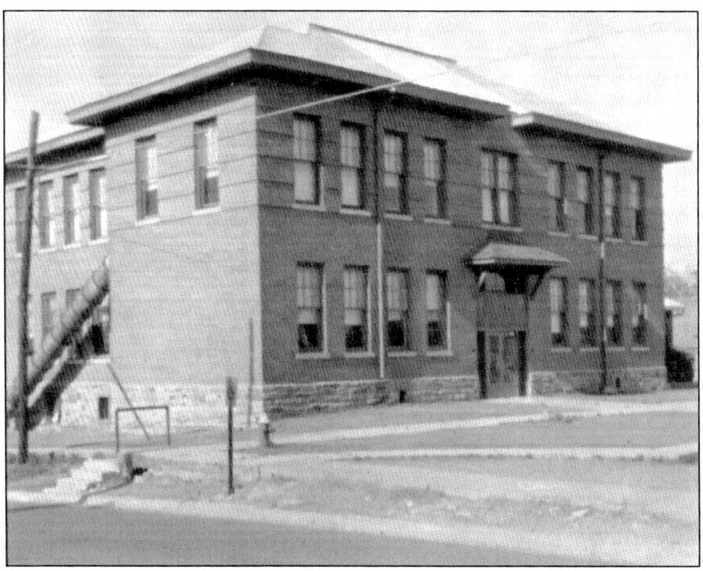

This is Searcy High School in 1908. People who treasured education were said to naturally migrate to Searcy, and by 1916, the population had grown to over 2,000. Sue Ellen Pride McDowell expressed in her book, *Cotton and Jasmine: A Southern Mosaic*, that her family moved to Searcy in 1890 in order for her to enter Galloway College and for her brother, Pinson, to enter Searcy Military Academy. (Courtesy Eloise Muncy.)

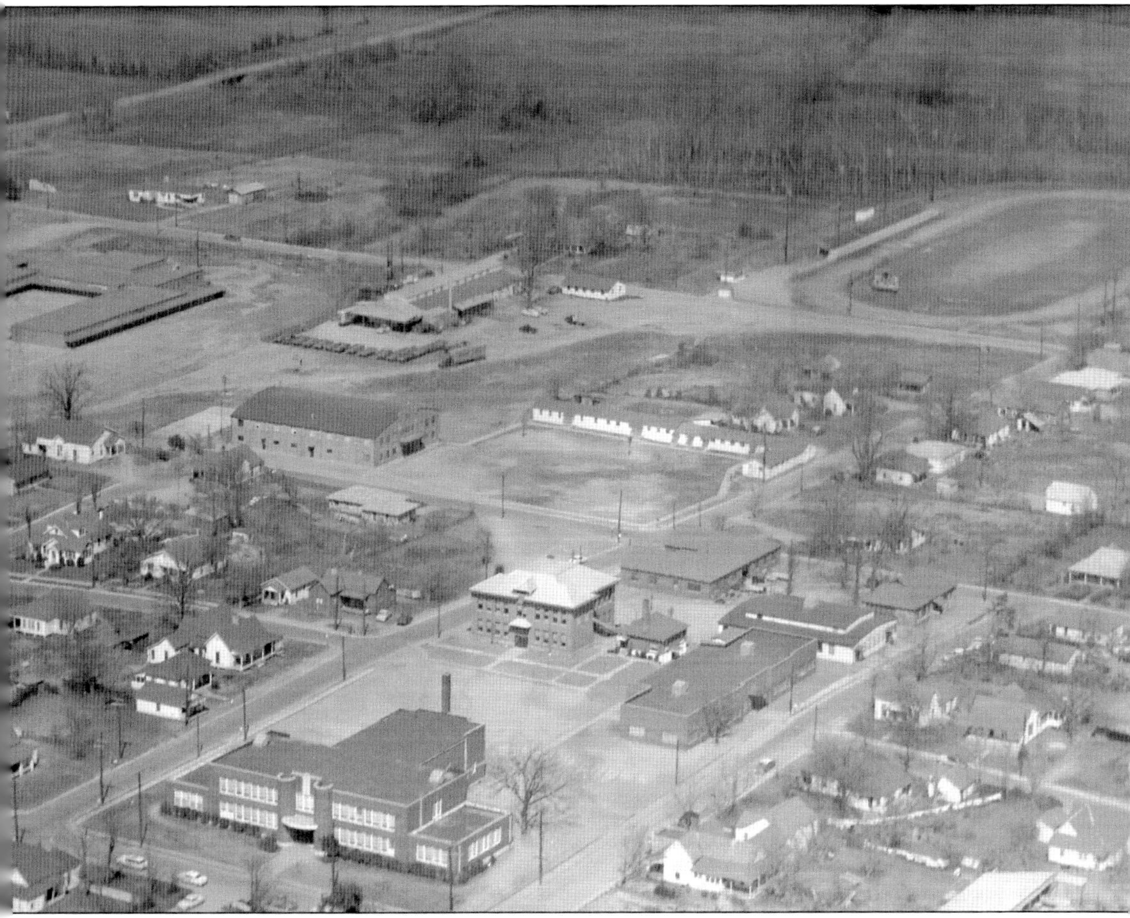

This is an aerial view of the area surrounding the former Searcy High School complex. The building in the forefront is the old high school, which later served as the junior high school until a fire destroyed the structure. Directly behind this building is a two-story building that once housed the elementary school and later served as the sixth-grade building (it has since been torn down). Other buildings of note include the old gym (center, left), which now serves as the maintenance shop. The long building behind the old gym (center, top), once occupied by the Birds Eye frozen food plant, was built during the Great Depression by the federal government's National Youth Administration (NYA), which provided employment for young people between the ages of 16 and 25. The old Lion Stadium was built in the open area that looks like a track at upper right. (Courtesy Searcy School Administration.)

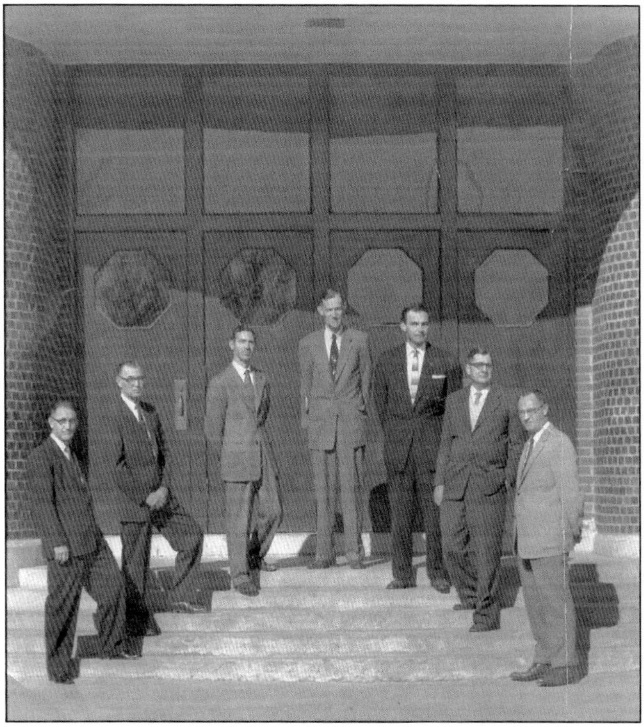

Searcy school board members and district administrators stand on the steps of the new Searcy High School building in 1956. They are, from left to right, Elmer Yancy, Hipp Gilliland, Principal Lee Yarbrough, school board president A.P. Strother, Supt. James Ahlf, Richard Deener, and Curtis Walker. (Courtesy Nancy Williams Showalter.)

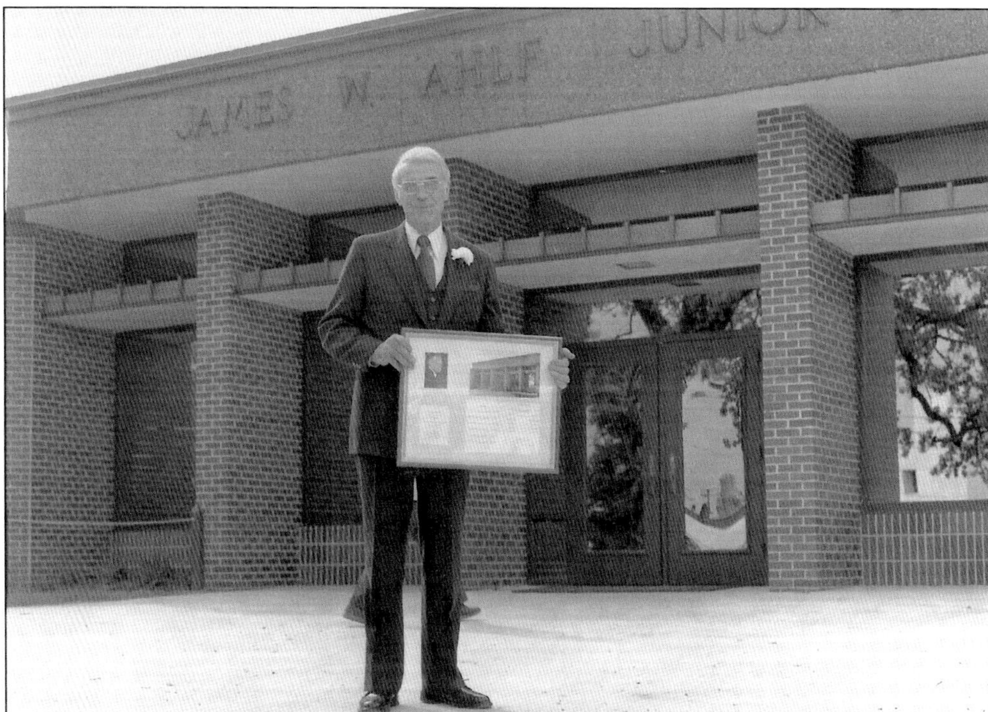

The new junior high school—erected after a fire destroyed the old building that originally housed Searcy High School and the junior high—was named in honor of Supt. James W. Ahlf. The new building opened in 1982. (Courtesy Frances Jo Ahlf.)

Harding Academy, which offers Christ-centered education from prekindergarten through high school, occupied this site on Park Avenue and Blakeney Street, beginning in 1924. The academy moved to a new building on Park Avenue in 1980. (Courtesy Bill and Billie Diles.)

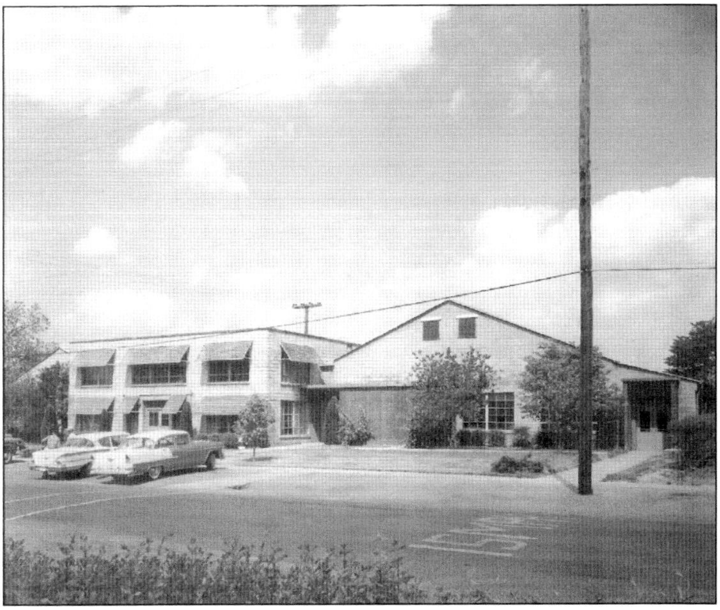

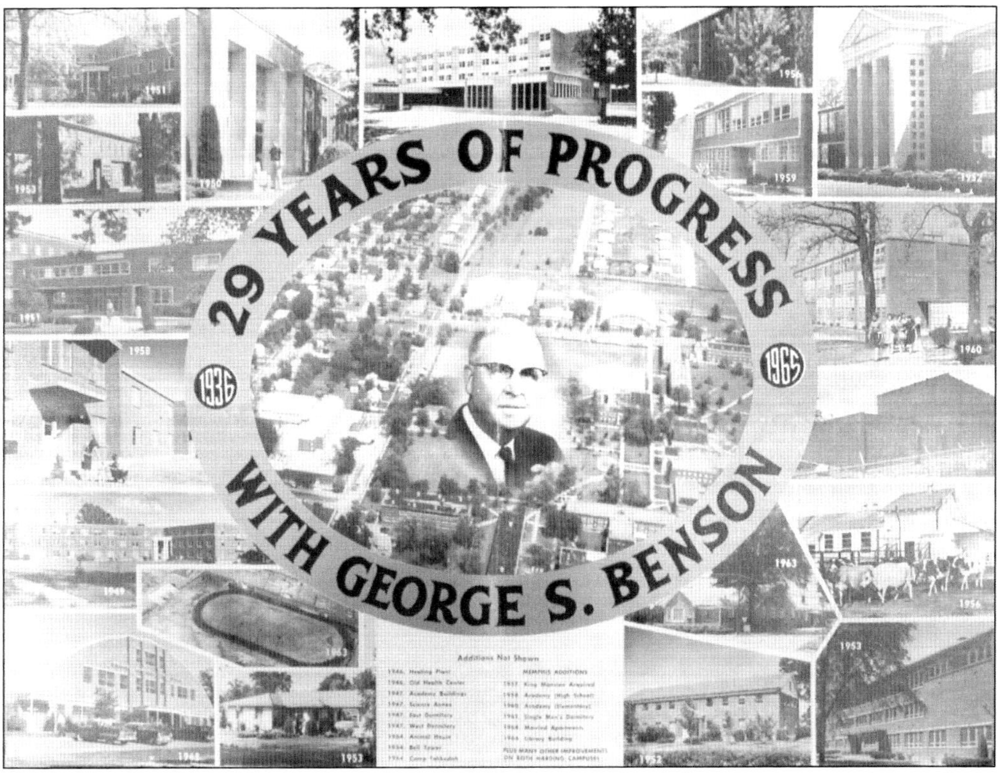

This composite shows 29 years of progress at Harding College, from 1936 to 1965. In 1979, it became Harding University. Other additions not shown include a new heating plant, a health center, academy buildings, a science annex, two new dormitories, an animal house, the bell tower, and Camp Tahkodah. Several additions were also made on the college's Memphis campus during this period of rapid growth. (Courtesy SRCC.)

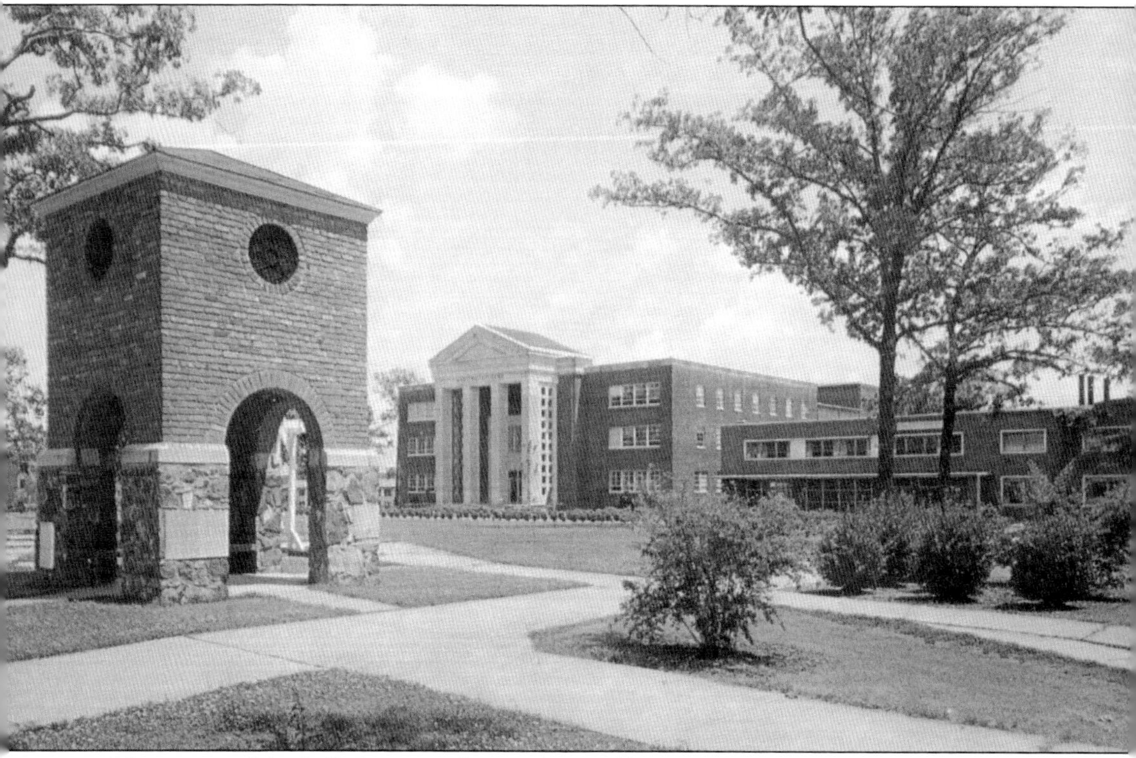

This image of the Bell Tower on the Harding College campus is a reminder of the old Galloway College and the Galloway Ghost. It is said that upon returning to her room in Godden Hall late one night, a young woman named Gertrude heard a sound and went to investigate the three-story elevator shaft. A bloodcurdling scream rippled through the halls, followed by schoolmates and the housemother finding Gertie dead at the bottom of the shaft. Some say Gertie's ghost has been seen many times in Godden Hall, some say she moved to the new Pattie Cobb Hall, and some just do not say. (Courtesy Jeff Montgomery.)

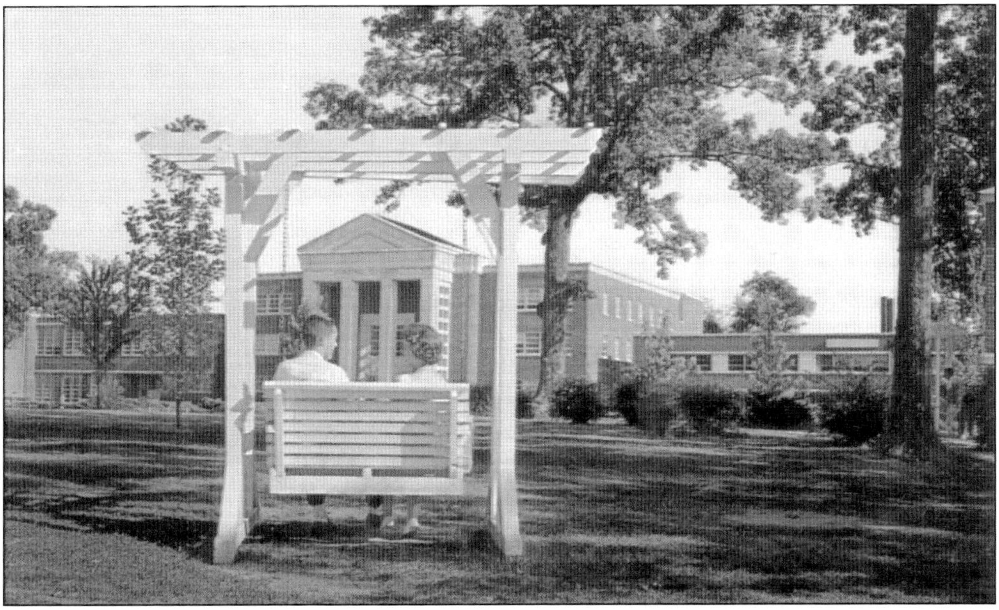

The Harding Swing was designed and built by Harvey Dykes in 1934. At first, school social regulations stated, "Sitting in swings, talking, playing tennis, etc. is permissible any time on the grounds during daytime, but couples could not walk in groups with fewer than six people, and they could ride in cars only with special permission, but they could enjoy a Harding Swing." (Courtesy Jeff Montgomery.)

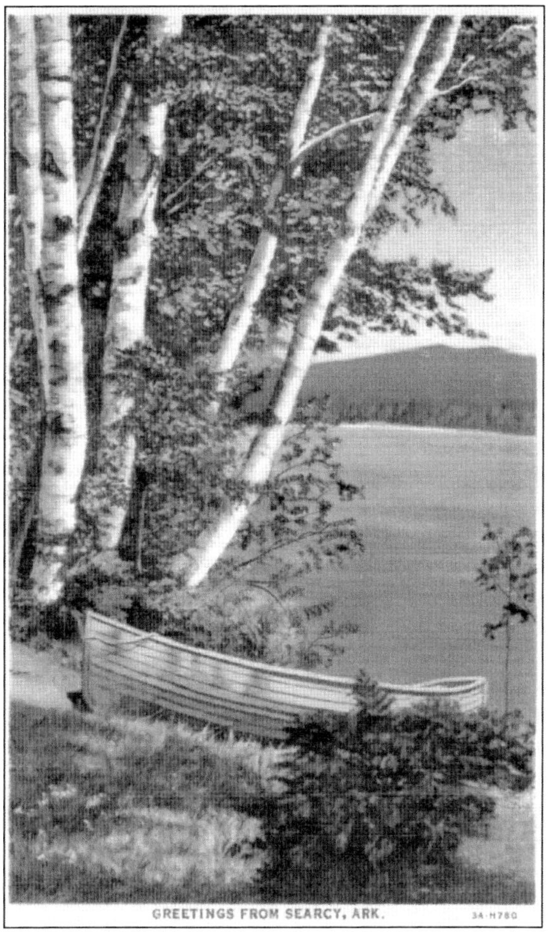

This postcard was postmarked on May 25, 1935, from Judsonia, Arkansas, with a penny's worth of postage from "Alva" to Glen Cornwell in Yukon, Oklahoma. It arrived without a street address, and zip codes had not yet been invented. The text reads: "Friday a.m.—This is one of the many similar scenes to be found in this country (not much overdrawn). Having good meeting. Eating strawberry shortcake twice a day. Mrs. H. and Mr. R are still up on white river." The final sentence is mostly illegible but looks like "Remember us to see she rests." The words "Remember" and "to" are clearly written. (Courtesy Carolyn Boyles.)

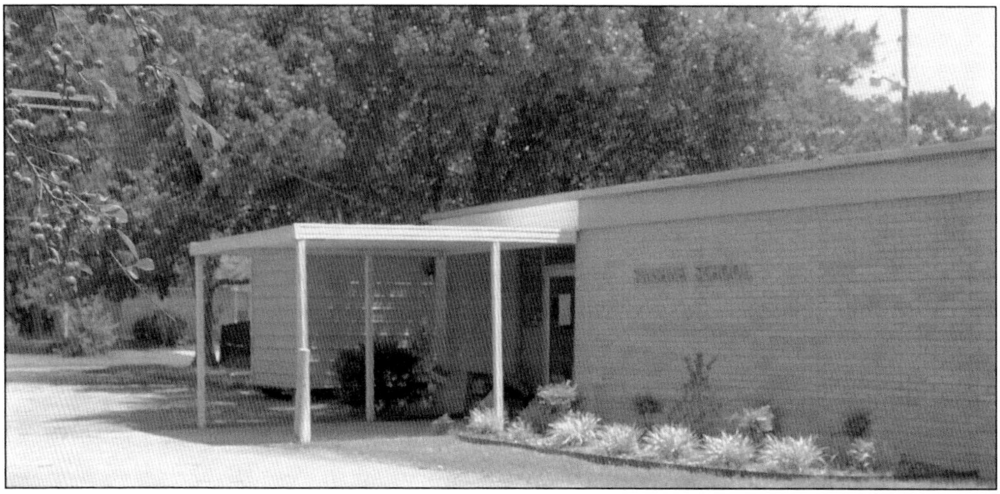

The Searcy Junior Auxiliary took on a project in 1964 that resulted in an Army barracks being converted to classrooms to serve seven developmentally disabled students. The project was named the Sunshine School. Ann Gardner was the first teacher. As enrollment swelled, it moved to this building, which served until growth necessitated additional space. (Courtesy Carolyn Boyles.)

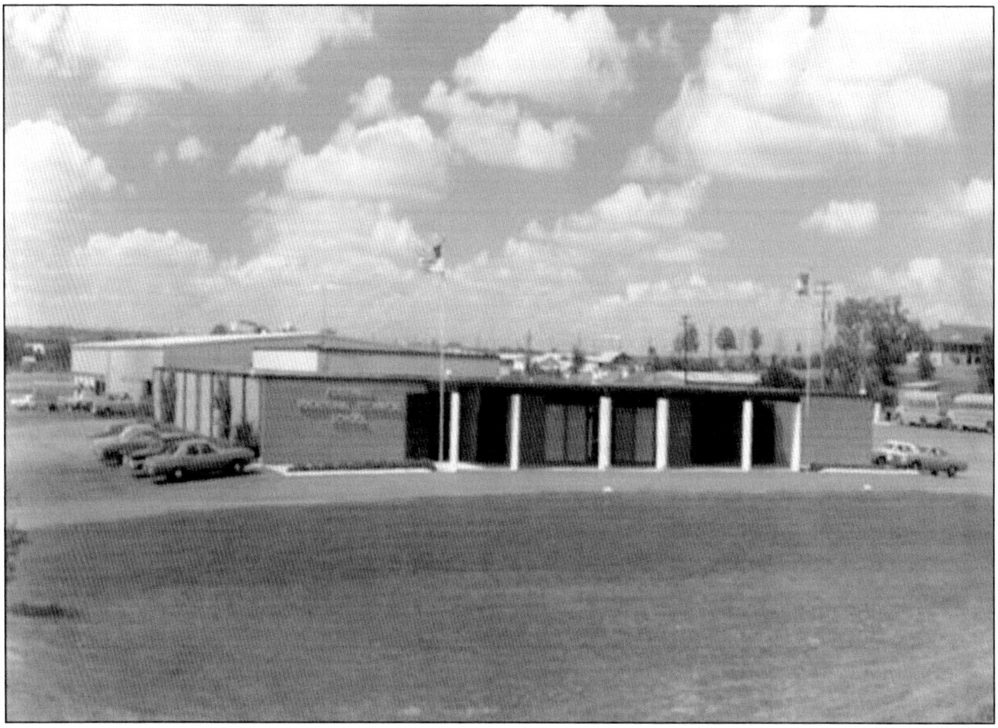

Foothills Vocational-Technical School was built in 1966 and dedicated by Gov. Winthrop Rockefeller. Vocational education was provided to students who were either in the workforce or who would soon graduate from high school. Luther S. Hardin was the first director of the school. Foothills became Arkansas State University–Searcy on July 1, 2003. Dr. Eugene McKay, Arkansas State University chancellor, and Foothills director Don Harlan said the two institutions had enjoyed a good relationship for several years and that working together they could better respond to the needs of students, business, and industry. (Courtesy Arkansas State University–Searcy.)

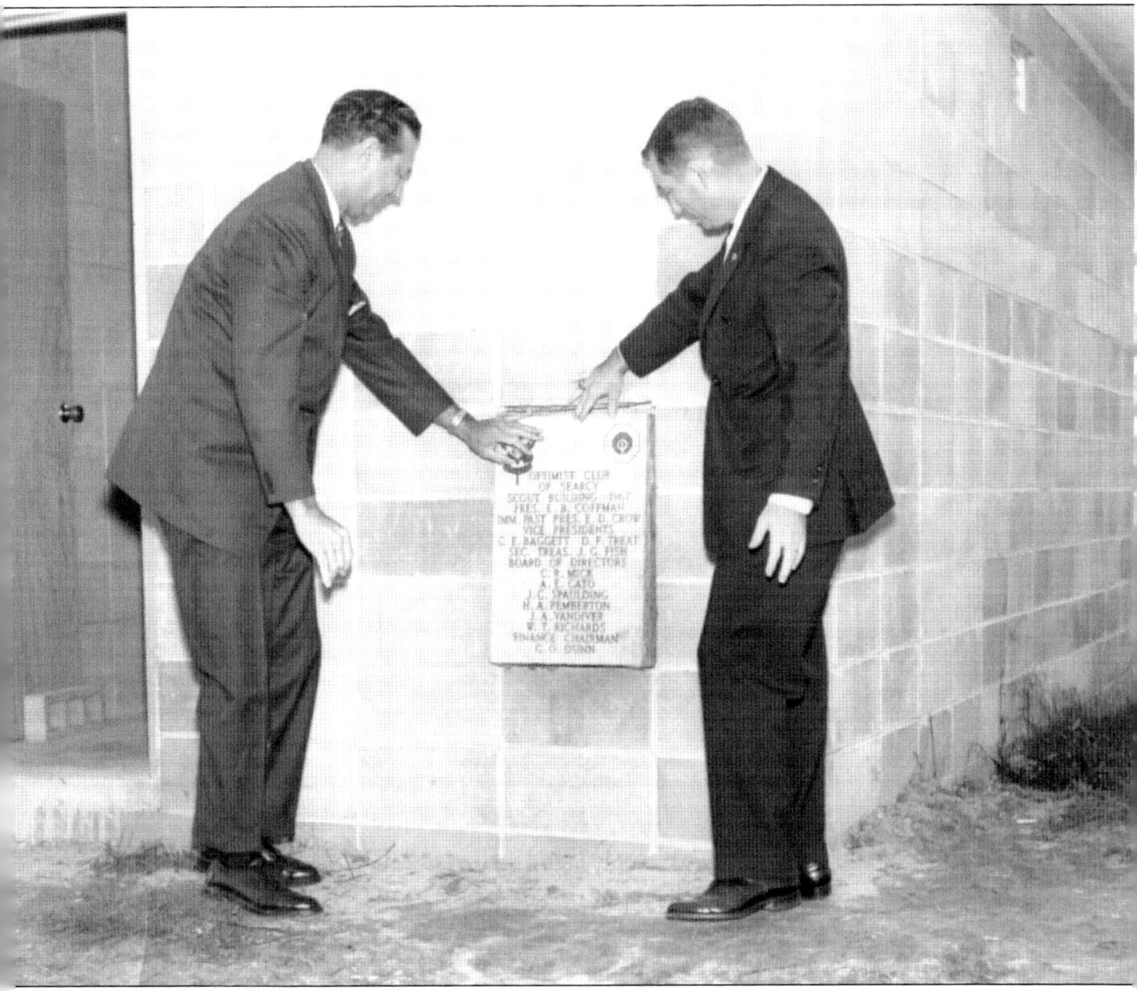

Around 1967, these unidentified men inspect a cornerstone that reads, "Optimist Club of Searcy Scout Building-1967; Pres. L.B. Coffman; Imm Past Pres. E.D. Crow; Vice Presidents G.E. Baggett, D.F. Treat; Sec. Treas. L.G. Fish; Board of Directors C.R. Mick, A.E. Cato, J.C. Spaulding, R.A. Pembertson, J.A. Vandiver, W.T. Richards, Finance Chairman G.O. Dunn." Dr. Raymond Muncy's definitive book about Searcy's history was published in 1976, and in that year, the local Optimist Club honored him with its Citizen of the Year Award. (Courtesy SRCC.)

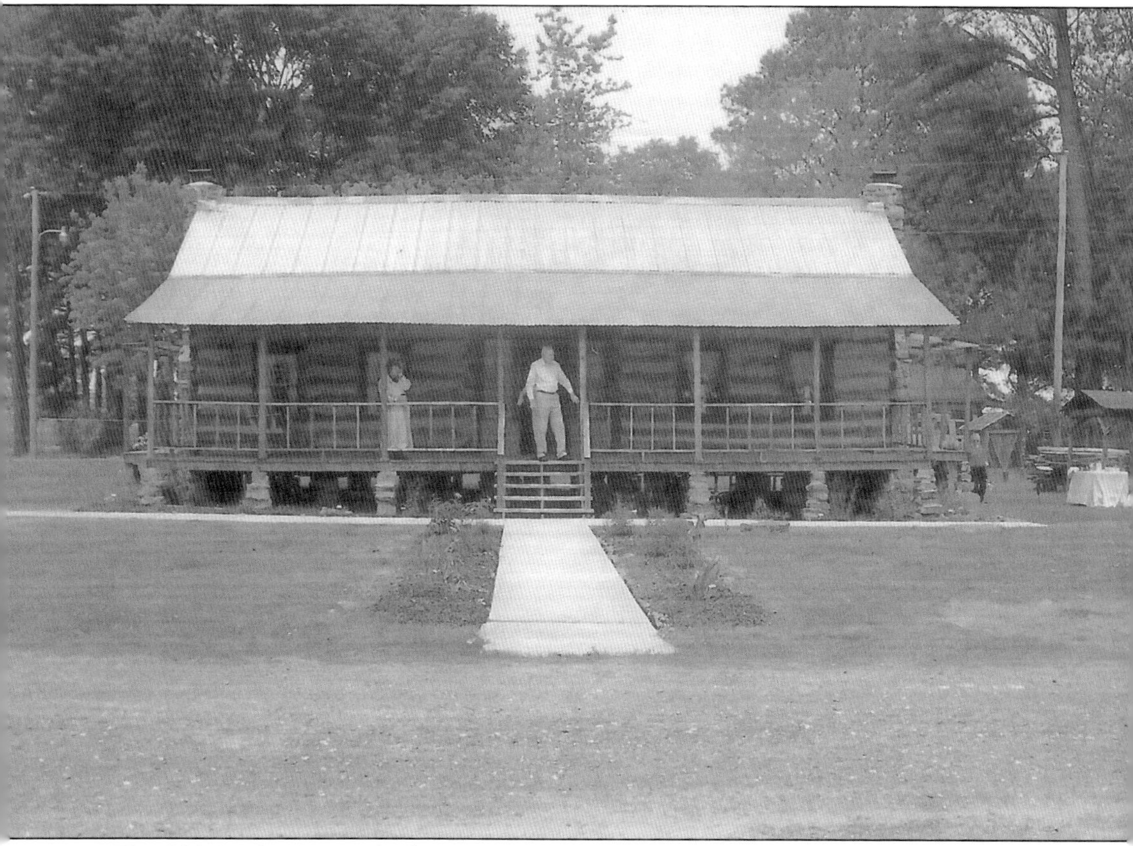

The Old Gordon House, built in 1884, was moved from the Providence community to Pioneer Village. Pioneer Village is located on Higginson Street, near the Searcy Events Center. The Old Gordon House is a one-and-a-half-story log house with two rooms and a dogtrot that is fully furnished in the style of the 1800s. (Courtesy WCHS.)

Four

Commerce

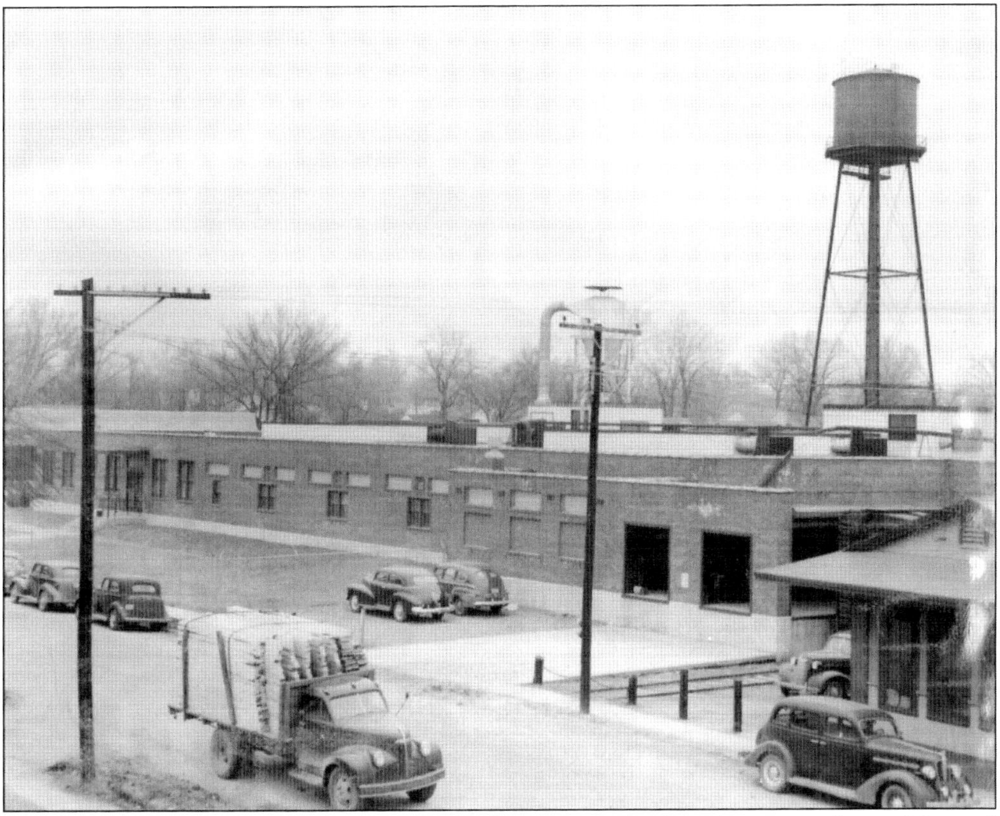

In the 1940s, citizens in Searcy joined in an effort to raise funds and attract industry. The goal was to raise $100,000 to erect this building and to bring International Shoe Factory, the second largest shoe manufacturer in the nation, to the city. The factory owners agreed to train about 450 local people for employment if the city would fund the building. The campaign to raise the money was led by R.G. Deener, chairman of the executive committee; H.M. Thompson of the site committee; and Ewing Pyeatt, president of the chamber of commerce. (Courtesy SRCC.)

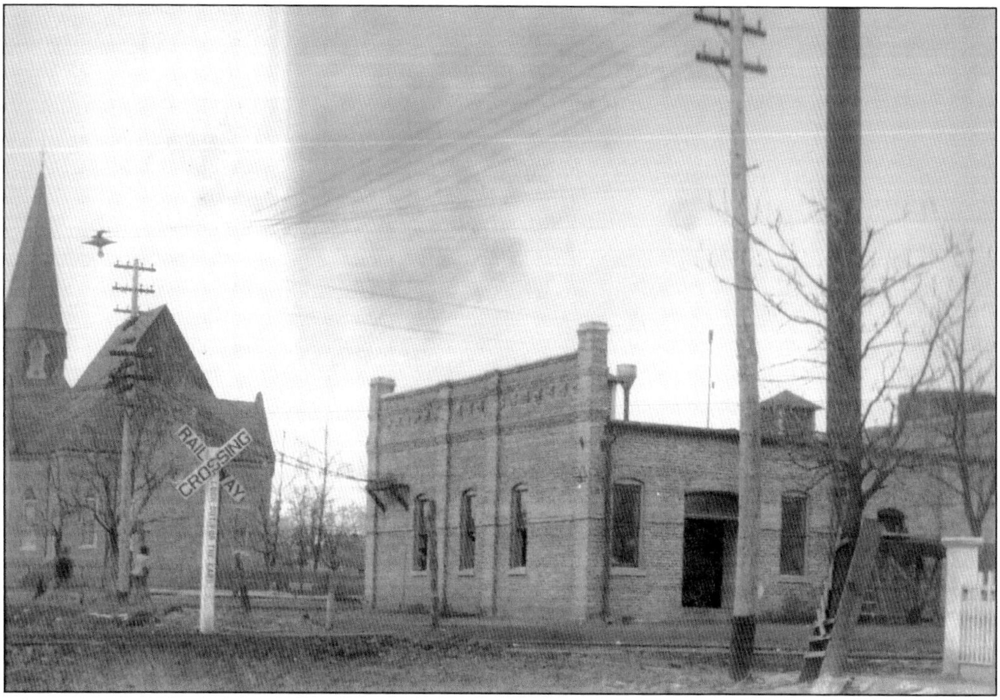

This c. 1920 image shows the first successful light plant in Searcy, which was located on the corner of Main Street and Pleasure Avenue across from Spring Park. It had a "wildcat" steam whistle that was used as a fire alarm. Arkansas Power & Light Company acquired the franchise in 1927. Coleman Office Equipment is now located on this site. The First Presbyterian Church was on the corner behind the light plant, which was once the location of Rendezvous Restaurant. (Courtesy Steve Barger.)

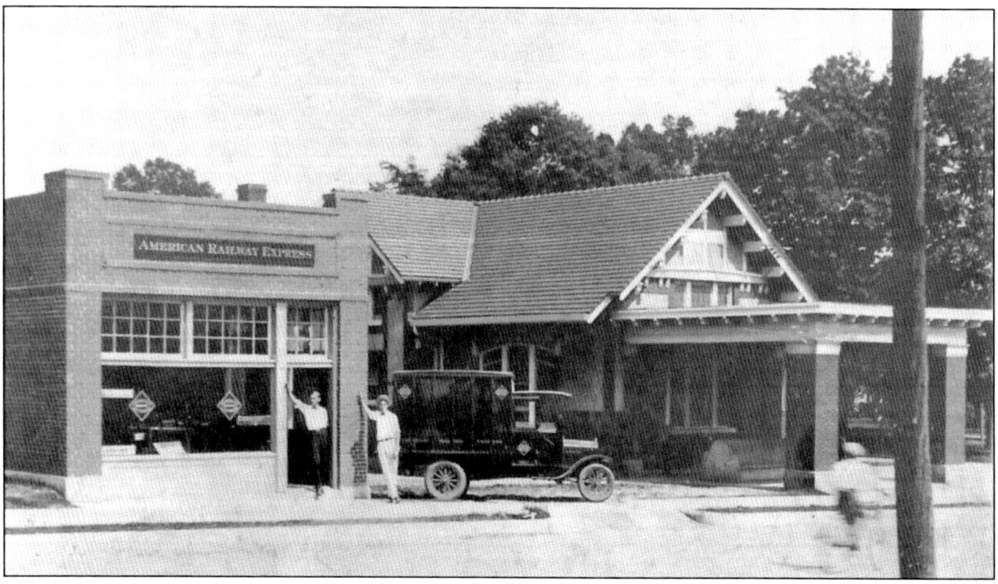

The American Railway Express agency was established during World War I as a fast and efficient way to send packages, money, and goods. The Searcy office was located on Spring Street and Pleasure Avenue, next to the Rock Island Depot. (Courtesy Main Street Searcy.)

Ray Albert Yarnell was the founder of Yarnell's Ice Cream Company. The history of the company goes back to 1923, when Ben Grissom moved his ice cream–making operations from Kensett, Arkansas, to Searcy. Yarnell went to work for Grissom in 1927. From 1927 until 1932, there were several owners of the company before Yarnell bought it from Southwest Dairy Products. Albert Yarnell, son of Ray Albert, actively managed the company for many years until his semiretirement around 2010. (Courtesy Albert Yarnell.)

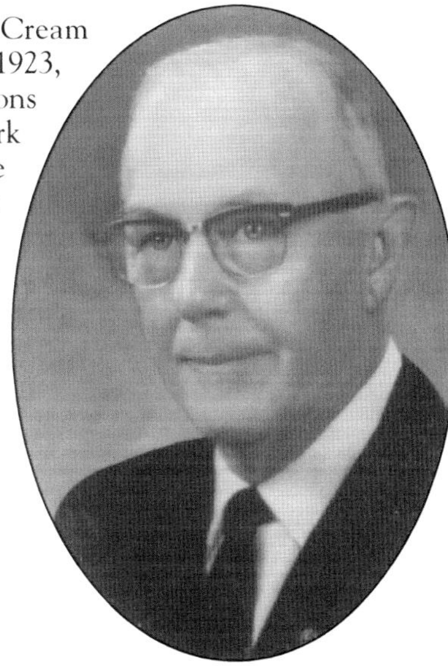

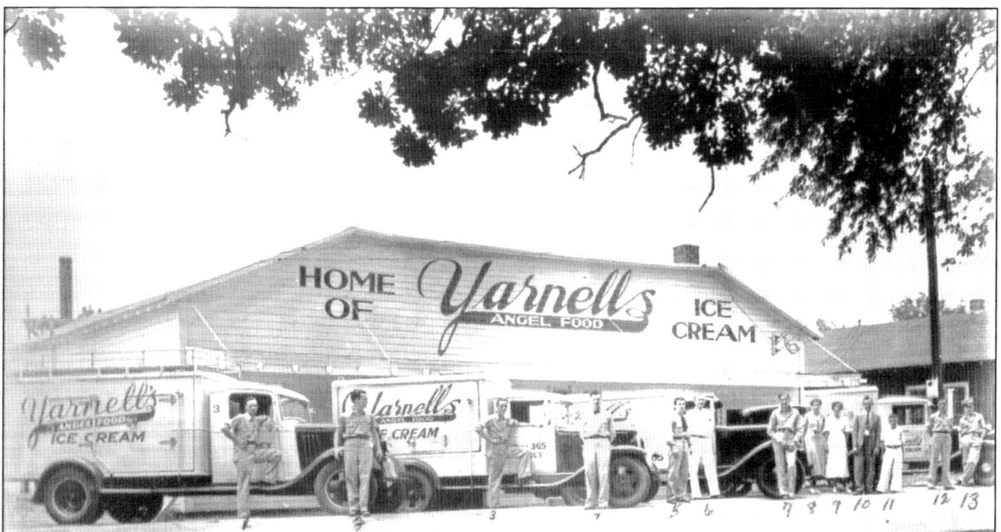

Employees of Yarnell's Ice Cream were photographed in front of the plant in 1934. They are, from left to right, R.L. Dacus, Coy Blankenship, Thomas J. Rogers, Howard G. Edwards, Fount Matheney, Jim Fortune, Wayne Morris, Helen Paxson, Hallie R. Yarnell, Ray A. Yarnell, Albert R. Yarnell, Stanley Coe, and Bubba Pembertson. The company's angel food vanilla ice cream was its flagship flavor. (Courtesy Albert Yarnell.)

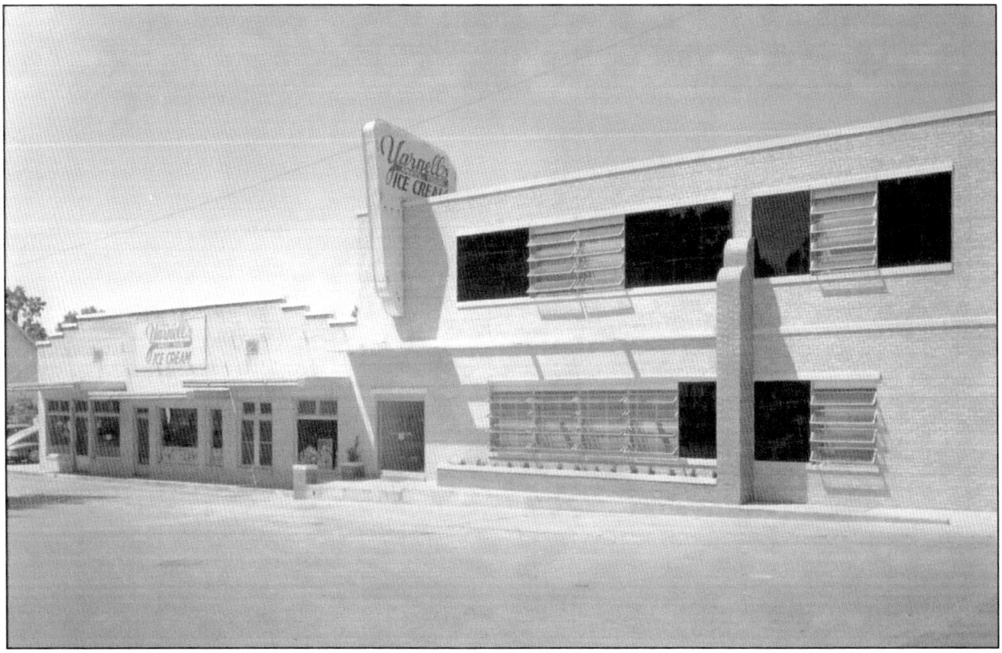

Yarnell's Ice Cream had become popular enough by the 1950s to necessitate the construction of another building. This photograph shows the completed addition. (Courtesy SRCC.)

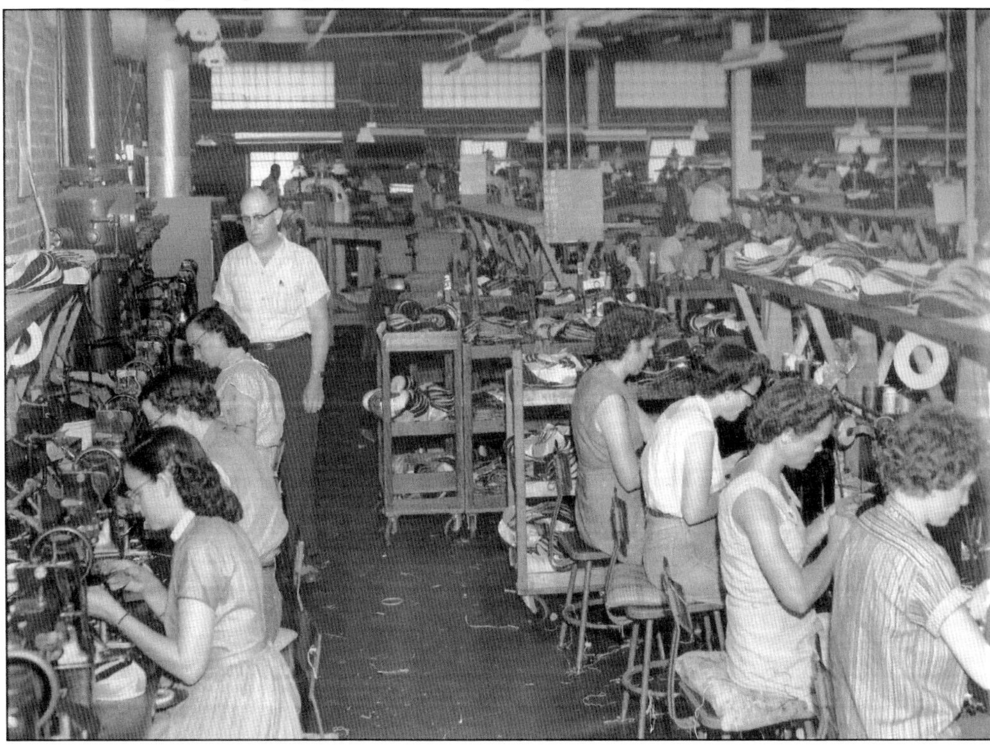

International Shoe Company had a good production record in the late 1940s and 1950s. The payroll for 1948 listed 280 employees. In 1957, the Searcy factory produced and shipped 1,638,321 pairs of shoes. (Courtesy SRCC.)

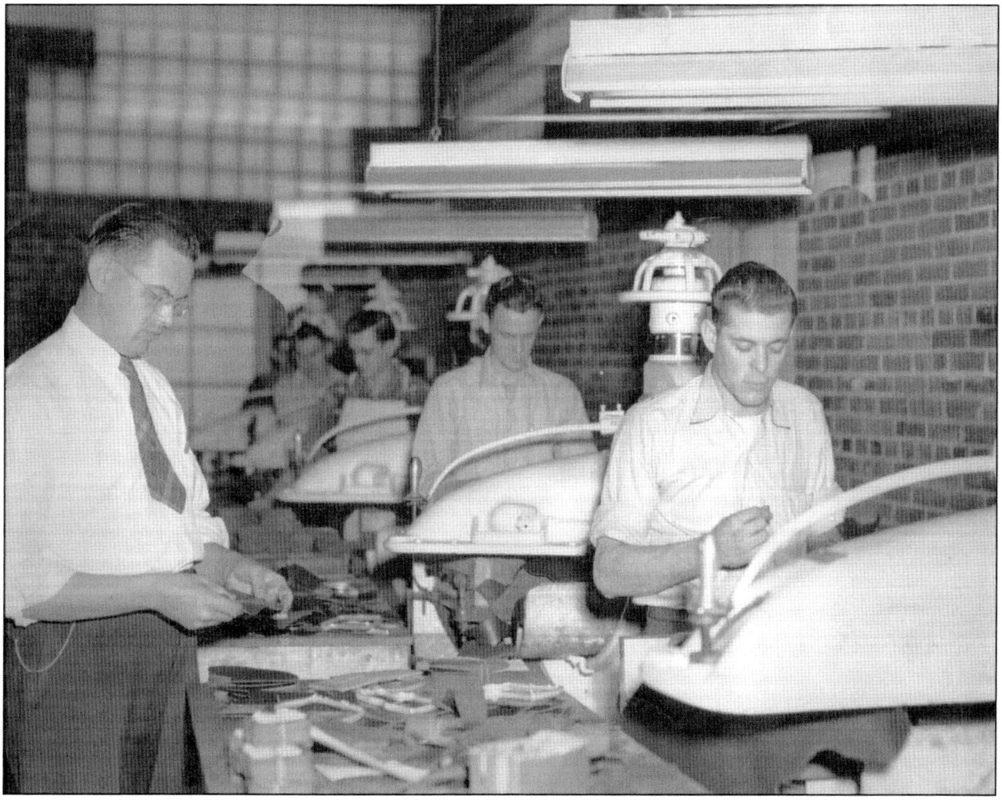

This is one of many photographs taken at the International Shoe Company in the late 1940s. The three men shown in the foreground of this picture are Roy L. Skaggs, cutting room foreman (left); Jefferson Rushin, first operator (center); and Willard Hill, second operator. Rushin and Hill work at cutting machines that contained metal dyes and were used to cut the various shoe parts from the leather skins placed on the block. Skaggs is examining some uppers that were just cut. (Courtesy SRCC.)

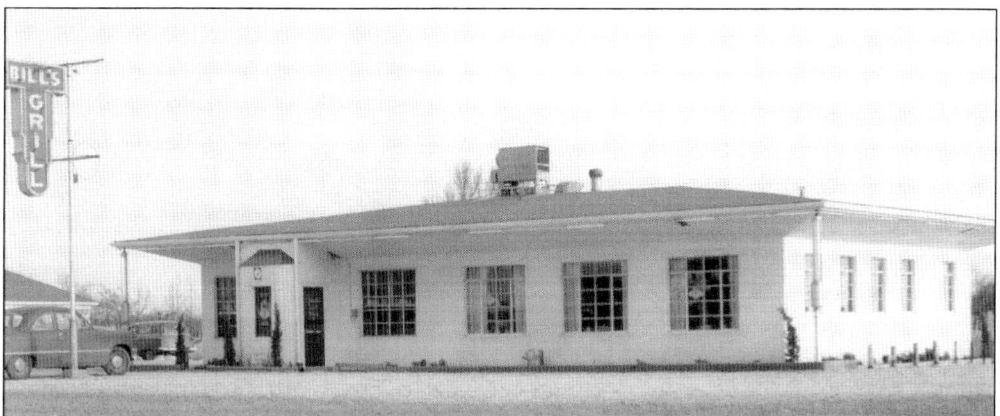

Bill's Grill, owned by Bill McMikle and his wife, was located on Highway 67 East/Race Avenue during the 1950s. It advertised curb service, counter service, telephone reservations, a private dining and conference room, and no parking problems. The grill also claimed that it was "North Arkansas's Finest and Searcy's Best Restaurant." (Courtesy SRCC.)

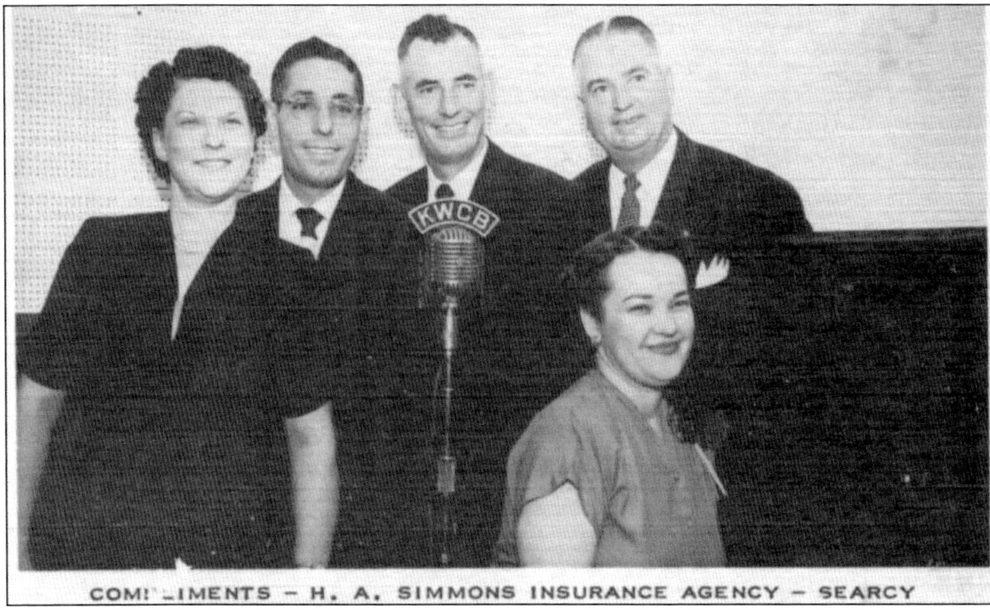

The Bradberry Quartet is pictured here in 1953. The members were, from left to right, Zoe Harlan, Truett Langley, Manuel Harlan, and Floyd Bradberry. Mildred Langley, Truett's wife, was pianist. They sang often on KWCB Radio in Searcy. The H.A. Simmons Insurance Agency in Searcy distributed postcards with a photograph of this talented group and its piano player. (Courtesy Jim Bradberry.)

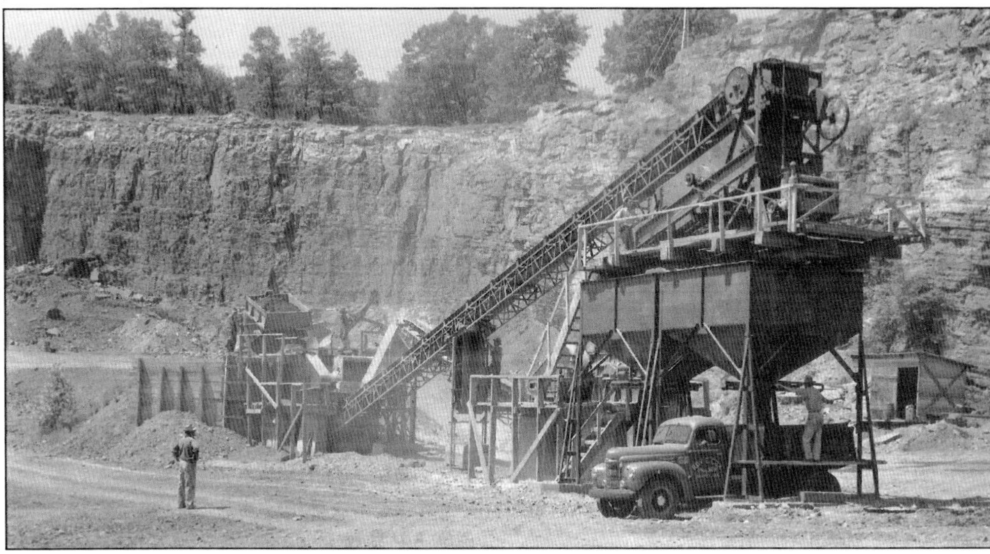

Searcy and White County's first rock crusher was set up at Bee Rock in 1947. Betty Thornton Ulrey wrote a piece for the *Arkansas Democrat* on July 1, 1951, about the early trails leading to the county seat and how they were cleared of trees and stumps to allow the passage of wagons and carts. She praised judge Floyd Bradberry for the graveling of 400 miles of county roads since the rock crusher's installation. Cloie Presley, noted historian, also wrote about the county's first roads being "just dirt" trails running in all directions and told about a proposal to have a Sesquicentennial Historical and Nature Trail near Bee Rock. Searcy's Riverfront Park is now located in this vicinity. (Courtesy Jim Bradberry.)

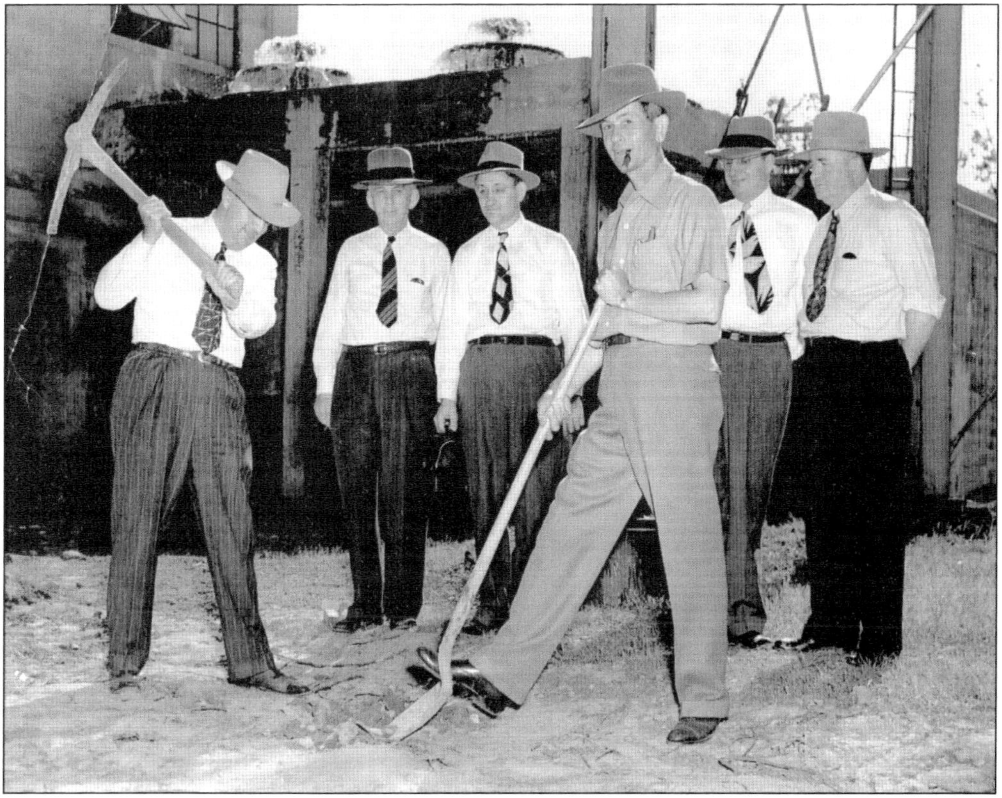

The board of directors for the Searcy Water and Sewer Company break ground for a new facility in 1949. They are, from left to right, E.P. Pyeatt, Mayor B.L. Oliver, Elmer Yancey, Cal Aclin, Richard Deener, and Hubert Smith Sr. (Courtesy SRCC.)

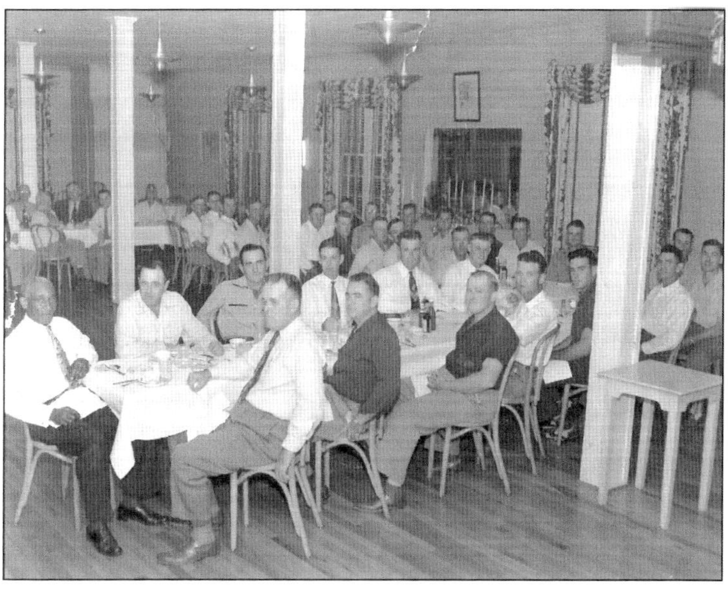

Employees and guests of the Searcy Water and Sewer Company enjoy a meal at Christmastime in the upstairs banquet room at the Rendezvous Restaurant around 1940. (Courtesy Searcy Water and Sewer Company.)

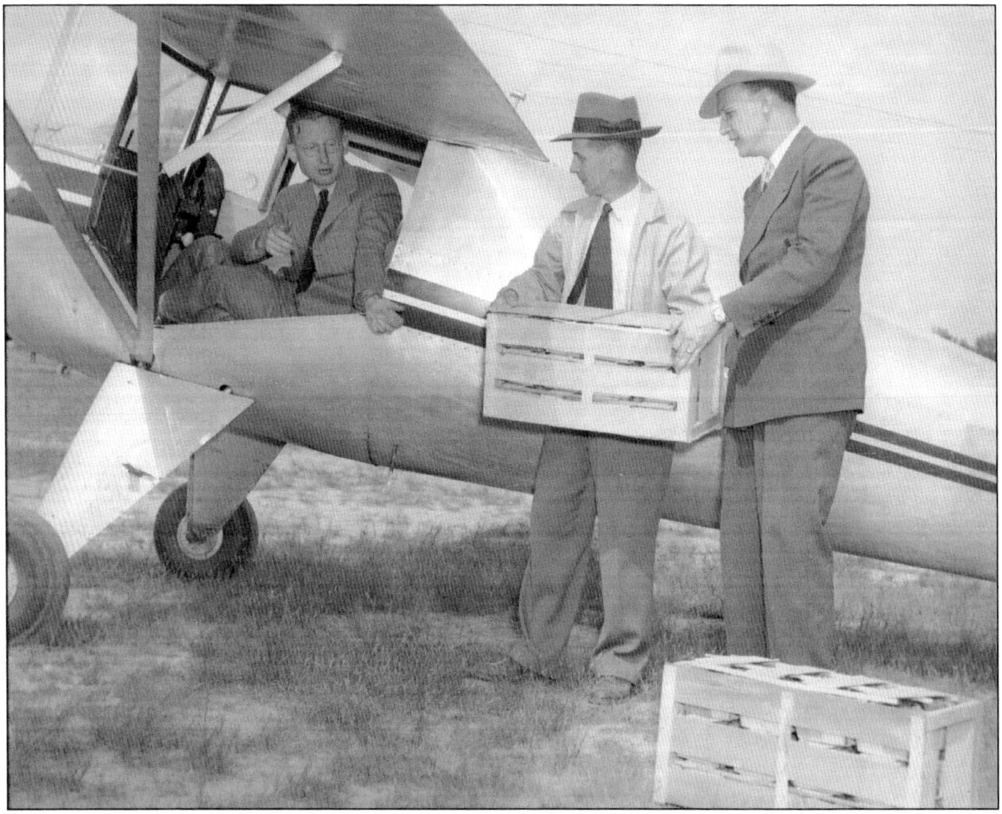

In 1947, a banquet was held in St. Louis to observe National Air Week. The menu at this banquet included one item from each of the 50 states. Henry Alt of St. Louis (seated in the airplane) flew into Searcy to pick up a crate of Arkansas strawberries. County agent C.D. Christian (left) and B.D. "Sy" Forsythe, secretary-manager of the Searcy Chamber of Commerce, pass the strawberries to Alt. (Courtesy SRCC.)

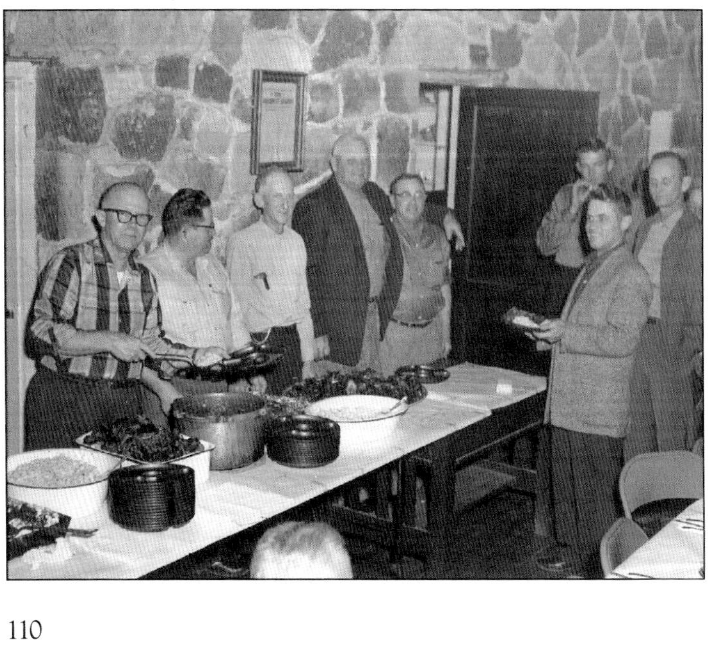

Identified at this c. 1950 dinner at the American Legion Hut are, from left to right, Elvin Hilger, J.W. (Red) Morris, ? Reiff, Ed Coward, W.R. (Reiser) Steward, Ed McDaniel, Clyde New, and Jake Moon. (Courtesy Nancy Williams Showalter.)

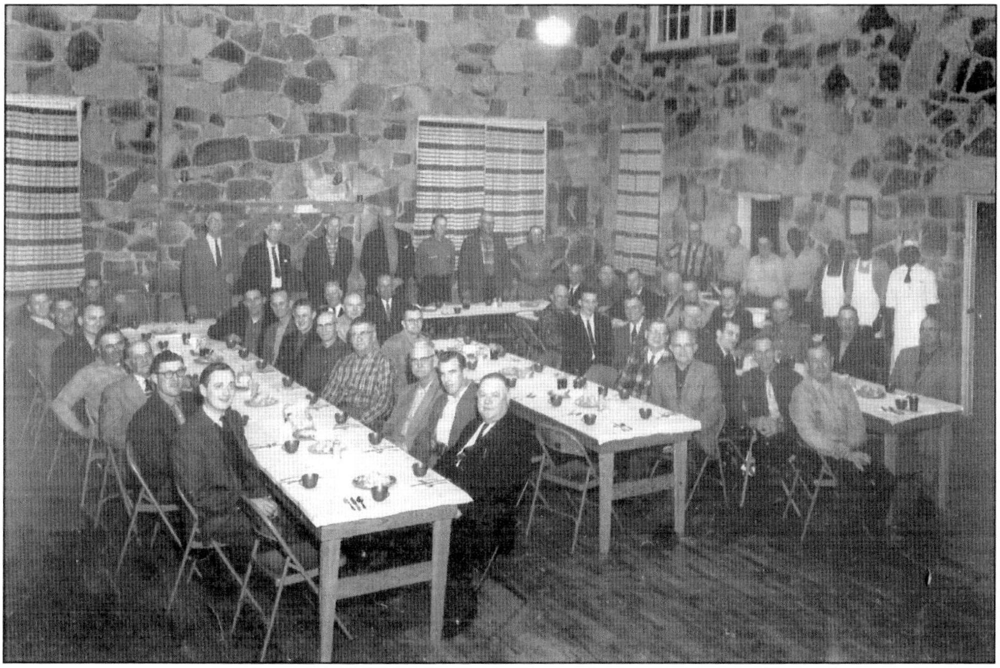

This unidentified group is ready for a meal in the American Legion Hut. Truman Baker, commander of the Searcy Legion Post, is standing at the far left of the photograph. A Searcy businessman, Baker was appointed by Gov. Homer Adkins as a lieutenant in the State Guard. He was also affiliated with the staff of the Veteran's Administration at Fort Roots in North Little Rock, a position he held until he was elected commander of the Gordon Gale Post of the American Legion in North Little Rock. He was also elected commander of the Sixth District and appointed as a member of the American Legion's National Security Commission for a three-year term. (Courtesy Nancy Williams Showalter.)

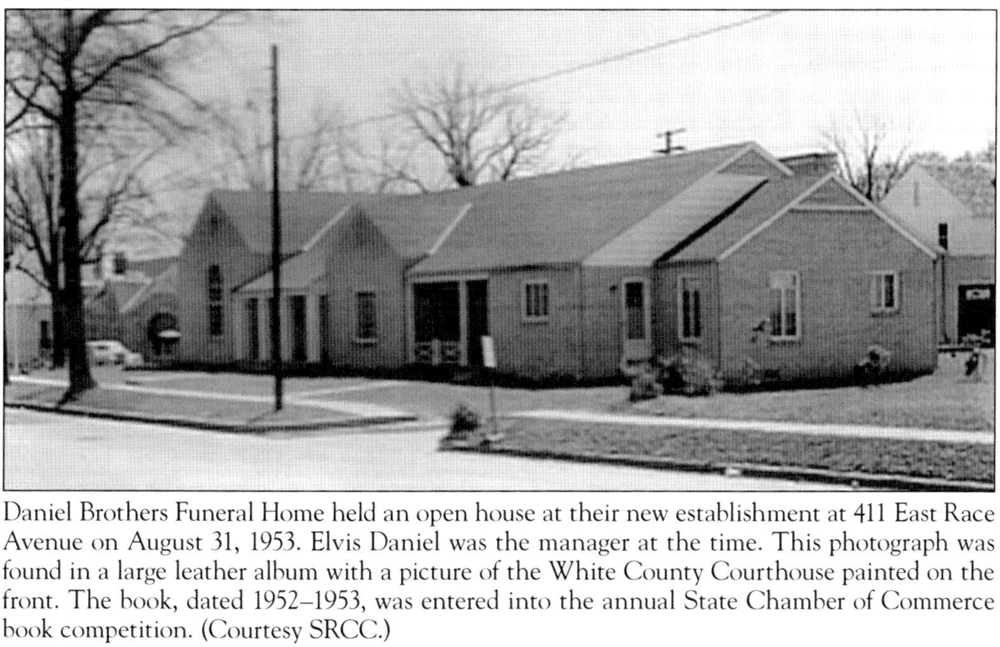

Daniel Brothers Funeral Home held an open house at their new establishment at 411 East Race Avenue on August 31, 1953. Elvis Daniel was the manager at the time. This photograph was found in a large leather album with a picture of the White County Courthouse painted on the front. The book, dated 1952–1953, was entered into the annual State Chamber of Commerce book competition. (Courtesy SRCC.)

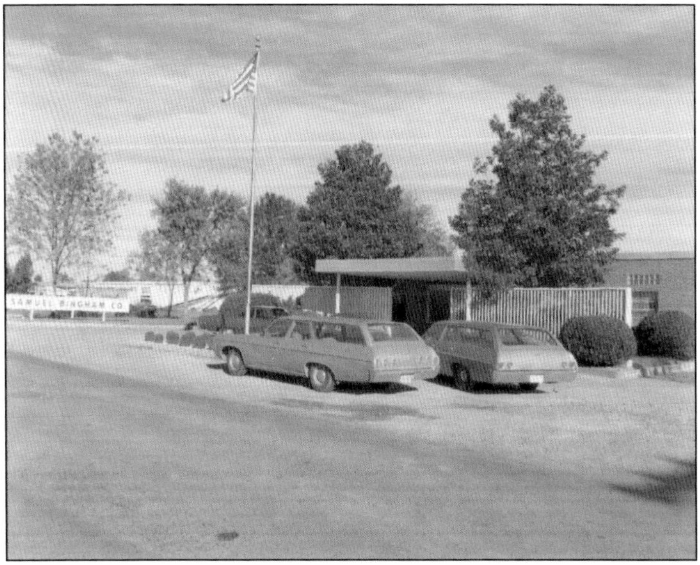

The Samuel Bingham Company announced a tentative contract to build a manufacturing plant in Searcy on September 2, 1955. The company built and reconditioned rollers for industrial manufacturing. It originally employed 20 people. Increased demand forced an expansion in 1961. In 1965, the plant employed 85 people and had the highest production rate of any Bingham plant in the country. (Courtesy SRCC.)

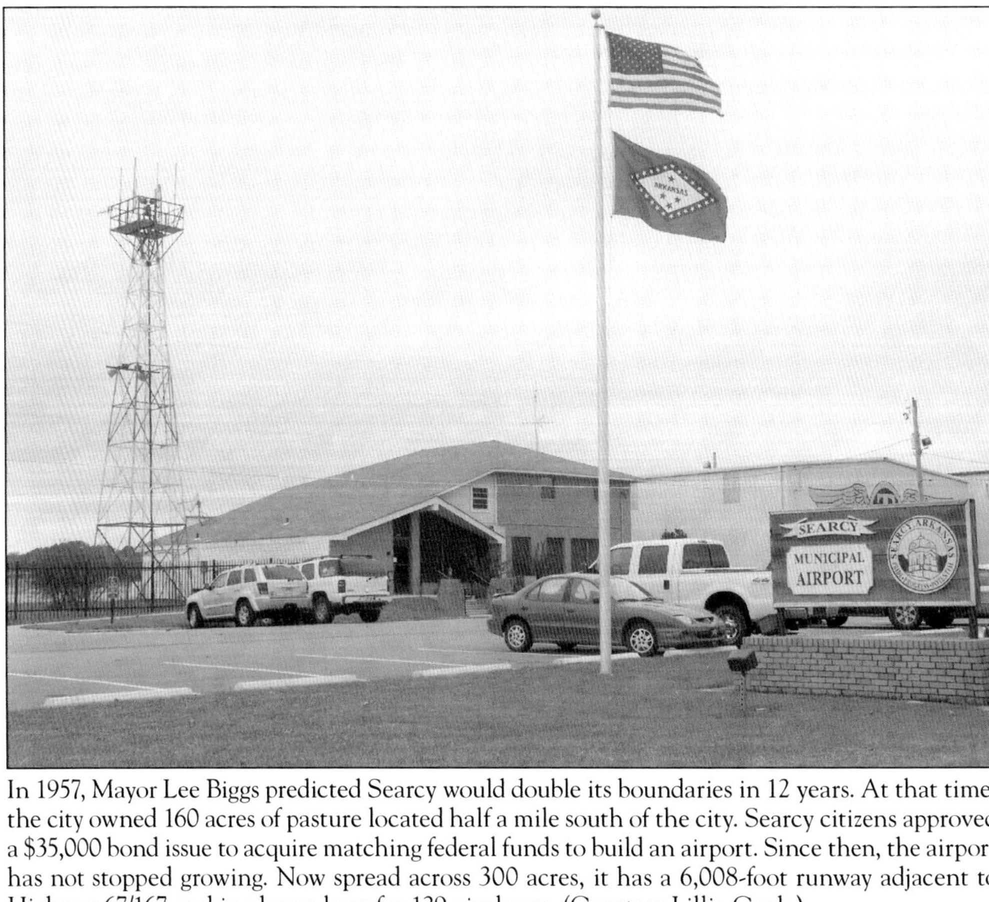

In 1957, Mayor Lee Biggs predicted Searcy would double its boundaries in 12 years. At that time, the city owned 160 acres of pasture located half a mile south of the city. Searcy citizens approved a $35,000 bond issue to acquire matching federal funds to build an airport. Since then, the airport has not stopped growing. Now spread across 300 acres, it has a 6,008-foot runway adjacent to Highway 67/167 and is a home base for 129 airplanes. (Courtesy Lillie Cook.)

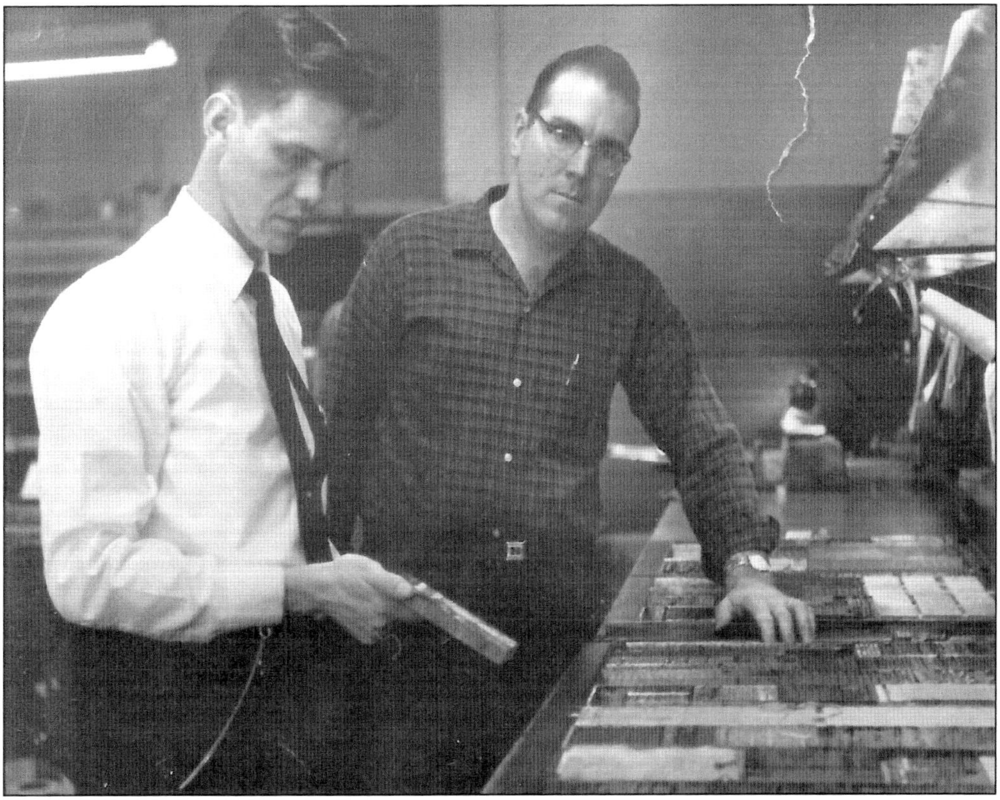

Perrin Jones (left), now editor emeritus of *The Daily Citizen*, shows an unidentified employee in the composing room how typesetting was done before the days of computers. (Courtesy Eloise Muncy.)

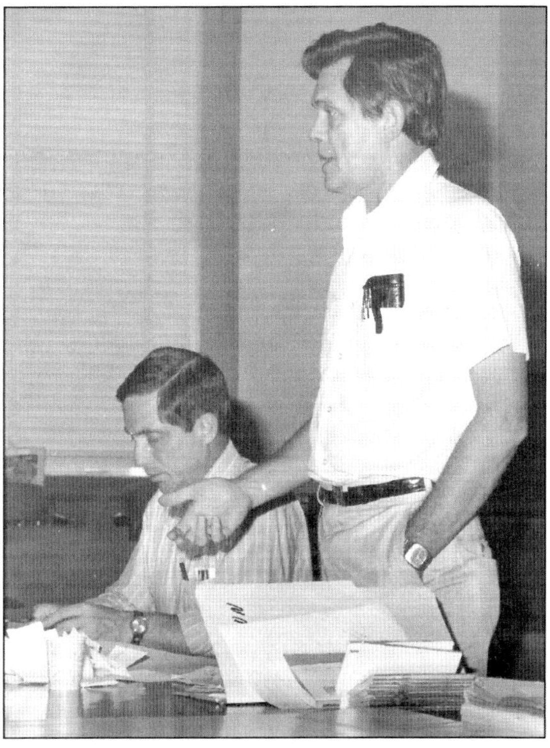

Jim Wilbourn (seated) and Perrin Jones conducted many meetings for the Democratic Party in Searcy. Jones was vice president of the 1970 State Constitutional Convention and was once considered as a candidate for governor. He withdrew when Orval Faubus decided to run. The gold pen used by Jones to sign the constitution in 1970 is in the local historic museum, along with the gold pen that Searcy judge Jesse N. Cypert used to sign the constitution when he and J.W. House represented White County at the 1874 State Constitutional Convention. (Courtesy Nancy Williams Showalter.)

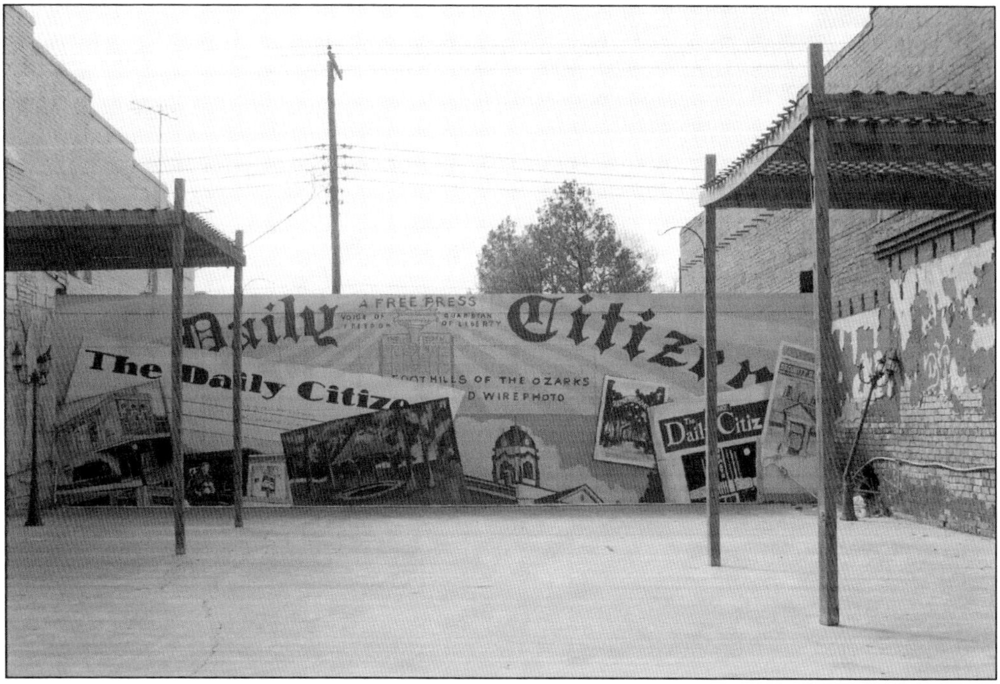

This "pocket park" in downtown Searcy is located where *The Daily Citizen* office stood for years. The newspaper is now owned by the Paxton Media Group of Paducah, Kentucky, and is managed by local residents. (Courtesy Carolyn Boyles.)

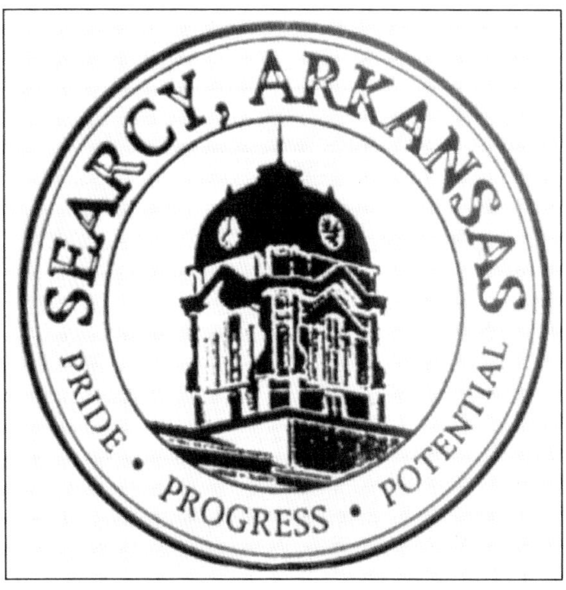

Chuck Hicks, assistant professor of music at Harding University, designed the Searcy city seal in 1974. Hicks designed the seal on a paper napkin while sitting in a chamber of commerce meeting in the upper room of Mrs. Harris' Cafeteria. The seal has been incorporated into official Searcy signage, such as the "Welcome to Searcy" signs (also designed by Hicks) and many of the city's street signs. Mayor David Evans was in his first term when this design became the city's official seal. (Courtesy Chuck Hicks.)

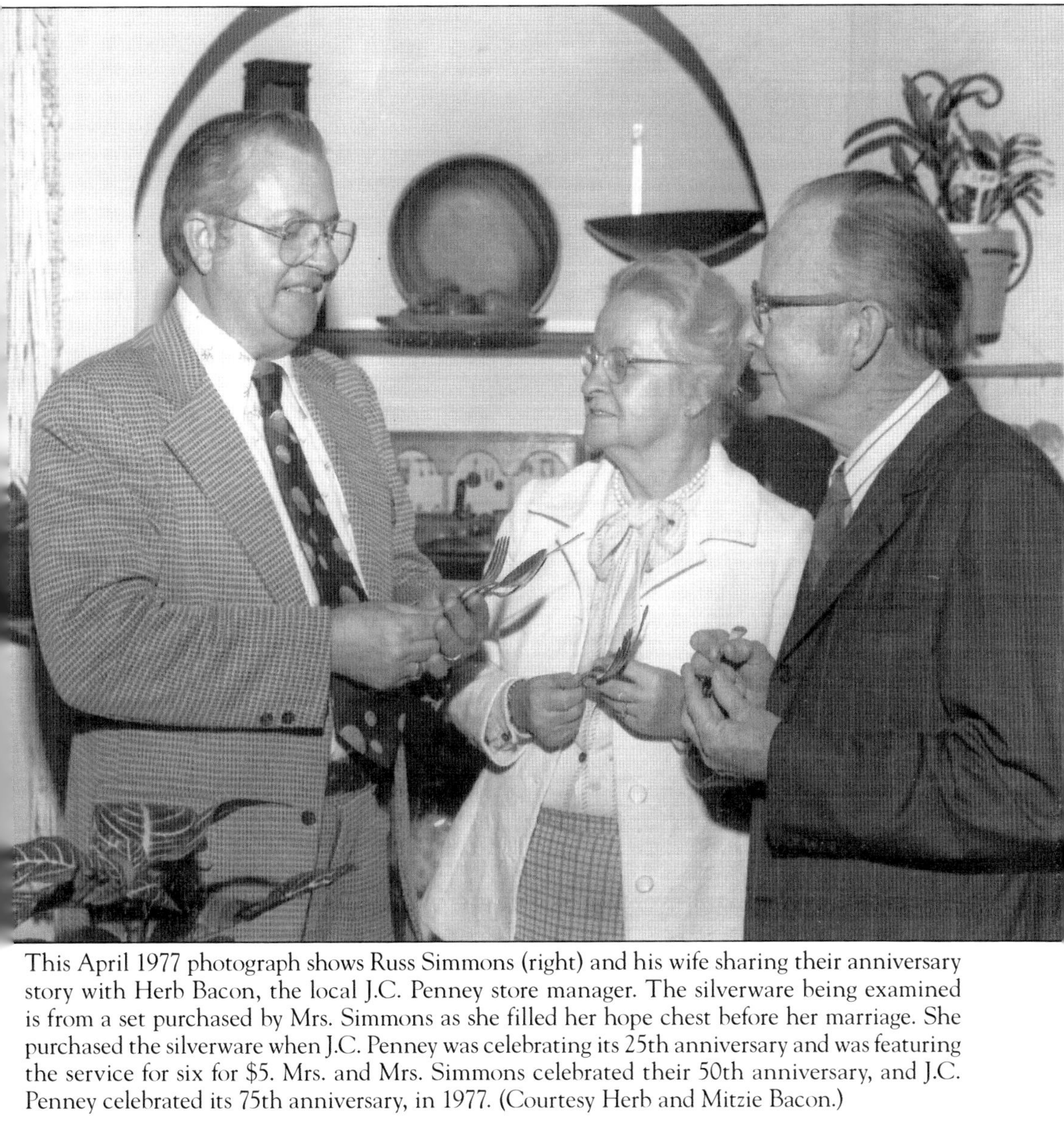

This April 1977 photograph shows Russ Simmons (right) and his wife sharing their anniversary story with Herb Bacon, the local J.C. Penney store manager. The silverware being examined is from a set purchased by Mrs. Simmons as she filled her hope chest before her marriage. She purchased the silverware when J.C. Penney was celebrating its 25th anniversary and was featuring the service for six for $5. Mrs. and Mrs. Simmons celebrated their 50th anniversary, and J.C. Penney celebrated its 75th anniversary, in 1977. (Courtesy Herb and Mitzie Bacon.)

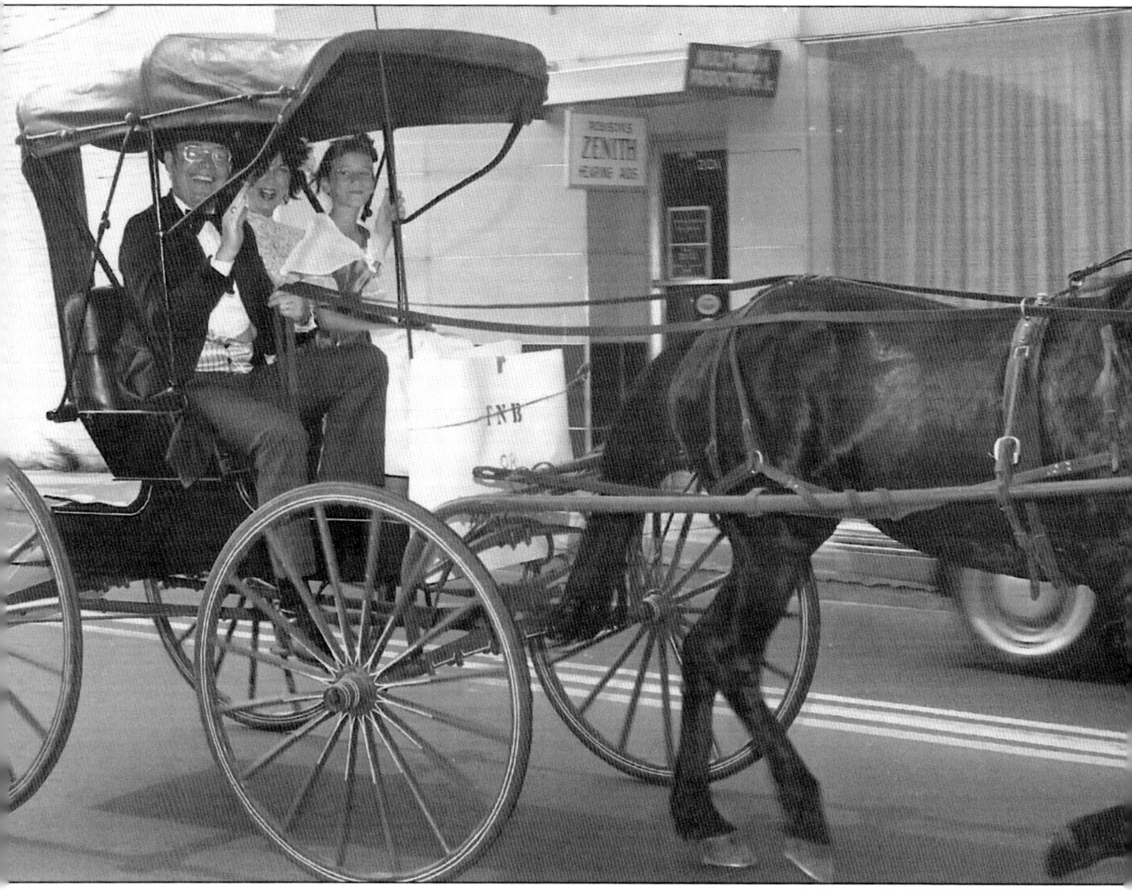

In 1979, First National Bank president Wayne Hartsfield—along with his wife, Suzy, and daughter Jenny—dressed up and rode in Ed Lightle's horse-and-buggy rig on the bank's 75th anniversary. The old Searcy Bank, established in 1904, is featured on the front cover of this book. (Courtesy Regions Bank.)

Five

PERSONALITIES

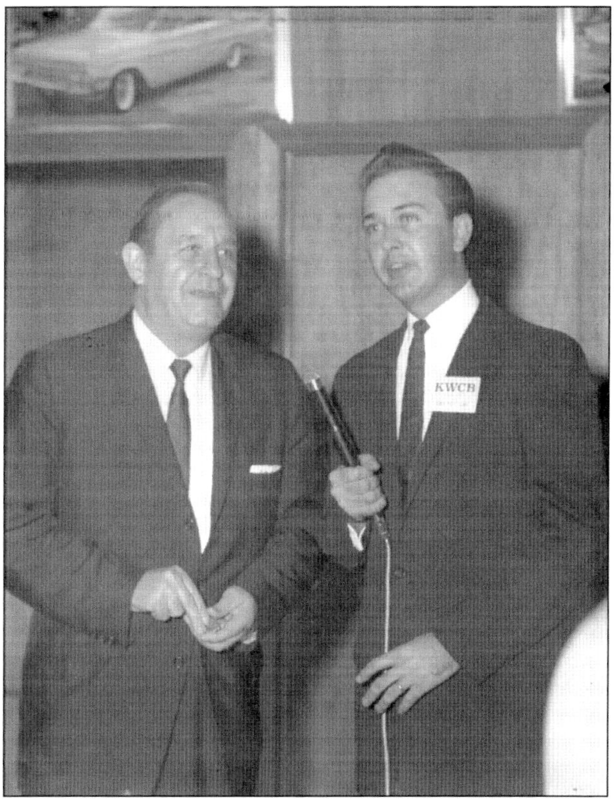

John Paul Capps (right) of Searcy radio station KWCB interviews Gov. Orval Faubus at the grand opening of the new Truman Baker Chevrolet showroom in Searcy in 1961. The building was on the corner of Race Avenue and Main Street, while the dealership's offices and parts departments were located in the old National Guard armory. Truman Baker Chevrolet occupied the entire block in 1961. Faubus is best known for his position against desegregation of Arkansas schools, ordering the Arkansas National Guard to physically prevent black students from entering Little Rock Central High School in 1957, despite a Supreme Court order. Capps was a longtime member of the Arkansas House of Representatives. He served as speaker of the house in 1981 and was later elected to the Arkansas State Senate. (Courtesy John Paul Capps.)

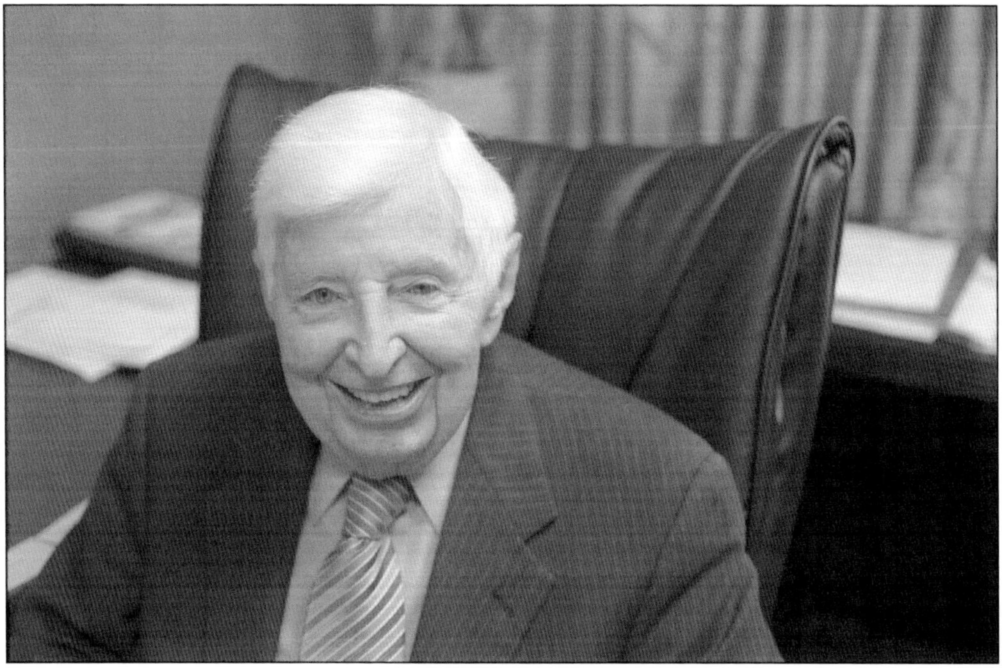

Dr. Jimmy Carr and his wife, Mary Stephanie Carr, moved to Searcy from Florida in 1970. They thought he was retiring, but he began working for Harding College as an assistant to Pres. Dr. Joe Pryor. At Harding, Carr also assisted two other presidents and managed the Elderhostel program. He tried retirement again in 1977 but was recruited to assist Ray Montgomery, administrator of White County Medical Center. Carr worked until age 95 in public relations. (Courtesy White County Medical Center.)

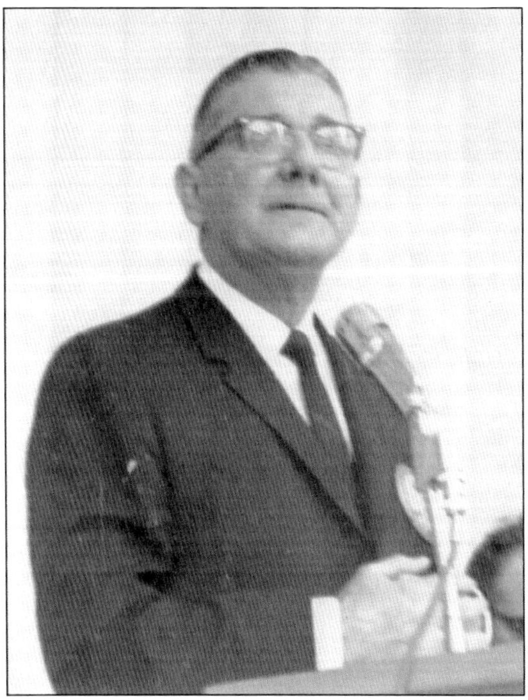

Wilbur Mills served as White County judge from 1935 to 1939 and in the US House of Representatives from 1937 through 1977. He was confirmed as an associate chief justice of the Supreme Court in 1939 and played a large role in the creation of Medicare. Representative Mills also pushed for an automatic cost of living increase for Social Security recipients. He campaigned for the Democratic nomination for president in 1972 but was defeated by George McGovern. Mills died on May 2, 1992, and is buried in nearby Kensett, Arkansas. (Courtesy SRCC.)

Gov. Ben Laney, who served Arkansas from 1945 to 1949, appears at a Young Business Men's Club "thank you" dinner in Searcy on March 30, 1948, held in appreciation for the paving of State Highway 16. Laney was a conservative Democrat whose most significant contribution to Arkansas was the Revenue Stabilization Act of 1945, which banned deficit spending. (Courtesy SRCC.)

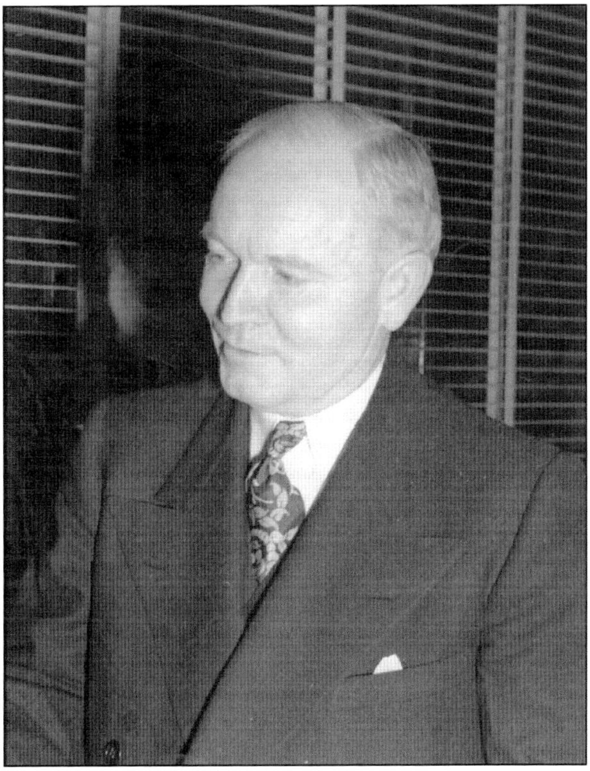

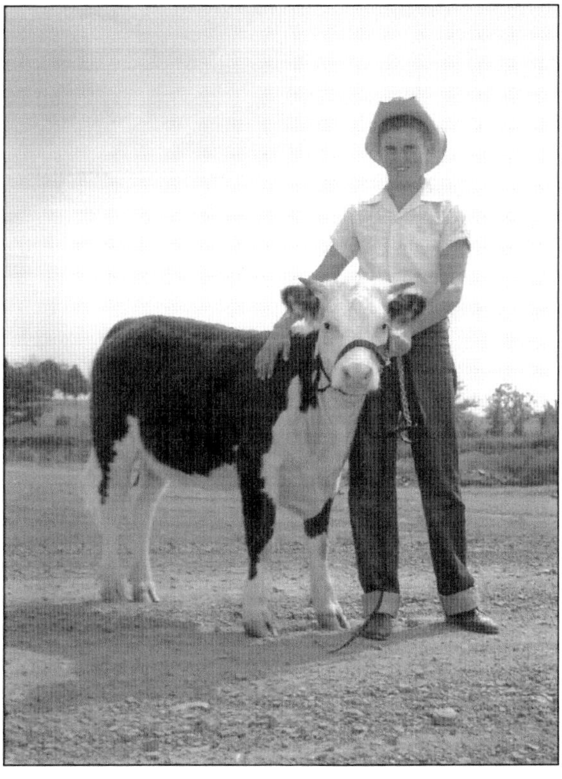

In 1954, Billy Roy Floyd showed his prize bull at the White County Fair. He graduated from Searcy High School in 1957. He worked for the Coca-Cola bottling plant in Searcy for many years and became known as "Mr. Coca-Cola." Floyd was involved in numerous local, civic and charitable activities. As president of the Searcy Chamber of Commerce in 1973, he was instrumental in bringing a Walmart Supercenter and distribution center to Searcy. His service to Searcy High School and the community was recognized by his induction into the Searcy Public Schools Education Foundation Hall of Honor. He died in 2007. (Courtesy Regions Bank.)

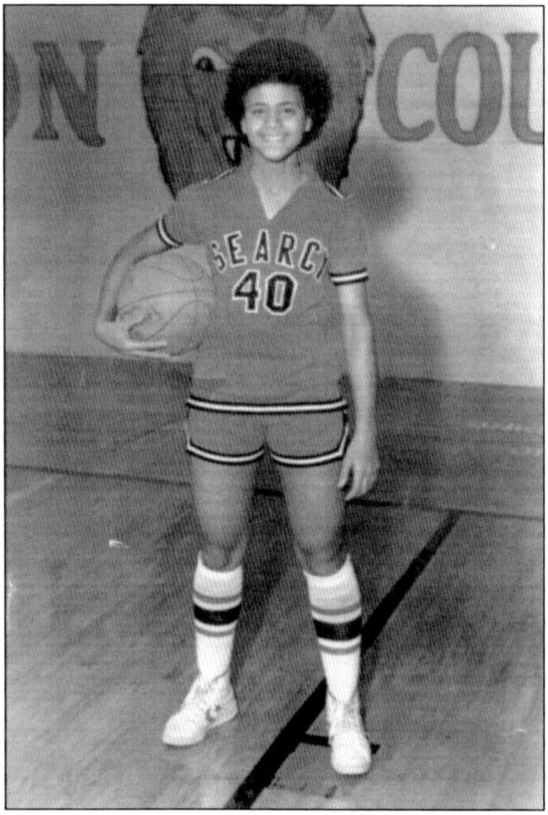

After a 20-year hiatus, Searcy High School reinstated basketball for girls in 1980. In 1981, the second annual Bo Baker Memorial Award for the most improved senior high school player was awarded to Paula Clay. The award was established by Bo Baker's mother, Bertha Baker. Bo was an athlete at the school. (Courtesy Paula Clay Cleveland.)

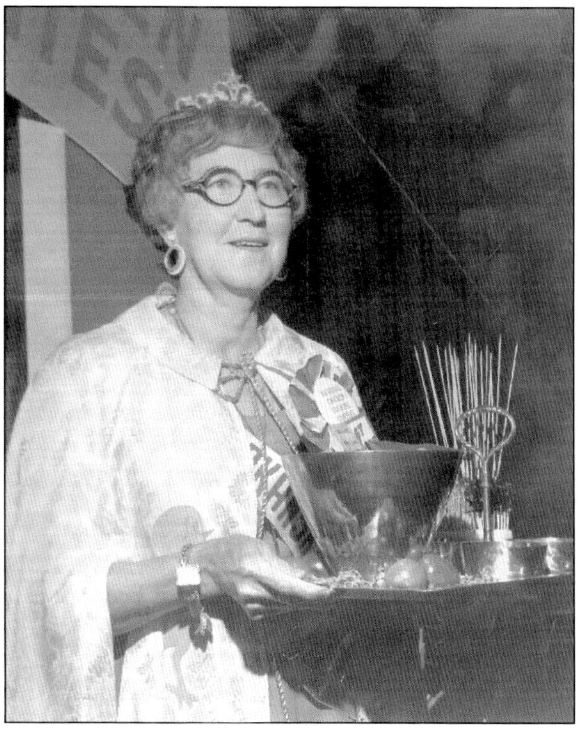

Norma Young won the Delmarva National Chicken Cooking Contest in 1971 with her "dipper nuggets." She received $500 cash, a $250 wardrobe, and an all-expenses-paid two-week trip to Europe, where she visited and shared her cooking skills with chefs and home economists. In 1963, she had been named one of the 10 best bakers in Arkansas by Pillsbury. In 1967, she came in 15th in the Grand National Bake-Off and was the Arkansas Poultry Cookin' queen. She won the Arkansas contest again in 1968. She attended the 50th Annual Poultry Festival on June 12, 2009, and celebrated her 100th birthday in 2011. (Courtesy Kay Young Wright.)

Ethel Bailey Shumpourd was 74 when she retired in 1974 after 51 years of service as supervisor of housekeeping at Porter Rodgers Hospital. She started her work as a cook in the Wakenight Sanitarium in 1923 and became a housekeeper when Dr. Porter Rodgers Sr. bought the sanitarium in 1929. During her career, she supervised and trained many hospital workers. Before integration, she opened her home to black maids whose employers were spending the night at the Mayfair Hotel. (Courtesy Everlyn Green.)

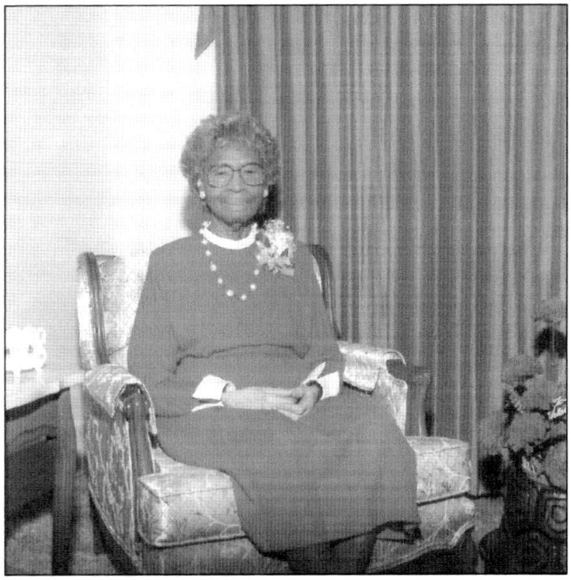

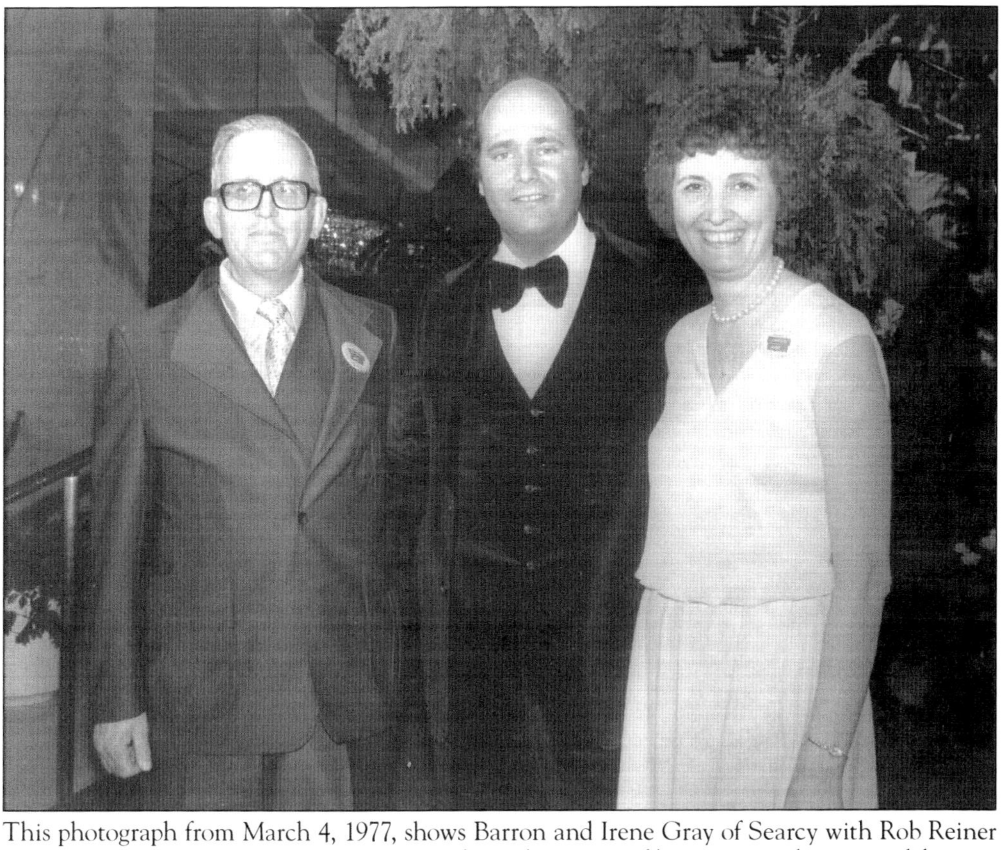

This photograph from March 4, 1977, shows Barron and Irene Gray of Searcy with Rob Reiner (center). The Grays won a trip to Los Angeles to be guests of honor at a gala party celebrating the 200th episode of *All in the Family*. While there, they were interviewed by Norman Lear, the developer of the popular television show starring Carroll O'Connor, Jean Stapleton, Reiner, and Sally Struthers. (Courtesy Irene Gray.)

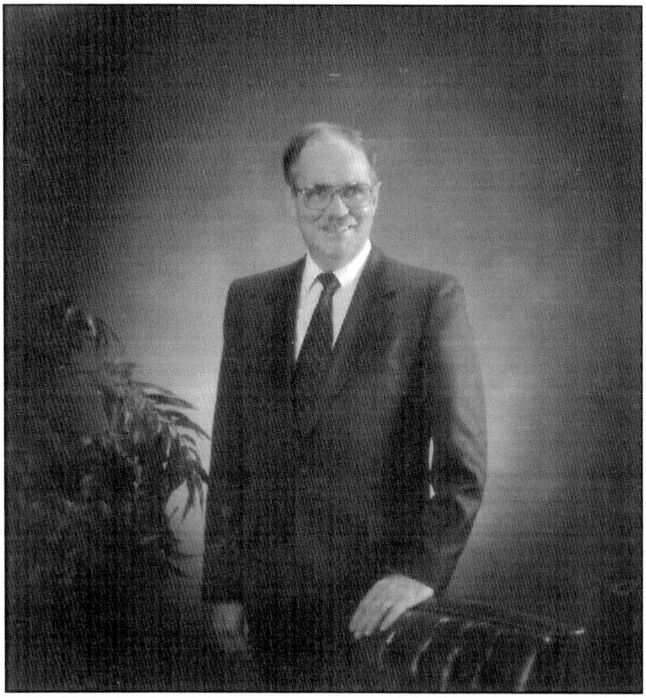

Raymond Lee Muncy, PhD, was a distinguished professor of history at Harding University and wrote *Searcy, Arkansas: A Frontier Town Grows Up With America* in 1976 as a bicentennial project for the City of Searcy. (Courtesy Eloise Muncy.)

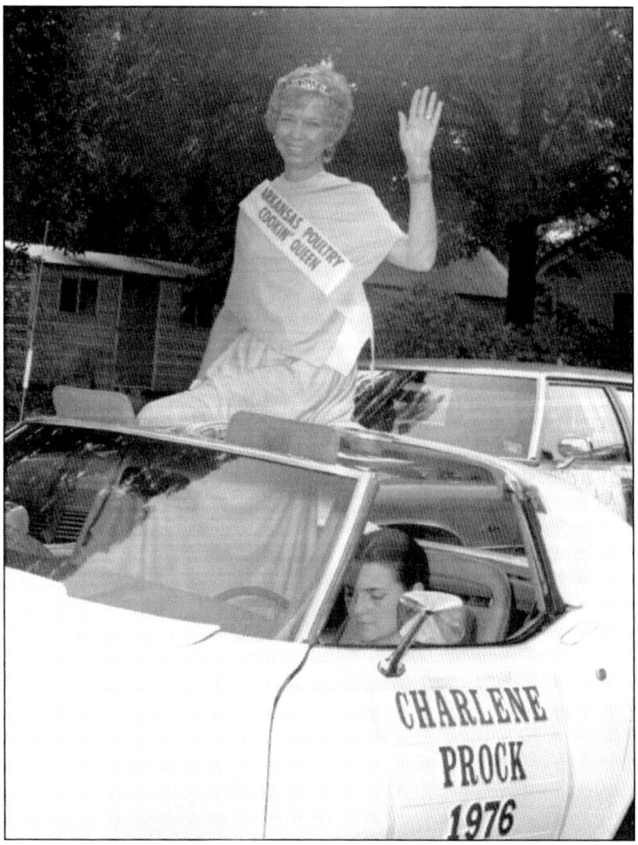

Charlene Prock was the 1976 Arkansas Poultry Cookin' Queen. Preliminary contests were held in Searcy for several years. Mary Ghent, also from Searcy, was the 1975 Poultry Cookin' Queen. Prock's winning recipe was for Heritage Chicken USA. (Courtesy Charlene Prock.)

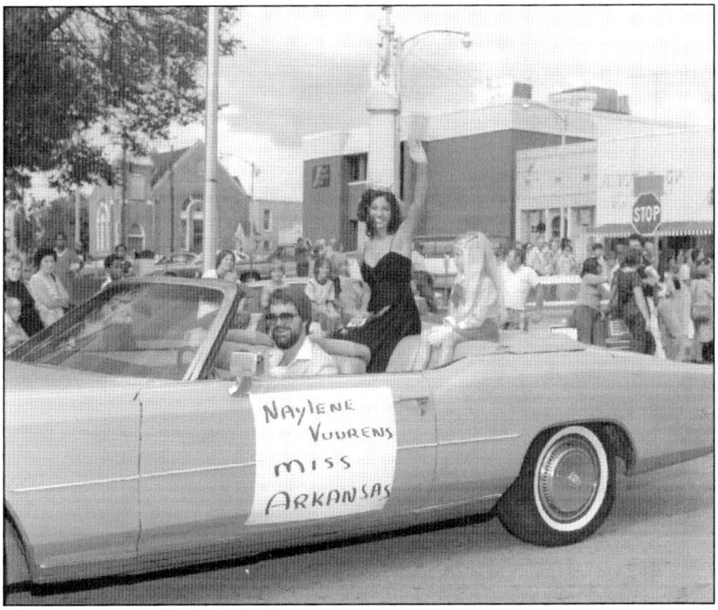

Naylene Vuurens of Searcy was Miss Arkansas 1978. Vuurens entered the Miss Arkansas Contest as Miss Diamond Lakes. Here, she waves to the crowd gathered to welcome her home in a convertible driven by Ron Van Hook. Vuurens was an employee of the Van Atkins Department Store in downtown Searcy. The young lady riding in the backseat is unidentified. (Courtesy Ron Van Hook.)

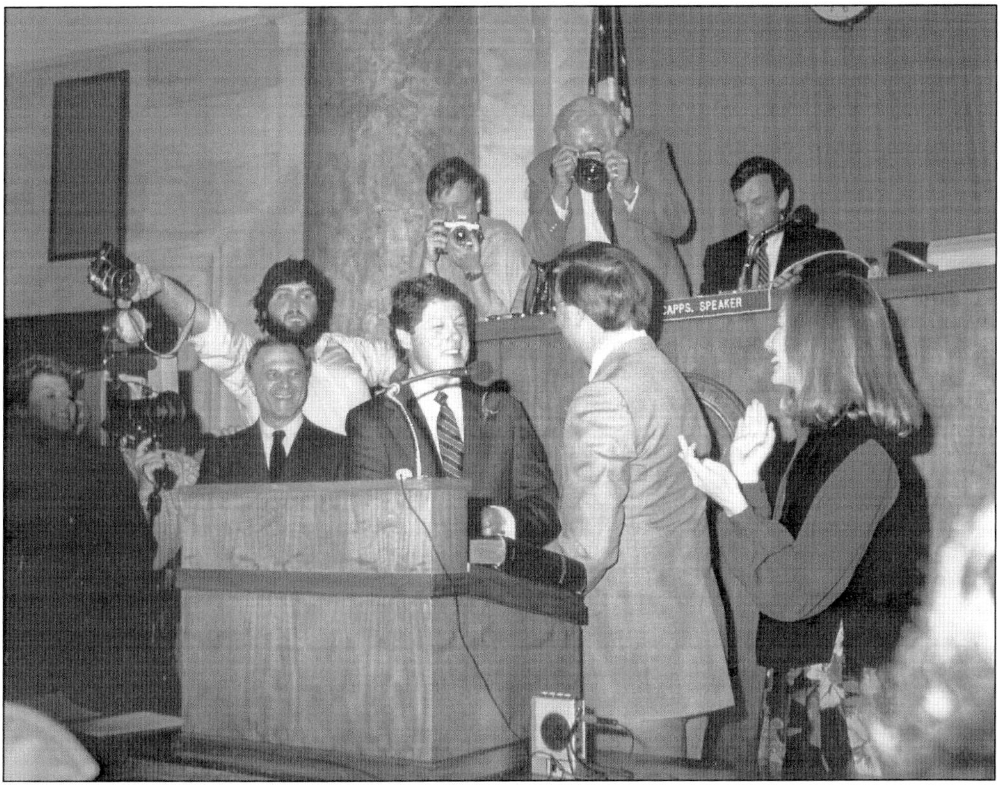

As speaker of the house in the Arkansas Legislature in 1983, Rep. John Paul Capps had the honor of giving Governor-Elect Bill Clinton the keys to the governor's office. Pictured here are, from left to right, (first row) Barbara Pryor, Sen. David Pryor, Clinton, Capps, and Hillary Clinton; (second row) three unidentified photographers and Secretary of State Winston Bryant. (Courtesy John Paul Capps.)

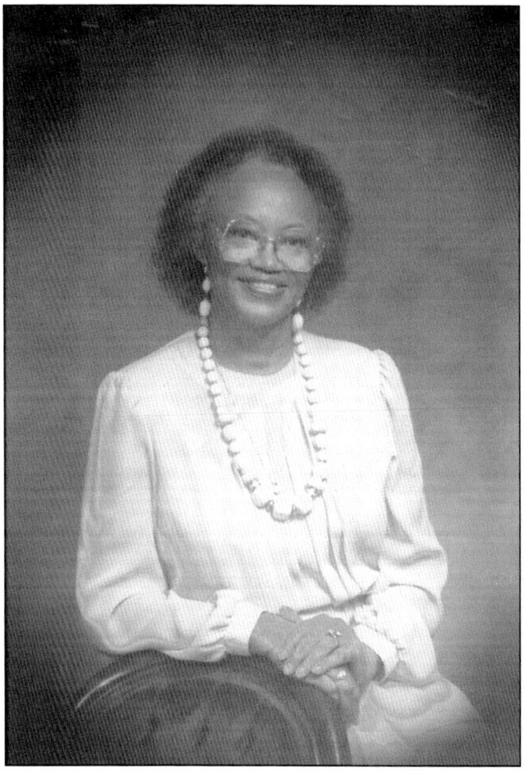

Everlyn Green, the daughter of Ethel Bailey Shumpourd, taught math in Searcy public schools for 43 years. She attended McKinley Junior High and graduated from Dunbar High School in Little Rock. Green continued her education at Dunbar Junior College and received her master's degree from the University of Arkansas. Her teaching career began in 1942 at White County Training School, and she retired from Searcy High School as its principal. Green was inducted into the Searcy Public Schools Community Foundation Hall of Honor in 2006. (Courtesy Everlyn Green.)

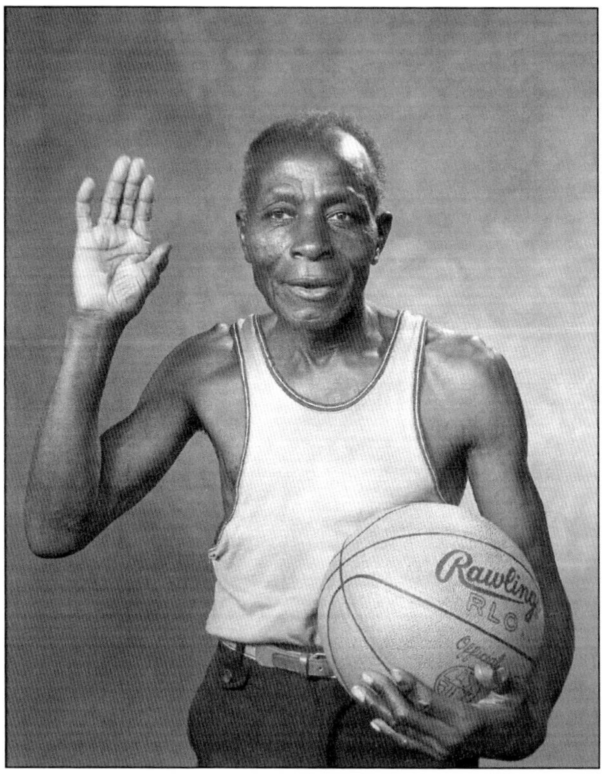

Arvada DePriest, a local man about town, was photographed by John Baker in 1983. Baker said DePriest might have been called a "fixture" in the community during the 1980s, as he was always there to watch any kind of sporting event. DePriest, a graduate of White County Training School, usually had his camera and took pictures at games. Sometimes he filmed sporting events at Searcy High School. (Courtesy John Baker Photography.)

Governor Mike Beebe and his wife, Ginger, have occupied the governor's mansion in Little Rock since the beginning of his first term in 2006, but they still call Searcy home. Governor Beebe began his second term in 2011 and continues to serve Arkansas with pride. Ginger Beebe (née Croom) was raised in Searcy, and the couple maintains a residence in town. (Courtesy Tiffany Dabbs.)

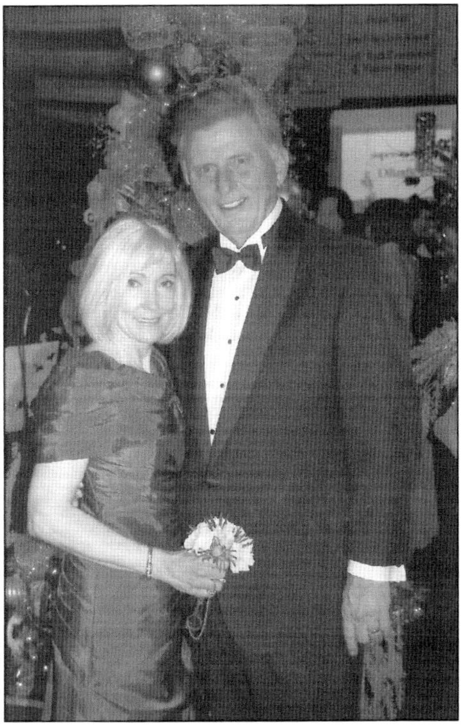

Brothers Dale (left), Leon (center), and Irvin Van Patten were photographed with Sen. Bob Dole during a veterans' tour in Washington, DC, in 2007. The three Van Patten brothers served in World War II: Dale in France, Leon in the Philippines, and Irvin in Germany. Senator Dole was badly injured while serving in Italy in World War II. (Courtesy Leon Van Patten.)

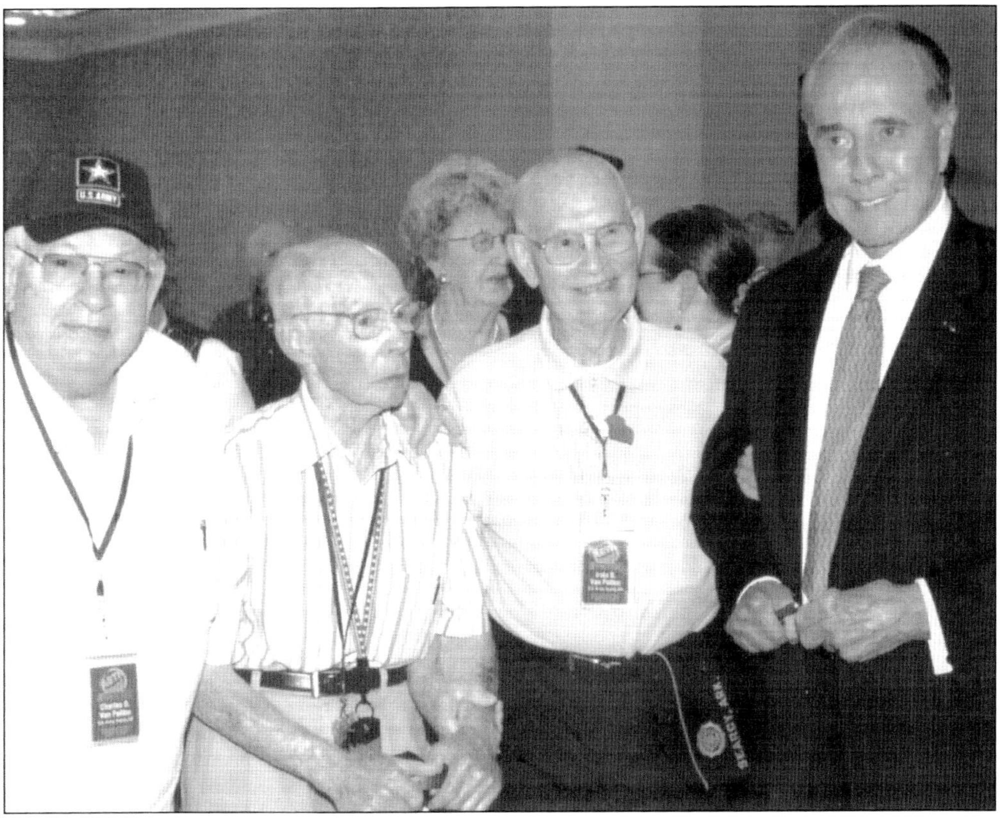

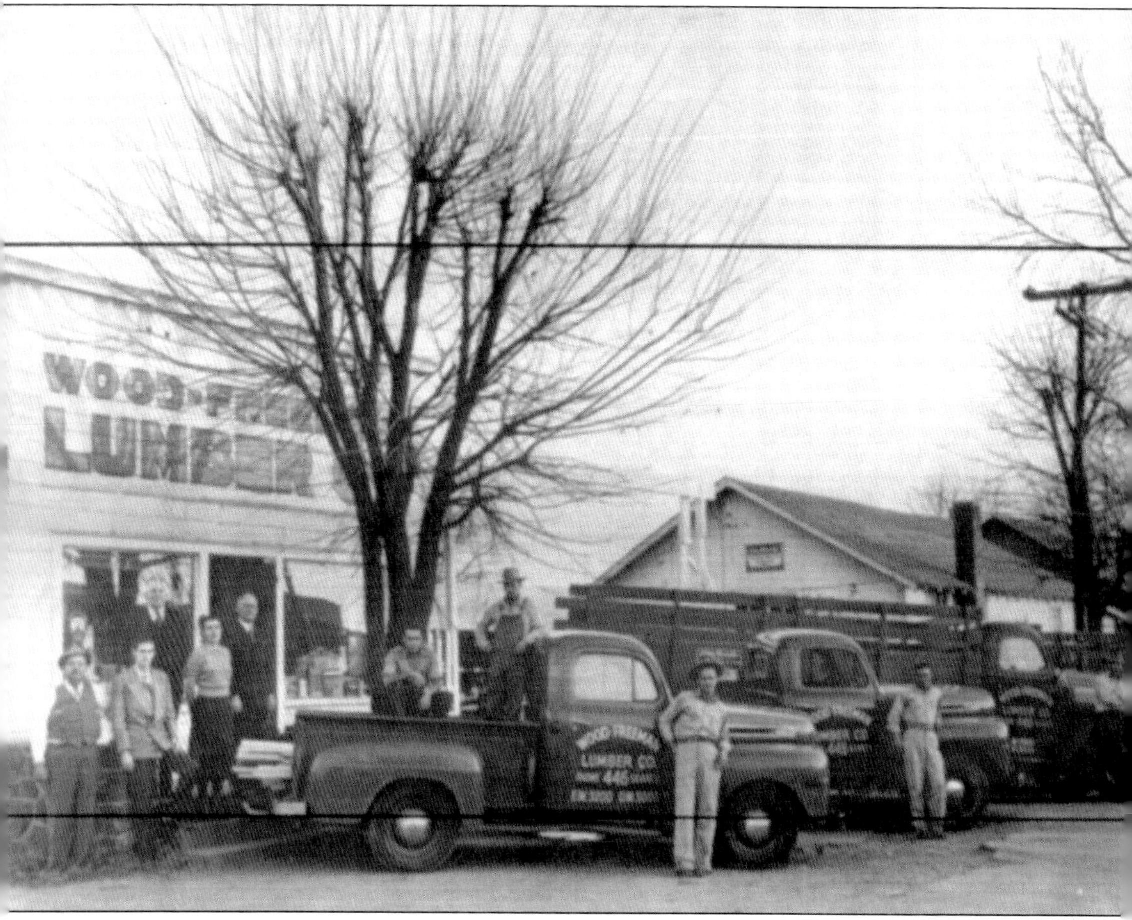

The Wood-Freeman Lumber Company was located at 400 South Locust Street in 1947. Employees were, left to right, Gordon O'Neal, T.R. Garner, R. Brown, Esther Smith, and J.H. Wiseman. The man sitting in the truck is unidentified; Opie Price is standing in the truck; Elden Brown is in front of the truck; and the man to the right is unidentified. Jim Berry Plant is standing against the truck on the far right. (Courtesy Jack Wiseman.)

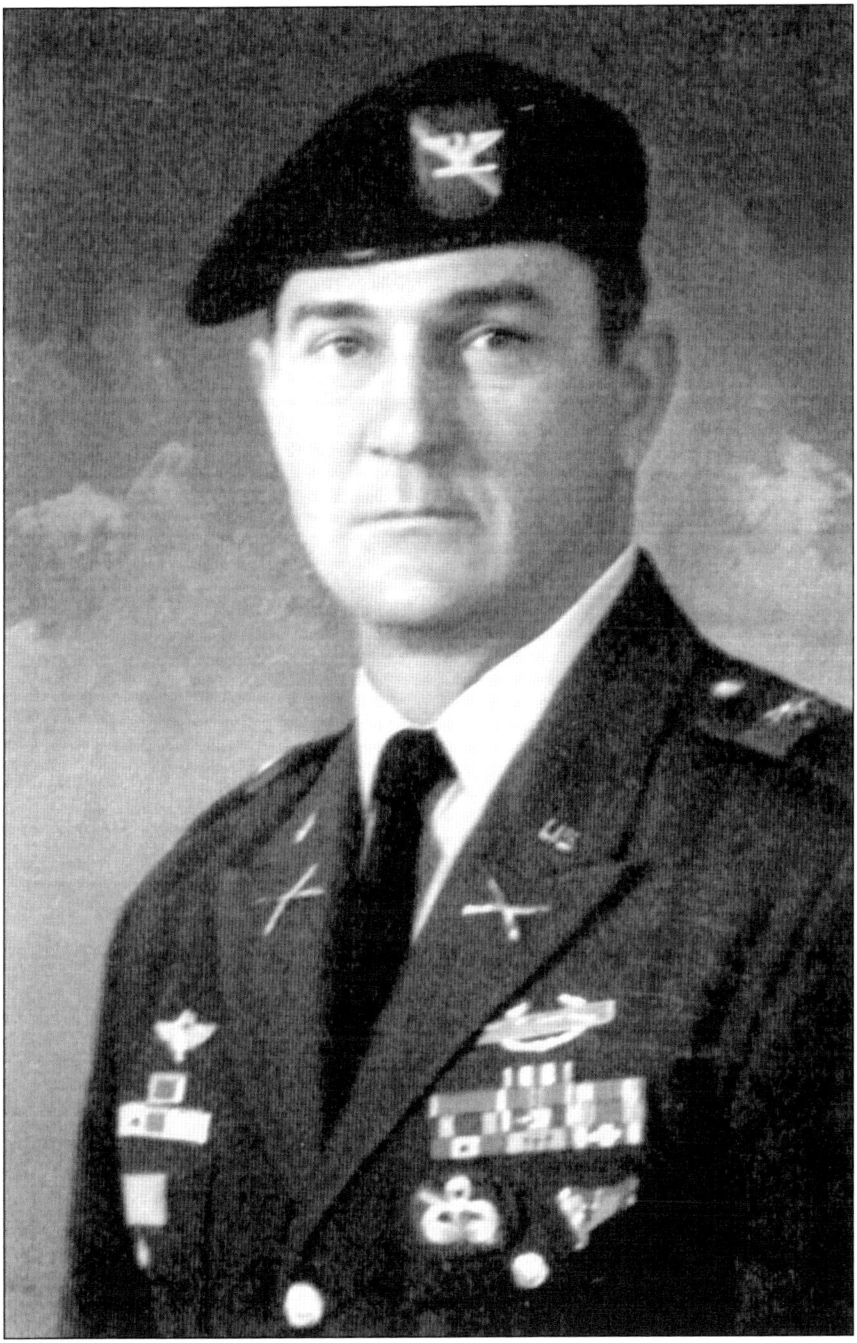

Col. A.J. "Bo" Baker grew up in Searcy and graduated from Searcy High School. He played football at the University of Arkansas before entering the Army. He became one of the first men to wear the Green Beret. He earned many medals for leadership in Korea, Vietnam, Panama, and Germany, where he died from a heart attack in 1980. An airfield in Germany bears his name, and the new National Guard Armory in Searcy was dedicated to him on August 4, 1996, in a service attended by his mother, widow, daughter, and many friends and relatives. US senator Dale Bumpers was among the many dignitaries who spoke at the service. (Courtesy Pam Wood.)